# Advanced Rock Climbing

## Mastering Sport and Trad Climbing

### Bob Gaines

Guilford, Connecticut

**FALCON®**

An imprint of The Rowman & Littlefield Publishing Group, Inc.
Falcon and FalconGuides are registered trademarks and Make Adventure Your Story is a trademark of The Rowman & Littlefield Publishing Group, Inc.

Distributed by NATIONAL BOOK NETWORK
Copyright © 2018 by Bob Gaines

All photos by Bob Gaines unless otherwise noted
Illustrations by Mike Clelland

British Library Cataloguing in Publication Information available
Library of Congress Cataloging-in-Publication Data available

ISBN 978-1-4930-3139-9 (paperback)
ISBN 978-1-4930-3140-5 (e-book)

♾™ The paper used in this publication meets the minimum requirements of American National Standard for Information Sciences—Permanence of Paper for Printed Library Materials, ANSI/NISO Z39.48-1992.

Printed in the United States of America

*Nicki Dyal leads Course and Buggy (5.11a) at Joshua Tree.*

PHOTO BY GREG EPPERSON

# Contents

# Foreword

Climbing for me was a doorway to a world that made sense. As a teenager rebelling against authority and boggled by the downright weirdness of city life, I opted out as much as I could. Dabbling in a number of sports, I never connected with anything—until I touched rock. Compared with the made-up rules of man-made games, climbing immediately brought me in touch with a real and wild world governed by the laws of nature. In that "Aha!" moment the million-volt light bulb switched on above my head and I realized: This isn't just sport; this is my new life!

Finding what you are born to do doesn't mean you can do it, though—not right away, at least. It did, however, provide me with enough fire in my belly to hurdle the obstacles and tackle the setbacks. Still, I could have used some help. I was living in western Canada when climbing hadn't yet become a thing. I scoured the library, but there were far more books on Sasquatch than on anything to do with rock climbing. Trying to learn when there was no one to teach obviously slowed my progress and presented me with all kinds of needless stumbling blocks and even do-or-die scenarios. Over time, though, I bumbled my way to a level of proficiency that allowed me to visit some of the greatest climbing areas on the planet.

What it brought me went way beyond what I expected. Searching for cliffs around the world, I've come face to face with mountain lions and Himalayan yaks, kangaroos and koalas, exotic birds and venomous snakes. But it is the climbing that has been the most mind bending, hair curling, and jaw dropping. And it is that intensity that heightens the senses and—I think—makes us better than who we are. Rock gymnastics above a thousand feet of air, needle-sharp summits against blue skies almost black from the altitude, and adventures so rich they turn climbing friends into blood brothers. Climbing alone, I even found some of that relaxed familiarity with an environment normally achieved by lizards and monkeys.

A lot has changed since I first started climbing. My initial roadblock was too little information; now you could say that there is too much. Anyone with a laptop can publish, whether it's a treasure trove of good insight or a Dumpster full of rubbish. The tough part now is finding that treasure.

I first got to know Bob Gaines down in Joshua Tree, where he owned and ran Vertical Adventures. That was over twenty years ago, and since then I have guided for him and, when schedules allowed, climbed with him. As a climber, he has some of the very best footwork, especially on that maddening off-vertical granite where the dinky smears and razor-blade edges lie right on the cusp of invisibility. I once tried to follow him on one of his new routes. Watching him go first, it looked downright

*Jeff Schoen leading The Prescription (5.11), Needles, California.*

PHOTO BY GREG EPPERSON

ix

casual, perhaps a good warm-up before getting on something hard. I started up with a head full of confidence. I was fit, I was experienced, I was sure this was a done thing—and I was wrong! Halfway up I slammed up against a baffling bit of blankness. I just couldn't grasp what kind of sorcery Bob had used to glide his way through it. There was no way I could crank through on finger strength either; there was nothing there. You clearly had to have a pact with the devil or possess insane technical skills. I had neither.

As a guide, Bob defines the gold standard. Simply put, he is the best I've seen. There is no one thing that makes a good guide, either. Of course there's the raw ability as a climber, but there is also a host of rope techniques, rock skills, and the nebulous realm of massive experience. He knows five times as many knots as I do—OK, so it's more like ten times. His résumé includes the first ascents of big walls, hard free climbs, and doubling for Captain Kirk on El Cap for a *Star Trek* movie. Who else can say that? He has risen to the point of instructing new guides. In other words, he teaches the teachers. He has also written widely on the subject, producing many how-to books. All of this is to say that he is a world-class communicator about climbing.

At the core of it all, though, is Bob's love of climbing coupled with his enthusiasm for teaching and inspiring. It is this that makes the adventure of learning come alive and take you places. Enjoy the trip!

Peter Croft
June 2017

*Peter Croft free solos, tips (5.12a), Yosemite Valley.*

PHOTO BY GREG EPPERSON

# Acknowledgments

First and foremost, I'd like to thank John Burbidge for putting it all together. Thanks to project editor Ellen Urban, copy editor Paulette Baker, and Melissa Evarts for the great layout and design.

Thanks to Peter Croft for writing the chapter on crack climbing. Peter is, without a doubt, the best crack climber on the planet and, as far as I know, the first climber to on-sight free solo a 5.12 crack climb. Peter can climb a 5.9 hand crack with about as much effort as it takes me to walk down a sidewalk.

Thanks to Wills Young for his contribution on steep face climbing techniques.

Special thanks to John Long for being an influential climbing mentor, and for all those insightful conversations we had while working together on the *Climbing Anchors* books.

Thanks to Greg Epperson for his wonderful photography.

Thanks to all those who graciously posed for pictures, including Patty Kline, Peter Croft, Tony Sartin, Terri Condon, Tony Grice, Mike Moretti, Todd Gordon, Erik Kramer-Webb, Tommy Romerro, Dave Mayville, Michael Baines, Steve Schwartz, Mike and Lori Satzberg, Lisa Rands, Kevin Jackson, Robin Depke, Adam Radford, Carmen Cendejas, Casey Stroud, Melissa Popejoy, Erin Guinn, Lori Shiraishi, Frank Bentwood, Francisco Kim, Alex Nunez, John Lauretig, David Kerner, Roddy McCalley, and Anne Marie Richardson.

Thanks to all my fellow guides and mentors, from whom I've learned a great deal: Erik Kramer-Webb, Chris Baumann, Marcus Jollif, Tony Sartin, Tony Grice, Dave Mayville, Wills Young, Pat Dennis, Adam Fox, Jon Tierney, Alan Jolley, Todd Vogel, Mark Houston, and Ron Funderburke.

Thanks to my wife, Yvonne, for her help with the photo editing.

I'd like to thank my climbing partners for all the great adventures and lessons learned along the way, including Ed Salazar, Tod Conover, Rich Piotrowski, Kevin Blackburn, Charlie Peterson, Dave Katz, Banny Root, Pat Brennan, Mike Paul, Roy McClenehan, Scott Cosgrove, Fred Becky, Jay Smith, Werner Braun, John Long, John Bachar, Peter Croft, John Mallery, Tony Sartin, Todd Gordon, Alan Bartlett, Dave Mayville, Tommy Romerro, Frank Bentwood, Kelly Vaught, Chris Baumann, and last but not least, my favorite partner of them all, and partner for life, my wife Yvonne.

*Eric Decaria on the Cobra Formation, Canyonlands National Park, Utah.*

PHOTO BY GREG EPPERSON

# Introduction

This book is written from an instructor's perspective. For more than thirty years I've worked as a professional rock climbing instructor and climbing school manager. Many of the techniques in this book were learned over these years—from other guides and from peer training and review I've received through the American Mountain Guides Association (AMGA). I'm currently an instructor and examiner for the AMGA's Single Pitch Instructor program, and many of the principals in this book are a result of my exposure to and collaboration with other AMGA instructors.

It's been said that to truly become an expert, no matter what field, you'll need to log 10,000 hours to fully master the subject. For example, if you want to be an expert crack climber, and you can get in 5 hours of crack work in a day's climbing, you'll have to crack climb for at least 2,000 days to reach expert status. There are no shortcuts. You must pay your dues, and there is no substitute for time on the rock.

What level you eventually attain will depend on your time constraints, level of motivation, and physical limitations, but you can accelerate your development by first building a solid foundation, mastering good fundamentals, and benefiting from good mentoring and coaching.

As a climbing instructor, I've got my 10,000 hours. My goal for this book is to convey the salient lessons I've learned over time—in particular, those key techniques and systems I've found to be most beneficial. My hope is that this book becomes your favorite reference for knots, systems, and fundamentals—the veritable "tools in your tool box" you can utilize in your pursuit to becoming an expert, and to do it safely.

Climbing can never truly be mastered; you're always learning, every step of the way. Enjoy the process, and enjoy the journey. In the end it's not important how hard you climb—it's about how much fun you have along the way.

Bob Gaines
July 2017

*Bob Gaines on the Lost Arrow Spire.*

PHOTO BY JEAN YURGALEWICZ

# Face Climbing Techniques

## Slab Climbing

When I began rock climbing in the early 1970s, the infamous "Stonemasters" ruled the Southern California crag scene. At that time, American and British climbers were setting the standards, and the Stonemasters were doing some of the hardest rock climbs in the world. Entrance to their elite clique was direct: You had to flash Valhalla, a three-pitch route at Suicide Rock, perhaps the first 5.11 edging climb in America. Back then, the best shoes were hard-rubber PAs and RDs, both totally unsuitable for difficult edging and smearing routes like Valhalla. Not until EBs came along did the ranks of the Stonemasters grow, although only slightly.

Everything changed when sticky rubber shoes arrived. Precise edging was out, and smearing was in—pasting the ball of the foot directly onto the rock, letting the edge, crystal, or merest rugosity "bite" into the boot sole. Some climbers referred to this new technique as "smedging." Around 1980 the Boreal Fire (pronounced FEE-ray) arrived, with a dramatically stickier rubber, and a slab renaissance ensued. Some of the old test pieces seemed a full grade easier in the new boots, and by 1985 almost every serious Suicide climber was a Stonemaster. I remember a slab boulder problem at the Camp 4 boulders in Yosemite that I had tried in vain hundreds of times but was able to do first try with my brand-new pair of Fires. Such is the part technology has played in slab climbing.

Extreme on-sight slab climbing requires quick thinking to unravel puzzling move combinations. Exacting footwork is essential, as is balance and relaxation under duress. Even the slightest quaking will send the boot skating away.

I like to work in two sets: handhold and footholds. First I scan the rock for the two best handholds. On edges I prefer the "crimp" grip (placing the thumb over the forefinger) for optimal power, digging the finger pads straight down onto the holds for the most positive purchase. On difficult slab routes the edges will generally be tiny—as thin as razor blades and one or two finger pads wide.

When no obvious edges are apparent, simply digging the finger pads into the most roughly textured area will help. Any downward pressure on the fingers is taking weight off the feet, making it easier for them to stick on sketchy holds. This is the key to hard slab climbing: maintaining points of contact and letting go with the fingers of one hand only to quickly latch the next edge.

Many of the most extreme slab cruxes consist of sidepull combinations, pulling sideways on vertical edges with arms extended in an iron-cross position. On low-angle slabs, palming is often the key and

*Beth Renn leads Vector Analysis (5.11), Grapevine Area, San Bernardino Mountains, California.*

PHOTO BY GREG EPPERSON

*Jay Smith on Hall of Mirrors, Glacier Point Apron, Yosemite.*

*Nose over toes. Carmen Cendejas on Leap Erickson (5.10b), Joshua Tree.*

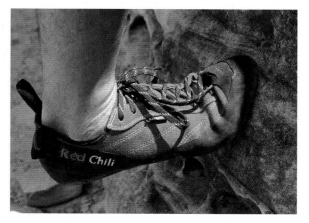

*Basic smearing profile. The heel should be lower relative to the toe. Angle the position of your foot to best take advantage of the shape of the smear. In general, you'll want your heel pointed away from the rock, but let the angle and shape of the hold dictate the position of your foot.*

helps keep the center of gravity over the feet. The idea is "nose over toes."

In my experience as a climbing instructor at Joshua Tree, a common client profile for guided climbing is a client with at least some gym experience but little or no outdoor experience on real rock. For this situation I typically start clients off on a slab, for several reasons. One is to get them used to "reading" the rock, looking for the subtleties and nuances of face holds, which can be tough for someone used to seeing colored holds on a gym wall. Another reason is that it begins the learning curve of valuable lessons on smearing: what will stick and what won't. Each move is a lesson and a positive building of trust and confidence in the

ability of the shoe's rubber to adhere to the rock. On a slab bereft of any obvious hand- and foot-holds, the client is forced to trust the friction of the boots while learning the subtleties of body position and center of gravity. Since footwork is the key to all climbing technique, even crack climbing, this builds a foundation that carries over to all other climbing techniques.

Watch a world-class climber and the first thing you'll notice is his or her fluid, ultra-precise footwork. Clients often ask me, "How can I have smooth footwork?" What I tell them is this: The first thing to do is mentally focus on it from the second you step off the ground. The goal is "quiet feet." If you're tapping or dragging your foot up the rock, you'll hear it. Climb with your eyes. Never take your eyes off the hold until your foot is set precisely on the hold, and consciously think about the best positioning of your foot on the hold. Never look for another handhold until both feet are set. Slowing down your movement will help you focus on precision.

Edges, sharp crystals, and protruding rugosities are the most obvious smearing targets. On low-angle blank slabs, often what you're looking for is simply a ripple or dimple that's slightly less steep. There are many friction climbs at Joshua Tree that are completely devoid of edges, climbed via a series of smears that resemble a miniature version of moguls on a ski run.

When things get steeper and the route has more defined edges, remember that you can use both the inside and outside edge of the shoe. The basic edging technique is for the level of the heel to be slightly higher than the toe.

To rest, if you're on a tiny stance big enough for only one foot, use your heel to stand on it, resting your toes, while you shake out the other foot. Then switch feet and do the same. Another resting

*Peter Croft demonstrates how to rest on tiny edges—hips in, knees against the rock. On Solid Gold (5.10), Joshua Tree National Park.*

*To rest on a slab, place your heel on the hold, then shake out your other foot.*

technique on a two-foot stance is to bend your knees and balance against the wall with your knees.

On traverses, crossing inside with the opposite foot works best, using the outside edge portion of the shoe that's crossing through to smear with. Ankle flexion helps maintain maximum surface contact between the rubber and the rock. Always focus on shifting the center of gravity to directly over the foothold you're stepping up on. A slightly dynamic technique with the lower leg will help you shift your center of gravity most effectively: Once

*Peter Croft demonstrates the crossover step, frontpointing on edges.*

shoe for hard slab climbing is actually one with a stiffer sole, not a soft slipper-like one. A stiffer shoe will allow you to edge better, frontpoint, and smear better on miniscule holds without tiring your feet as much as a softer boot will.

For optimal performance of climbing sole rubber, temperature is key. This is especially true for hard friction climbs. Modern climbing rubber smears best at between 45°F and 55°F, so take on that slab test piece in the cool shade. Any dirt on

*Peter Croft using proper edging technique on a steep slab—weight out and over the feet, heels slightly higher than the toes, heels in to the rock.*

the upper foot is set, bend the knee of the lower leg slightly and push off the lower hold as you shift your center of gravity to the upper foothold. This won't work for super high steps where you're most extended, but it will work most all the time and is a key fundamental that makes slab moves far less tiring on the legs.

On extremes slabs (5.12 and harder), where only the tiniest of edges, slightest ripples, or merest dimples mar the slab plane, frontpointing on microsmears is called for. Here, just the very front tip of the shoe is smeared, with the heel held relatively high. Contrary to popular belief, the best

Climbers on Pywiack Dome, Tuolumne Meadows, Yosemite, California.

your boot sole will be extremely detrimental, so meticulously clean your shoe soles before attempting that hard slab pitch. Rub off any dirt or grime, and clean the soles if necessary with a little water and a toothbrush. When properly clean, your soles should make a squeaking sound when you rub them hard with the palm of your hand.

Once shod, never walk around in the dirt. Dirt-impregnated soles are never the same. And never put chalk on your shoes—it greatly reduces your traction. Climbers discovered this fact in the 70s while working on a route called Hall of Mirrors on Glacier Point Apron in Yosemite. Many of the cruxes were as smooth as glass, and the first ascensionists discovered that any chalk dust on the footholds made it impossible for the feet to stick. By not using chalk, and subsequently not getting any chalk dust on the holds, they found that the smears worked.

On many of the old-school classic slabs, runouts of 15 to 20 feet are common. Leading these gems is an exercise in poise and mind control. Staying relaxed while facing a big fall is a tough proposition, but here are some tips. Focus on your breathing; steady, deep breaths will help you stay calm. When you get to a foothold where you feel comfortable, take advantage of it; shake out each leg, one at a time. On difficult routes I give myself a one-word mantra: "Relax." After each move I'll say it to myself: "Relax," mentally monitoring what muscles I'm firing the most and not tensing up more than I need to. After each move I'll think "relax"; do another move, "relax"; another move, "relax." Before I know it, I'm through the crux.

Today, with so many climbers learning technique in a vertical-walled gym environment, slab climbing has become somewhat of a lost art. But footwork is the foundation of all technique, and confidence in smearing establishes your connectivity to the rock, even on steeper routes.

Any aspiring trad (traditional) climber can benefit greatly from a long apprenticeship on the slabs. The subtle tricks of balance and footwork, well learned from trial and error and time on the rock, can be applied later to steeper test pieces, where footwork still is the key to success.

For the expert, extreme on-sight slab climbing demands a quick mind to solve the puzzle, mental poise, and steady resolve for the long runouts, plus the exacting footwork and balance of a dancer. Successfully climbing what looks impossibly blank might be the sweetest victory of all.

Perhaps Royal Robbins summed it up best in his book *Basic Rockcraft*: "Slab climbing is a special art different from face climbing and crack climbing. Strength is less important, although strong fingers and sturdy foot muscles help. The expert slab climber is distinguished by grace and a cool mind. He keeps his weight over his feet and moves calmly and deliberately, as if he were only a foot off the ground. He does not rush. He looks ahead, carefully calculating his tactics, and acts with resolution. His footwork is neat and deft, for he realizes the importance of precise use of holds. And he concentrates totally on the problem in front of him."

## Extreme Slab Climbing

One of the most difficult slab climbs I've ever done was a new route on Saddle Rock in Joshua Tree. It's a three-pitch route called Silver Spur, with the crux being the third pitch. The route was done ground up, and after the twelve protection bolts on the crux pitch were meticulously installed while hanging precariously off hooks, I knew that to free climb it, I'd have to perform way beyond my previous limits.

Success came from applying sport climbing tactics to a slab climb. While the pitch had no one single show-stopper move, it was seriously sustained, with a 5.11+ section after each of the first seven bolts. The difficulty was a cumulative effect: performing 100 feet of intricate moves with exacting precision, and without tiring out.

I always love a good project—something to aspire to, dream about, visualize, and train for. Success took me many tries over several years to have

*Bob Gaines leading Field of Dreams (5.11d), Tahquitz Rock, California, 1995.*

PHOTO BY SAM ROBERTS

it all come together, but I learned some good lessons about extreme slab climbing. One of the most important things was temperature. The optimal temperature for hard slab climbing is around 45°F. This is the best temp not only for your boot rubber to stick to the rock but also for your finger pads to contact the rock.

One year, with the temperature about 65°F in the shade, I made it past the crux and was mentally celebrating. But unbeknownst to me, one of my fingertips had been sliced on a razor-sharp edge and was bleeding, causing it to slip off a sidepull higher on the pitch. I hung there momentarily, suspended on my tippy toes, until the sudden shift in balance sent me hinging out from the wall, then losing all points of contact. Temperatures only got warmer and warmer until summer arrived. I'd have to wait for the fall season before ideal conditions would come around again.

To train for the climb, I made a list of all the V3 slab boulder problems I could find at Joshua Tree and frequented them as often as possible. Doing laps on these was a confidence booster, and my finger pads toughened up from all the crimping on minuscule edges. When I couldn't climb for a few days, I used a pet rock with a sharp edge and worked it as a pinch grip to keep the finger pads tough.

*Tony Sartin on Silver Spur, Joshua Tree National Park (5.12).*

On my initial attempts, it felt so thin, precarious, exposed, and scary that my jitters always sent me sliding off the holds. Strength wasn't the issue; it was performing such thin and balancy sequences with the fear of falling creeping in. I needed to relax and maintain composure. The key to success was simply to warm up properly, physically and psychologically: Practice the moves, then perform the sequences without getting nervous or scared. To warm up on the pitch, I'd hang and rest on each bolt until I was able to climb the entire pitch up to the anchor. I'd be doing all the moves, but resting in between.

Once I reached the anchor, I tried to toprope the pitch without falling, and made tic marks with chalk on all the key holds. Once I accomplished a no-falls toprope ascent, I pulled the rope for the redpoint.

On hard slab routes, tic marks can be extremely effective simply because the edges and holds are often very difficult to see. They can make a huge difference when the holds get ultrathin and nebulous. Just take the time to brush them off with a soft toothbrush after you're done so that the next climber can experience a tic mark–free, on-sight experience if he or she so desires. After all, what you consider your ultimate test piece might be just a warm-up for the next climber. As I often say, "One man's ceiling is another man's floor."

After many years trying, I finally redpointed Silver Spur in 2005. I've never been back up there, and I can't envision getting psyched enough or motivated enough to do a repeat ascent. As Royal Robbins once said, "The lure of the first is strong." As far as I know, it hasn't had a second ascent, but I'm sure the day will come when some virtuoso slab climber will flash the route on-sight.

## Steep Face Climbing

In my work with the AMGA's Single Pitch Instructor Program, I've served as an examiner for their Single Pitch Instructor Assessment. It's a two-day exam where the candidates are tested on a variety of categories, including technical scenarios, client care, risk management, and teaching skills. On day two the candidates are presented with clients and the goal is to accurately assess their abilities in a group setting in their role of instructor/guide.

Before this exam day I give candidates a list of potential topics and ask them to pick one for a lesson they'll present to the students. In one exam I had the opportunity to assess Wills Young, whose lesson was on face climbing technique. I've seen a lot of lessons on technique over the years, but Wills's stood out.

Wills was born in California but grew up in England, where he began face climbing on Gritstone. He moved back to California, living in Bishop for fourteen years where he honed his face climbing skills on the granite of the Buttermilks boulders. He migrated to Chattanooga, Tennessee, where he runs an outdoor guiding/indoor coaching business along with Lisa Rands out of the High Point Climbing and Fitness gyms.

I've often said that you don't need to run 100 meters in 10 seconds to be a great track and field coach—but it helps, especially if you can effectively convey your knowledge verbally and with demonstration. Wills is one of those coaches. He's one of the only humans to solve a V13 boulder problem, and he is able to clearly and effectively communicate the fundamental mechanics of advanced techniques to his students.

When Wills gave his presentation on face climbing techniques, I took notes. I can honestly say that it was one of the best presentations on climbing techniques I've seen, and I've seen a lot of them. I dug out the notes I'd scrawled down years ago.

Wills broke it down into these main principals:

1. Grip
2. Hip Position
3. The Push/Pull Principle
4. The Deadpoint Principle

When I began writing this book, I contacted Wills, who added some additional insights:

"I think what made/makes me a good face climber is the experience I gained as an older climber learning to excel on face and slab climbs before the climbing gyms changed the scene and steeper climbing became the fad. I was always baffled by overhangs because while I had strong fingers and good face-climbing technique, I had not developed the bigger muscles for the steeper boulders. But through extensive gym climbing and training I'm better at them now!"

"The ability to climb well on near vertical, roughly two-dimensional walls defines face-climbing skill. Flexibility of the hamstrings and hip turnout are key components to mastery. These components enable high-steps to be made between chosen footholds. Turnout is the ability to rotate the knees and toes outward to bring the hips closer to the wall, and is one of the most important attributes of a good face climber. This flexibility along with that of the hamstrings can be improved with practice and exercise. Static stretching ability is only half the battle: Look to strengthen your legs while climbing on easier terrain by stretching up onto the tips of your toes and raising your feet to high holds in order to build and maintain necessary muscle, and muscle memory, not just in your calves and thighs and butt, but in your obliques, and abs."

"Of course strength is slow to build, while technique can make a difference in a matter of days, hours, or even minutes! In order to get the most from the strength you have when face climbing, always identify key footholds, figure out how to get your weight on them, and make your legs do as much of the pushing as you possibly can. In this respect you might say face climbing resembles slab climbing, only steeper."

"The more I've learned about teaching technique, the more I realize how everything is interrelated and that technique is just a different kind of strength. Working technique builds the strength needed to use that technique."

## Face Holds

### CLOSED CRIMP

This is by far your strongest grip, formed by placing your thumb alongside, and slightly over, your forefinger. Your finger pads should be directly on top of the hold, with the fingers flexed and bent at almost a 90-degree angle at the knuckle joint. On difficult face routes you'll generally be able to only get two fingers on the holds, so the crimp is key to exerting maximum power.

*The basic crimp grip.*

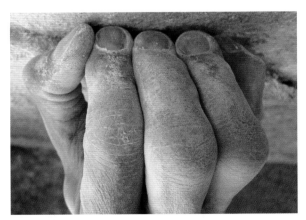

*Crimping a large edge. For maximum power, position your thumb at the tip of your forefinger, as shown here, or put your thumb on top of the tip of your forefinger.*

## OPEN-HANDED GRIP

For sloping holds the open-handed grip allows you to get more of your finger and hand skin in contact with rock, thereby increasing friction. The key is to stay below the hold to properly utilize it; you'll generate more friction when the elbow is down and against the wall and your weight is below it.

For training purposes, the open-handed grip is useful in that it puts less stress on the joints of the fingers, thereby reducing chances of developing finger joint problems and tendinitis.

*The open-handed grip is most useful on big, rounded, and sloping holds.*

*Climber on a steep face at Verdon Gorge, France.*

*John Long using the open-handed grip on heinously sloping holds. Stoney Point, California, 1983.*

## Hip Position

Hip position is the key to effective climbing technique for vertical and overhanging face climbing. Keeping your hips in to the wall takes weight off your arms—it's that simple. The goal is to put as much weight on the feet as possible throughout the climb. In most situations it's as easy as arching your back and consciously focusing on the position, much like the cobra position in yoga.

Focus on your center of gravity and how it changes when you shift the position of your hips. When doing a high step, lead with your hips, shifting them in to the wall and in the direction you're stepping, until your center of gravity has shifted to that upper foothold. Being aware of your hip position is one of the easiest ways to improve your performance on overhanging face climbs.

"Regarding hips being close to the wall," says Wills Young, "a point to understand is that when resting on face climbs, the hips need to be over the feet. But you need to create space between the hips and the wall, if possible, before you make your next move. As you move, you drive your hips toward the wall. This is critical, as a beginner mistake on big moves is to start a big movement with their hips very close to the wall. From that position, the momentum/trajectory of center of gravity can only be outward."

### HIP ROLL

If your hips are facing the wall, you're limited on how far you can reach up with one arm. For extended moves, you can gain a few inches by

*Ron Fawcett, perhaps the best British climber of the 1980s, with a classic hip roll on Crank City (V4) at Joshua Tree, 1984.*

*Hip and back flexibility is an asset for overhanging face technique, allowing you to put more weight on your feet and less on your arms.*

turning one hip into the wall. If you're reaching up with your left arm, turn your left hip in to the wall. You'll be able to reach several inches higher than if both hips are parallel to the wall. The opposite hand can be pulling straight down on a hold, or on a sidepull. If you're reaching up with your left hand, the left foot will naturally want to be positioned on the outside edge of the shoe.

### DROP KNEE

If you have knee problems, you'll want to be careful with this technique. It allows you to position your hip very close to the wall, using footholds that otherwise would seem out of position. If you're reaching up with your right hand, you can use a high

*Erik Kramer-Webb performs a drop knee on Big Mo (5.11b) at Joshua Tree.*

right foothold (using the outside edge of the boot); you swing your knee downward and roll your right hip in to the wall. Your left foot should be on the inside edge of the shoe. If you're utilizing a sidepull with your left hand, this technique will maximize your reach and keep your weight on your feet as you make the move.

### Push/Pull Technique

The combination of pulling with your arms while at the same time pushing off with your legs is another key for success on difficult face climbs. If you draw an imaginary triangle from your two upper handholds down to a single point in the plumb line, that is the spot you'll want to plant one of your feet, especially if the wall is devoid of edges for your feet and you're utilizing a smear. Paste your foot in that line and push with your leg as you pull with both arms.

You can also use your arms in a push/pull combination, pressing down with the lower arm as you pull with the upper arm.

Wills offers these valuable tips on the mechanics of advanced face climbing technique:

"One of the basic face climbing moves is front stepping, where you move your foot up to a foothold with the knee of that active foot pointing slightly or wholly out, thereby weighting your big toe or the inside edge of your climbing shoe as you step up. Hip turnout particularly helps in front stepping by allowing you to shift your weight sideways and to bring your butt over your heel to weight your foothold."

"In order to reduce strain on your hands when your weight is over your foot, use your trailing foot to help. With one foot placed high on the key hold, and the other hanging down against the rock, work the hip flexor of the lower leg to push inward on the rock with that low foot. This action turns your upper foothold into a fulcrum, rotating your upper body via your tightened core toward the wall, thereby allowing you to relax your grip or move your hands."

"This concept can be extended to slightly steeper face climbs, whereby you grip and pull with a high foot while pushing into the wall with a lower foot. The lower foot does not need to be placed on any specific hold to gain a benefit in this push-pull scenario. Always try to place that low foot in a position on the wall whereby you can make the move to the next handhold without having to drag the lower foot too much. If the handholds are large enough to allow, lean back, and place your lower foot high enough against the wall (with leg bent at the knee) so that that leg/foot can push you to the next hand hold, utilizing that same fulcrum concept."

"Likewise with the hands! Never forget your lower hand can push down while your upper hand pulls. It is a beginner mistake to

immediately let go with the lower hand as soon as a higher handhold is gained. The climber stuck between positions with one arm waving up into the air while the other arm strains to maintain position is a common sight though, even with experienced climbers. Better, in most cases, after reaching up to a new hold, is to maintain pressure or grip on the lower hold in order to move the feet to a new position or, by keeping that pressure, pushing downward on the lower hand, while pulling with the upper. This push-pull spreads the strain between your arms, utilizes different muscles, and will often help you gain enough height in precarious positions, to finally stabilize on the upper foot, let go with the lower hand and make a grab for the next available hand hold."

"Look for footholds with 'bite,' a rough texture, or a sharp or pointed edge, something that will dig into the sole of your shoe and provide tremendous grip. These are your go-to holds whenever possible; take advantage of them. Such

*Good technique on an overhanging arête—arms straight, hips in to the rock, pushing with the left foot.*

*1. John Long, dyno sequence at Stoney Point, 1983. First he plants his right foot and eyes the target hold.*

**2. In a single, powerful, fluid motion, he pulls with his arms and momentarily lets go with his left hand, latching the upper hold at the deadpoint.**

**3. After successfully latching the hold, it's time to reestablish footholds and carry on.**

edges don't have to be big; even small ones will provide a secure foothold. I will often choose a hold with bite over another that is twice its size if getting as much weight on that hold is critical."

### The Deadpoint Principal

Toss a ball up in the air. The moment the ball stops its upward progress and begins falling downward is the deadpoint.

In rock climbing, you can use this principal of physics to your advantage for dynamic moves. With perfect timing, at the moment the deadpoint occurs, you'll feel a sense of temporary weightlessness, albeit for a microsecond.

The deadpoint principal works when you're reaching up with one hand or attempting to dyno with both hands. In both instances, lead with the hips; as you pull with your arm or arms, focus on coordinating the upward movement by thrusting the hips in, toward the rock.

If making a move with one hand, unweight your hand momentarily, timing it to coincide with the deadpoint, then, at that very moment, latch the top hold.

For full-on two-handed dynos, focus also on your footholds, bending the knees slightly and pushing off with both legs to give you more of an upward trajectory.

The best way to master the deadpoint principal is in the bouldering arena, practicing dynamic moves.

### Mantles

For classic ledge mantles, look to see if the ledge slopes downward one way or the other. If the ledge is slightly lower to your right, it will be easier to get your right foot up on the ledge, which means the easiest mantle will be a left-hand mantle with your palm flat on the ledge, fingers pointing right. If the ledge is tiny, you can often make the mantle much easier by reaching up with the opposite hand (in this case the right hand) and finding an edge to crimp and pull down on.

If the ledge slopes downward to your left, it'll be easier to get your left foot up on the ledge, using a right-hand mantle, palm down on the ledge with your fingers pointing left.

If the ledge is wide enough and flat, it really doesn't matter what foot you step up with, and you can use both hands, about a foot apart, with palms pressed down and fingers pointing toward each other. Depending on the hold, sometimes it's best to flip the hand so that the wrist faces the wall and the fingers point outward.

## OVERHANGING MANTLE

Overhanging mantles involve a more dynamic technique. Grab the mantle hold with both hands and set your feet as high as possible, focusing on precision with your footwork and keeping as much weight as possible on the feet. In one fluid motion, pull hard with both arms; then, at the moment you're high enough, flip one elbow high enough so that the palm is pressing down. On difficult mantles with sloping and tiny holds, positioning the base of the palm opposite the thumb utilizes the small

*1. On an overhanging mantle, be especially cognizant of your feet as you move up, placing the feet precisely on the holds.*

*2. As soon as you're high enough, in one quick motion, rotate your elbow up and flip your palm onto the mantleshelf.*

**3. Lock your arm and lean in so that your upper body's center of gravity is directly over your palm.**

**4. Then step up. Flexibility will pay off on difficult mantles.**

bones at the base of the wrist. These bones are roughly shaped like a horseshoe and can be hooked on the best part of the hold.

## TRAINING FOR MANTLES

If you do a lot of gym climbing, mantling technique may be one of your weaknesses, since unlike bouldering, you're rarely topping out on a flat ledge. Training for mantle strength is all about triceps strength. Two exercises to isolate the triceps and develop mantling strength are triceps extensions and dips. A solid triceps extension routine is three sets of eight repetitions several times a week. Adjust your weight so that you're barely able to complete the last rep. For dips, if you can easily do three sets of fifteen reps, hang some weight from your waist for extra resistance.

# CHAPTER 2

# Crack Climbing, by Peter Croft

Crack climbing is the most mysterious of all climbing techniques. While face climbing roughly resembles ascending a ladder—in essence, grabbing onto the rock—cracks are all about plugging in. From birth, we viscerally have the idea of pulling on things—to get out of a crib, to scramble to the top of a tree, to climb out a window, or to escape from prison; it's an instinctive act.

Cracks, on the other hand, involve inserting our hands and feet in a variety of configurations into a variety of fissures—from the thinnest of fingertips, where much of the fight is about squeezing a meager amount of finger meat into mere slits, to chimney-width spelunking endeavors, where the physicality of Greco-Roman wrestling is mixed with the fun and games of claustrophobia.

Whatever size we're talking about, though, the prime directive in crack technique is to jam our digits and limbs whenever possible. When done properly, this means that when hanging off the rock, we are hanging off our skeleton more than our muscles. Instead of inserting our hands and fingers and trying to crimp the inside of the crack, we look for v-slots to jam our fingers or hands like a stopper, look for ways to use torque to add traction, and/or work to expand our hands into the jams by flexing key muscles—in much the same way a chuckwalla lizard flexes its belly to avoid being dragged from under a rock by a hungry coyote.

The central idea is attaching ourselves to rock less by clinging and more by camming our appendages into the rock. Done right, this involves using less strength than grabbing onto a hold. That a perfect hand jam, for example, could be a better, less-strenuous hold than a perfect jug may be a tough concept for a crack newbie to grasp. Think about it, though: Even a hyper-fit spider monkey must exert some effort to hold onto a branch. A pebble or a boulder jammed in a crack uses none. An imperfect analogy, perhaps, but it is essentially the concept we're after.

Even for those who have no ambition to become a crack climber and little desire to visit areas like Yosemite or Indian Creek, there are still reasons to become competent in these techniques.

On a trip to France, I visited one of their famous limestone crags to sample some of their sport routes. The route to do at this one cliff was a severely overhanging wall of small crimps and pockets marked at half height by a horizontal slash. When I arrived, a tall muscular German named Heinz was hard at work, going for his third attempt of the day. Impressed, I watched him savagely yard his way up on the initial tiny holds; but when he slapped for the horizontal he failed to clasp it and flew off, cursing mightily at the cliff and his cowering belayer. Over the course of the next hour, he tried it a couple more times but was unable to even

*Ron Kauk leads New Dimensions (5.11b) in Yosemite Valley.*

PHOTO BY GREG EPPERSON

momentarily stick the horizontal—clearly the crux move. From the ground it looked different. To me it appeared as though it would be possible to slot a decent hand jam. With the furious German done for the day, I tied in and started up. The initial wall was as fierce as it looked, powerful cranking on barely good enough fingerholds. Setting up for a long reach to the horizontal, I swung up and sunk my right hand deep into a lifesaving jam. Perfect! Forearms cooked from the bouldery climbing below, I simply switched off hand jams back and forth till my forearms had de-pumped, and then surged through to the top. Back on the ground, I made the mistake of making eye contact with Heinz, who was red in the face and looked ready to hit someone or anything. To him it just made no sense. What for him was the illusive crux move of the route turned out to be the one place I could cop a rest; that, in turn, allowed me, with fresh arms, to punch through to the top.

The act of jamming ourselves into the stone is a weird, maybe even creepy image to absorb, but it is an essential technique if one aspires to many of the great routes of the world. I know what you're thinking. You're adding to that creepiness the grit-your-teeth expectation of pain—most likely a lot of it! This brings us to a cardinal rule of jamming technique:

## Pain Avoidance

One of the essential skills of the seasoned crack climber is the ability to find jams that are relatively pain-free. I've heard all sorts of pseudo-experts say that you just have to deal with the pain, even embrace it. I've even heard that pain is just fear leaving the body; that one's a real pearl! It's all bunk, though! Sure, there will sometimes be some pain—just as with walking barefoot on the beach—but by treading carefully, we try to minimize it. Think how you wince and tense up when you step on a sharp rock; indeed, whenever you experience any pain. Usually that tensing up doesn't exhaust you too much because you can stop what you're doing and deal with it. On a long, strenuous hand crack, though, that suffering will unnecessarily cost you a lot of extra strength. And unless you've got the mind control of a Shaolin monk, there is no ignoring it—and certainly no embracing it!

## Footwork

Although the same principle of pain avoidance applies to the feet, the methods are different. The biggest mistakes, pain-wise, that people make with their crack footwork are over-jamming and wearing soft shoes.

Over-jamming the feet is a common mistake largely because people forget they have sticky rubber on the sides of their shoes. That means you can twist your feet into what looks like a marginal slot and they will likely stick. Experimenting by placing them closer to the outside of a foot slot will quickly teach you how secure these foot jams really are, how comfortable they can be—and how you might avoid being the stuck-foot guy who needs a rescue. Don't laugh; it's happened before!

The key to effective foot jamming is to insert the foot with instep facing up. This makes it easy to get our weight right over our feet. Watch someone try it the other way, with the outside edge of the foot facing up, and you can see that it pushes their weight off to one side—off their feet and onto their arms.

Although you can find all kinds of photos in magazines, books, and online showing crack fiends advocating pumping cracks in soft slippers, it does not mean this is the way to go for all jamming routes. Those pics are of seasoned climbers on particular routes where ultrathin slippers are an advantage. Watch those same climbers on a hand, fist, and off-width route, and they will be wearing something different and telling a different story. For the aspiring crack climber, a more comfortable (toes

*Foot jamming in a hand-size crack. Practice will help you find the line between over-jamming and security.*

able to lie flat) and stiffer shoe will help you climb more and harder with a smile on your face. On top of comfort, a shoe fit like this means a lower toe profile (than a slipper with bunched up toes), which translates into being able to insert your toe deeper and more reliably into a slot.

## Milking the Jam

No, this is not about adding dairy to raspberry preserves. This is about initial contact between hand and stone. A classic mistake that newbies make is to toss a hand at a sharp jam and immediately tug on

it. That would be wrong. Instead you want to take the time to feel inside the crack and experiment with a number of slight variations that still feel secure—milking it—until you find a jam that is at least relatively pain-free. Once the groping is complete, set your hand firmly in place—and yard on it! Without the effort of cringing, you can reach further with less effort. You will also look way cooler and smoother in case anybody is watching.

That brings us to another cardinal rule:

## Don't Be So Awkward

Do any activity awkwardly and, as with pain, you will expend extra effort. Stand, walk, or sit awkwardly and you will lose strength. Guys: Think how much embarrassing effort it takes to be awkward around pretty girls!

Although it is possible to pretzel ourselves into gimpiness on all sorts of climbs, it seems especially common on crack climbs. Part of this may be the way a crack system leans or because of the barn-door effect of having to place each limb in a direct line. It might also be due to the angle at which the crack slices into the rock or when the crack pinches off and we simply get crossed up by picking a bad sequence. No matter how we arrived there, once we established awkwardness, the clock started ticking faster; in other words, we began losing strength a lot quicker.

Much exhaustion (and drama) can be avoided by doing things you should already be doing when you face climb. Plan ahead: Look for stemming opportunities, footholds, potential rests and sequences. In short, don't rush into a junk show or dead end that you'll have to battle out of. Another handy technique from sport climbing is to flag one of your feet out for balance. This is helpful in all sorts of crack climbing situations but is especially helpful in cracks that go straight up and where each hand and foot is placed directly above each other. Many climbers think that is what you are supposed

to do—and sometimes it works. It's crack climbing, so just use the crack. But sometimes, as the previously mentioned barn-door effect comes into play, the body feels like it's about to swing sideways. At this point, or preferably just before, throw one foot out for balance, not on a specific hold but just far enough to prevent any tendency to barn-door around. Staying plugged solely into the crack and fighting the barn door is picking a fight you don't need to have.

## Finger Cracks

Of all types of jamming, finger cracks are the easiest for the face climber to become proficient at. Often the slots and pockets we find in these fissures resemble the pocket climbing found on many sport routes. Also, when the crack becomes too thin to jam and/or becomes offset, lieback moves—kissing cousins of side holds on face routes—will often see us through.

Finger cracks cover any size from ones you can barely get a bit of fingertip skin into all the way to the ones where the finger can be inserted all the way to the third knuckle (where the finger meets the hand). Clearly this will vary from person to person. Although everyone hits a bad size now and then, this is definitely a type of climbing that favors those with tiny hands. A nice and secure finger jam for a spider monkey is going to be an impossible fingernail seam for a gorilla.

As with other types of cracks, milking the jam will unleash its full power. What at first might feel loose and sloppy or just a bit too thin can, once the milking is done, feel completely locked in. This makes such a difference because of the variability of how uniform the insides of the crack are in conjunction with the irregularities of our own fingers. It could be as subtle as a bit of finger callous getting a bit more bite on a crystal or as lifesaving as a pinky jam finally sinking past the first joint—taking the crack from desperately marginal

*In ultrathin cracks, even if you can't get your toes in the crack, torqueing the rand of your shoe against any offset or into any pocket in the crack can make a huge difference.*

to comparatively bomber. In essence, milking allows us to get more meat in and also make it as comfortable as we can.

There are two basic ways to jam finger and hand cracks: thumbs up and thumbs down.

### Thumbs-up Jamming (Listen up; this is important!)

In all kinds of climbing—hell, in all types of movement—it is essential that we move in a way that allows us to move as our bodies are made to do, in a way that allows us to maximize our potential. When climbing finger and hand cracks, the cornerstone of efficient jamming is going thumbs up as often as possible. In climbing how-to literature, there is a lot of waffling as to which is best: thumbs up or down? The implication is that perhaps it doesn't make a whole lot of difference. This could not be further from the truth.

Watch any person walking. The way he or she swing the arms? The palms face inward (toward the other hand). If the person swings the arms up high enough, the hands are in a thumbs-up position—more or less, ready to jam. Not a good enough analogy? How about if you watch someone do a one-arm pull-up or a one-arm hang? That's right, the hand is essentially in a thumbs-up position. To belabor the point, imagine a fingerboard that has jams instead of fingerholds. Now imagine trying to do a pull-up with both hands thumbs down; after a certain point of awkwardness there is that nagging sensation that either your elbows or your shoulders are going to blow. Now picture trying that same pull-up with both hands thumbs up. By comparison, it feels like some kind of mellow yoga that's good for you. Basically, this is how your skeleton likes to move—so you should too!

Another bit of wonderfulness about thumbs up is that it allows you to reach farther and with less effort. Done thumbs down, a sinker hand or finger jam is good for pulling down to approximately face level, maybe a little bit more if you grit your teeth. Try that same jam thumbs up and you can easily take it down to mid-chest; if you pivot off it and turn it into an undercling jam, you can take it right down to your unmentionables. With practice, this technique can allow us to reach close to a body length—a nice trick to have if the crack pinches off for 5 feet or so. This also means that you can do a jam crack in far fewer moves and in far less time. Say, for example, that you have roughly 20 minutes of strength left on a 5.10c hand crack, and going thumbs down took you 25 minutes. Well then, you pump out, you fall, and you lose. Now you take that same crack and same fitness and go thumbs up. This time pulling, say, 30 or 40 percent fewer moves, you're up in 15 minutes. That's right—you

win! Now couple that extra reach with the fact that a thumbs-up jam requires less strength. Remember the fitness buffs showing off that one-arm pull-up power in what is basically a thumbs-up configuration? They do that because it is the most ergonomic—and easiest—way to do it.

Long story short, with thumbs-up jamming you can go farther, faster, and with less effort.

### Thumbs-up Finger Jamming

As the name implies, this is when we insert our fingers with the thumb pointing up. Apart from the benefits listed above, this is usually advantageous

**Thumb-up finger jamming in an offset corner.**

in very thin cracks where we are trying to wiggle the thinnest parts of our skinniest fingers into the tiniest of slots. Wiggling (milking) that jam often allows us to at least get that first knuckle in. Once that is achieved, it allows more of our weight to hang off our skeleton instead of just our muscles. These ultrathin crack scenarios are often referred to as pinky jamming, meaning we are primarily using our pinky and neighboring ring finger, as these digits are thinner than our index and middle fingers. Thumbs-up is also useful in situations where the crack is offset. For instance, when jamming a straight-in crack where the right facet of that crack sticks farther out, the right hand would be inserted thumbs up and the left thumbs down. This allows both hands to articulate without the offset getting in the way.

### Thumbs-down Finger Jamming

Sometimes the crack is simply more suited to a thumbs-down jam. For instance, when a crack angles up and right, it is usually easiest to go thumbs down with the right while going thumbs up with the left. There will be other times when the particular shape and size of the slot simply demands the camming action of the thumbs-down jam to make it secure. Experimentation will give you the answer.

Thumbs down also gives us extra torque, which is especially useful in cracks that are on the verge of being a bit too big for our digits. By inserting our fingers in this way, the natural camming action that occurs when we pull down in effect makes our fingers a little bigger, making the jam more secure. Off course we can use thumbs-down jamming in any finger cracks where we want the extra camming, but in the thinnest jams the benefits of that camming are outweighed by the fact that the primary jammers in thumbs down are our thickest fingers.

At the outer limits (size-wise) of finger cracks are the rattly finger cracks. These can be anywhere from less than 1 inch to 1.25 inches, depending

*The great Japanese climber Hidetaka Suzuki thumbs-down finger jamming on Yosemite Valley's Cosmic Debris (5.13a) in 1987.*

on the size of your fingers. "Rattly" means that no matter how much you adjust or milk the jam, you cannot make it solid; it just feels rattly. In these situations, you almost always go thumbs down; but before you add the extra torque and twist down on it, try to squeeze your thumb under your index and middle fingers. Once your thumb is inserted as well as possible, twist down on it. This camming action expands this three-finger combo, hopefully making it stick. This is called a "finger stack," or "ring lock." Because there is not that much finger flesh in contact with the rock, this is one of the most precarious

*The finger stack, or ring lock, seen from inside the crack.*

jams—and therefore one of the most difficult to become proficient at. This is also the zone where finger jamming often merges into hand jamming. In other words, it is a size of crack where you often need to choose between finger stacking and thin hand jams. Because of the extra surface area of your hand in contact with the rock, thin hand jams will be more secure.

## Hand Jamming

Simply put, hand jams are the king of jams. Become proficient at hand size and you will find that they are not only the best jams you can find but also the best hold of any type you can find on the rock. It is the best jam you can find because there is more surface area and more of an expansion ratio than in finger or fist jams. This ability to expand the size

of your hand is mostly due to the (relatively) large muscle in your hand that articulates the thumb. When you draw the thumb across the hand toward the pinky finger, that muscle fattens up. When this is done inside a crack, the hand expands to fit the crack, lodging it in place. This jam is also the best type of hold because, while even the best jug is only good for a downward (and perhaps outward) pull, a good hand jam is good in every direction—up, down, sideways. You are truly plugged in.

A common mistake is trying to make the jam secure by bending the fingers and pressing the fingertips against the rock. This makes proper execution of the hand jam a bit awkward, as well as making it difficult to fully flex (expand) that thumb muscle. It also unnecessarily tires the fingers. Simply put, it will exhaust you faster.

Adding to the security of these jams is the fact that these size cracks make for easy and quick placement of the feet, more or less wherever you want to place them. This makes it convenient if you want to have a secure foot jam low—say, for placing gear—or high if you want to make a big reach to bypass a thin section or simply to move fast. Because of these factors, hand jamming allows us to climb a long pitch faster than any other type of jamming. This isn't about bragging rights regarding what a fast climber you are. It's about the ability to move efficiently (and rapidly) up a stretch of stone, which means you will be able to spend less time in strenuous situations, which in turn means you will be able to go farther with less effort.

There are different types of hand jams—from thin hands, where it is barely possible to squeeze in a small portion of our hands, all the way to the rattly wide hand scenarios where nothing seems to stick.

### Thin Hands

Right away, we have to decide whether to go thumbs up or thumbs down—thumbs up for extra reach or thumbs down for extra camming action. With a dodgy jam, the extra camming action seems

*Crimson Cringe (5.12a), a classic Yosemite Valley hand crack. Climber: John Mallery.*

like a good deal, and sometimes it is, but going thumbs down also effectively makes the jamming portion of the hand a bit thicker, meaning we can't squeeze in quite as much meat. Experimentation and practice—a lot of it—will make the decision easier. Whichever configuration we pick, milking that jam will be the key to making it solid enough to pull on.

## Wide Hands

Once again we have to pick between thumbs up and down, and once again the answer is usually thumbs down. While it is possible to go thumbs up, the only way to add security to the sloppiness is to press our fingers against the rock—too much effort! The camming action as we pull down on that thumbs-down wide hand jam tries to rotate the hand into a fist jam; when the hand can't rotate anymore, it cams in place and locks us in.

# Fist Jams

As the name implies, these are jams in which we use a clenched fist. With these jams, however, it is a choice of palm up or palm down. In other words, the sides of our fists are in contact with the rock. As the solidity of these jams is roughly the same either way, and the ability to make a long reach is similar as well, it is more of what feels less awkward. Depending on the angle and/or the diagonaling nature of the crack, one might feel better than the other. In general, though, it usually works best to go palm up on the lower hand, palm down on the upper, and shuffle them upward in that method.

Because there is some variability in how big or small you can make your fist, there will be some variability in the sizes of cracks you will be able use for fist jams. Past the outer limits of your own fist size are what some call rattly fists, which aren't really fists at all. That size is the beginning of what is perhaps the most mysterious (and terrifying) type of crack climbing: off-widths.

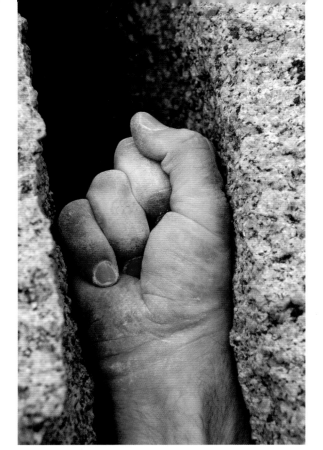

*Palm-up fist jam.*

*Palm-down fist jam.*

## Off-widths

These are cracks in the netherworld between fist jams and chimneys. No fist jam will stick, and you can never quite get your whole body inside.

While hand and finger cracks have most face climbers scratching their heads at first, off-width cracks add gut-wrenching nausea to the picture. This is because every part of your body comes into play. Go to failure in an off-width is like battling a giant anaconda—and losing. Whereas in face climbing finger, hand, and fist cracks, we use just our hands and feet, in off-width cracks (and chimneys) we use the works: knees, heels, shoulders, butt cheeks, and anything else that works. With so many options, it is easy at first to pick the wrong combination and get so crossed up that you end up battling yourself. A common mistake is to try make the same big moves we use in face climbing or, say, hand and finger cracks. In off-widths it is important to make much smaller moves in order to make progress.

Once the crack gets too wide for fists, we need to pick which side we want to go in with. Next, the easiest option is to insert a leg, aiming to get the knee in, if possible, and then the whole arm. Now bend the forearm, aiming to bring the fist back toward the shoulder. This flexing of the arm muscles should be a bit thicker than your fist and will jam securely in that rattly fist size.

As the crack gets wider, it is possible to get in a little deeper and use the "chicken wing." Basically, this means performing the previous maneuver but trying to get the heel of your palm on the edge of the crack in front of you. Once planted at around shoulder height, this will lock you in place. The

Tony Sartin on Pratt's Crack (5.9), Pine Creek, California.

*Erik Kramer-Webb displays a classic "chicken wing" on Hobbit Hole (5.10), Joshua Tree, California. Note the heel-toe jam.*

outside free hand simply grips the outside crack edge. The outside foot should stay low in the crack. On this size crack you should be able to easily insert the inside knee, bring it up high in the crack, bend it, and lock yourself in place.

*Heel-toe jam.*

*Dual heel-toe jams.*

As the crack gets progressively wider, it becomes possible to use our feet in a heel-toe position. This involves putting our foot toe down into the crack and then, once lightly wedged, pushing down on our heels. This is one situation in particular where stiffer (and hopefully high-top) shoes are a godsend. This heel-toe action locks our feet into a solid platform. In all, there are too many configurations to list here.

Now, as the crack widens a bit more, we can wiggle our whole body inside. This where the crack becomes a chimney.

## Chimneys

Once we are able to get completely inside, the battle isn't over, but in general it does become a bit easier. This is due in large part to there being a lot more surface area in contact with the rock. In narrower chimneys, we should be able to use the previously mentioned heel-toe jam to great effect. The chicken wings we used in the wider off-widths also become useful in narrower chimneys. Once the chimney gets wider, we'll use variations of this move, bringing our arms below our shoulders, cocking the elbows closer to waist height against the wall behind us while camming the heels of our hands against the wall in front.

As the chimney widens further and becomes too wide for the heel-toe jams to work, we need to cock our feet behind us and wedge our knees in front. This is where knee pads would come in handy, but for the most part it's not actually the kneecap we use (which would hurt as much as it sounds) but the head of the quadriceps, which is much more stable and comfortable. In this manner we can use counterpressure, squirming frog-like. In fact, if you've ever seen a frog (or, better yet, a bat), take note—they are excellent chimney-ers.

As the chimney widens and it is possible to look around, take note of any footholds. Remember, though, because the name of the game is

*Roy McClennehan wriggles up 1096 (5.10d) in Yosemite Valley.*

*Erik Kramer-Webb demonstrates both heel-toe and knee-foot combinations on a flared chimney.*

counterpressure, even the smallest of shallow friction scoops can be used for footholds in opposition to firmly planted butt cheeks on the wall behind you. Alternating hands pushing in front and behind in combination with the feet is the technique here.

When the chimney widens further yet, we need to span the two walls by stemming between the two, one hand and foot on either side—as airy as it sounds! As with other types of chimneys (and off-widths), smaller moves will be the key to more-secure moves and less-strenuous movement.

## Liebacks

This technique is used mostly on inside corners, both hands pulling on the edge of the crack while pushing against the wall in front with the feet. Although a relatively simple technique, this is strenuous stuff—it effectively pits your arms against your own legs, working in opposition. Adding to the burl factor is that your feet will feel more solid

*Carmen Cendejas liebacks on Norm, (5.10a), Joshua Tree, California.*

**Back in the EB and swami-belt days, Charlie Peterson demonstrates good liebacking technique on Wheat Thin (5.10c), one of Yosemite Valley's classic liebacks.**

the higher they are; but the higher they are, the more weight is on your arms. Twisting the inside foot into the crack whenever possible and looking

for any footholds for the outer foot will allow you to keep your feet lower (less strenuous). Because of its strenuousness and the fact that the very nature of liebacking pushes us away from being able to look in the crack, makes it hard to stop and place gear. This is why the less-strenuous, although often more-technical, jamming is preferable (whenever possible) when leading. No matter what, before launching out on that lieback, spy out what you're heading for: a ledge, a good foothold, a hand jam—anything that allows you to stop, rest, and get that gear in.

## Placing Gear

For those with minimal leading experience, take note of something that helped me survive my early climbing years. Whenever I stopped to place gear, immediately after getting something in and clipped, I would place another piece. That way I'd have the confidence of two good pieces, side by side, in case I misread a sequence or didn't find the rest hold I was hoping for.

One of the great things about crack climbing is that often you can place gear where you want rather than having to punch it to the next bolt. Another plus is that you can usually place gear where it's easy to place and clip. The mistake many people make is trying to place gear too high. This makes it much more strenuous. Imagine making peanut butter sandwiches on top of the fridge for the whole family—not a rest-day activity! How about at a waist-height counter top? Easy-peasy! Placing gear way up high also means it's easier to pick the wrong size, and it requires way more effort to clip the rope. As much as possible, place gear hanging off straight arm (thumbs up if you can), right in front of your face. It's easier to get it right on the first try and a lot easier to clip.

## Practice Makes Perfect

When venturing into any foreign activity, it is essential to start easy. This is true whether learning a new language or becoming an astronaut. We start at a very basic level, and maybe one day we'll get to the moon. Climbers often try to be the exception to the rule, reckoning that if they can climb, say, 5.10 face, they should be able to jump on 5.10 cracks. Wrong! All that is gained by this approach is a crushed ego and lots of scar tissue. The reason we learn by baby steps is that we acquire skill by repetition—lots of it. Hurling ourselves at something that is far too difficult is akin to learning Russian while hanging on a fingertip edge—we don't have enough time and/or strength to learn much of anything. Much better to err on the side of something being a bit too easy and then pumping laps.

We don't teach a child to ride a bike while chucking rocks at her. Likewise, we don't need the extra drama of having to lead while acclimatizing ourselves to the weirdness of jamming. Toprope when you can. Remember, lots of repetition is the key to something becoming instinctual. That is when your climbing jumps to another level—that point where instinct takes over from conscious thought.

# Taping Up

Crack climbing can be brutal on the hands, especially in a place like Joshua Tree. Taping up will help you milk the jams without ripping your skin. Tincture of benzoin (Cramer Tuf-Skin comes in a spray-on version) will help the tape job stick.

Rubber crack gloves are becoming more popular; modern designs are thinner and better than the clunkier versions of the past.

If you tape your hands too tightly, it will impede circulation and you'll get pumped faster. In this sequence, Joshua Tree guide Erik Kramer-Webb demonstrates one method of taping that allows good hand circulation.

*1. Start with a strip across the knuckles.*

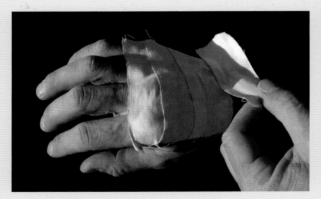

*2. Continue laying tape down toward the wrist.*

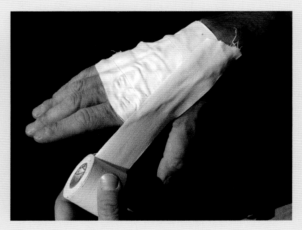

*3. Lay a strip down between the thumb and forefinger.*

*4. Bring it back around between the thumb and forefinger.*

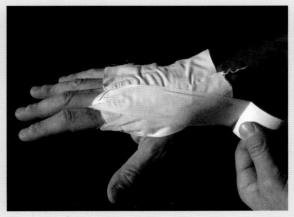

*5. Smooth out the wrinkles.*

6. Make a strip between the pinky and ring finger.

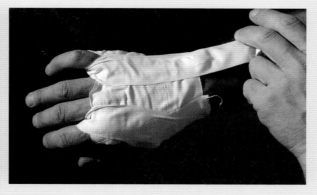

7. Bring the strip back down to the wrist.

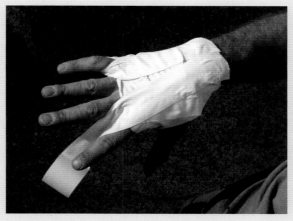

8. Make another strip between the index and middle fingers.

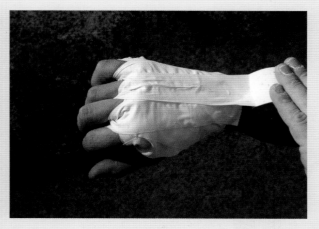

9. Make another strip between the middle and ring fingers.

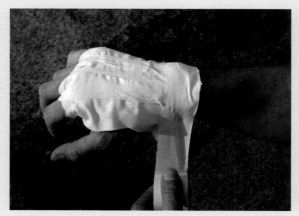

10. Wrap the tape around the wrist, but not so tightly as to compromise hand circulation and wrist flexion.

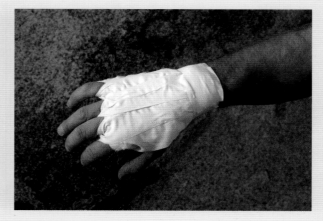

11. Good to go!

# CHAPTER 3

# Rope, Slings, Cord, and Carabiners

## Rope

### History

Mountaineering's first golden age ended abruptly on July 14, 1865. For Edward Whymper, who led a team of seven climbers up the first ascent of Switzerland's Matterhorn—at the time the last great unclimbed peak in the Alps—both triumph and tragedy were his fate on that great and dreadful summer's day. Theirs was the first ascent of the icy pyramid—the greatest achievement in alpine climbing at the time, and for Whymper perhaps the sweetest victory, for after a dozen attempts he now stood on the summit, jubilant, gazing down on the tiny gingerbread town of Zermatt far below.

The euphoric climbers, all seven tied together with manila ropes, began a tedious descent. One of the party suddenly slipped, pulling several of the others off. While Whymper held fast, clinging to a rock outcrop to avoid being yanked into the abyss, the rope broke, sending four climbers to their death. The three survivors were saved from a tragic fate by the weak rope, since they were unanchored and had no belay. Some speculated that the rope had been cut with a knife, but a formal investigation and inspection of the rope revealed that the cord had simply parted—broken under the strain.

The fallen were later buried in the Zermatt cemetery; the Matterhorn soars above as their tombstone for all time.

Through the late nineteenth and early twentieth centuries, climbing ropes were made from natural fibers like hemp, manila, and sisal. While strong enough for many applications, these ropes were ill-suited to the rigors of climbing and were subject to mildew and rot.

Nylon, also known by the generic name polyamide, was developed by the DuPont company in 1935. Modern nylon climbing and rappelling ropes that could actually hold up to the forces generated by leader falls were first manufactured in the 1940s, coinciding with the availability of high-quality "nylon 6," allowing the construction of lighter weight ropes that could stretch to absorb great forces and hold more than 2 tons. Nylon is still by far the best material for rock climbing ropes due to

*My first rope—the classic Goldline.*

its ability to stretch and absorb the forces created in a fall, making it superior to any other yarns currently available for this application.

Polyester, patented in 1941, has less stretch than nylon; it is widely used today in the manufacture of low-stretch ropes used in applications where dynamic properties are not required.

My first climbing rope, which I bought in the 1970s, was a three-strand nylon rope with the brand name Goldline. The three-strand twisted construction (called laid construction) consisted of three strands of twisted filaments spiraled into a singular rope. These ropes stretched considerably under body weight, and if you were rappelling or prusiking without contact to the rock, the spiral construction resulted in a dizzying spin.

## Kernmantle Ropes

The big step up in rope technology came in 1953 with the advent of the first kernmantle rope, made in Europe. The kernmantle design consists of an outer, tightly woven sheath (mantle) over a core of twisted, parallel fibers (kern). The core of the rope provides most of the rope's strength; the sheath protects the core from abrasion and damage, and reduces friction as the rope runs through carabiners

**Deconstructed kernmantle rope showing the braided white interior core under the more tightly woven sheath.**

and rappel devices. The kernmantle rope handles better and is more durable than a rope with laid construction.

During the 1950s and into the golden age of big wall climbing in Yosemite during the 1960s, Goldline ropes were still the standard, as they were about one-third the price of kernmantle ropes. By the late 1960s and early 1970s, having become more widely manufactured and distributed, with a correspondingly lower price, kernmantle ropes had become the standard climbing rope worldwide.

Today the kernmantle rope is the standard design used in climbing, rappelling, caving, canyoneering, vertical rope access, fixed lines, rescue, and life safety ropes. These ropes are made from nylon, polyester, or a combination of these and other synthetic yarns.

There are three basic types of kernmantle ropes: dynamic, low-stretch, and static. A dynamic rope is required for situations where a high-impact force can be generated—such as in a leader fall—and therefore is the standard rope for rock climbing, ice climbing, and mountaineering, where the rope will be used for belayed climbing and rappelling. A dynamic rope will typically stretch about 26 to 36 percent during a leader fall (dynamic elongation) and around 7 to 11 percent under body weight (static elongation).

## Unicore Ropes

In 2013 the Beal Rope Company introduced a line of ropes called Unicore, where the sheath is permanently bonded to the core. This new design prevents sheath slippage and, if the sheath is cut, prevents the sheath from fraying or unraveling. Beal manufactures both dynamic and low-stretch Unicore ropes. I've used the low-stretch version extensively for toproping in my climbing school at Joshua Tree, an area with extremely coarse granite that can easily fray and cut rope sheaths, and found these ropes to be very durable. I've also found the low-stretch Unicore design supple enough to

# Dynamic Rope Types

Dynamic ropes are sold in single, double, and twin configurations.

A **single rope** (marked on the label with a "1" inside a circle), the most commonly used rope for rock climbing and rappelling, is used as a single strand.

A **half rope** (marked on the label with a "½" inside a circle), used primarily for alpine rock climbing and mountaineering, consists of a pair of ropes; both are tied into the leader, who alternates clipping one strand at a time into protection. This configuration reduces rope drag through protection and allows the leader to belay two followers at the same time, each of whom is tied to one strand. It also provides two full-length ropes to facilitate a rappel descent.

A **twin rope** (marked with two overlapping circles), used primarily in alpine climbing, should only be used with the two strands together; each climber ties into both strands, and both strands are clipped into points of protection. The big advantage is that a twin rope allows for retrievable rappels for the length of the rope; it also is lighter than a half rope. A single strand should not be used alone, however.

exhibit good handling characteristics, and it holds knots well.

The Unicore rope would be a good choice for big wall climbing, since the lead climbing rope is typically tied off and used for jumaring as the second cleans the pitch. Any fixed line is more susceptible to being cut over an edge, and high up on a wall, this could be disastrous.

## UIAA and CE Certification for Dynamic Ropes

Dynamic ropes sold for rock climbing are tested and certified to UIAA (Union Internationale des Associations d'Alpinisme) and CE (Certified for Europe) standards and should bear the UIAA or CE certification on the label. This means the rope has been tested and certified by a "third party" at one of three UIAA-approved testing facilities to meet the European Norm (EN) 892 and UIAA-101 standard for dynamic rope. To receive this certification, the rope sample must survive *at least* five UIAA drop tests. This test is done by taking an 80 kg (176 lbs.) weight, attaching it to one end of a 9-foot length of rope, then raising it 8½ feet above the anchor and dropping it 15 feet over a 10mm diameter bar (similar to a carabiner) that is anchored approximately

1 foot above where the rope end is anchored. This simulates a fall factor of 1.7 (total distance of the fall divided by the length of rope in the system), which is a very severe fall in climbing situations.

For a single rope, during the first drop the peak impact force on the rope is measured and must be less than or equal to 12 kilonewtons (kN) (8 kN for a half rope with a weight of 55 kg), with a corresponding stretch of less than or equal to 40 percent. Twin ropes have the same requirements as a single rope but must survive at least twelve drops without breakage. In addition to the stringent drop test requirements, sheath slippage can be no more than 1 percent, and static elongation under an 80 kg (176 lbs.) load can be no more than 10 percent for a single rope and no more than 12 percent for a half or twin rope.

To the best of my knowledge, the only documented rope failures among UIAA-certified ropes were ropes that were cut over sharp edges and one rope with known pre-exposure to sulfuric acid.

## Static and Low-Stretch Ropes

For many years the term "static rope" was used to define any low-stretch rope typically used as a rescue rope or as a fixed line for rope access,

*Climbing shops sell static and low-stretch ropes from spools, cut to the length you desire.*

with virtually no stretch under a person's body weight rappelling down the rope. For example, the Sterling Rope company's ½-inch diameter HTP Static rope stretches only 0.8 percent with a 300-pound load and has a safe working load (SWL) of 908 pounds, which is one-tenth of its MBS of 9,081 pounds.

A static rope, by definition, is just that—static, with *very* low stretch; think of it almost like a wire cable. Because of their stiffness, static ropes generally have poor handling characteristics and are typically used only for fixed lines and haul lines, where dynamic properties are not required. A static rope should never be used for lead climbing or toproping, where it may be subject to any impact force; it should be used only for applications where stretch is not required.

## LOW-STRETCH ROPES

The Cordage Institute defines low-stretch as a rope with an elongation between 6 and 10 percent at 10 percent of the rope's MBS. Since a low-stretch rope has relatively little stretch (usually 3 to 4 percent under body weight) compared to a dynamic rope, it is a great choice if you're using it just for a fixed line or hauling. Low-stretch ropes are an excellent choice for rigging extensions for toprope anchors, toproping and fixed-line rope soloing, where some stretch is desired to add an element of shock absorption to the rope system.

## CE EN 1891

On both static and low-stretch ropes manufactured in Europe, the CE label indicates the rope has passed testing in accordance with EN (European Norm) 1891. There are two types of EN 1891 certifications: Type A and Type B. To receive an EN 1891 Type A rating, the rope must have a minimum diameter of 10mm and be able to hold at least 22 kN (4,495 lbs.). A Type A rope must also be tested to withstand five factor 1 falls with a weight of 100 kilograms (220 lbs.) on the end of the rope. The

rappelling, and life safety. As rope manufacturers developed new techniques and technologies to create better low-stretch ropes, the terms "static rope," "low-stretch rope," "low-elongation rope," and "semi-static rope," often used interchangeably, became somewhat ambiguous, especially since all ropes have some stretch, so a more precise definition was needed.

The Cordage Institute, an international rope industry association that disseminates industry standards, defines two categories of non-dynamic ropes: static and low-stretch.

## STATIC ROPES

Static is defined as rope with a maximum elongation of less than 6 percent at 10 percent of the rope's minimum breaking strength (MBS). New technology allows manufacturers to create ropes fall factor is the total distance of the fall divided by the length of the rope that comes into play during the fall.

What is a fall factor 1? Let's say you're standing on a bridge. You are tied to one end of a 200-foot rope and the other end is attached to the bridge at the level where you're standing. You step off the bridge and fall the length of the rope. You've fallen 200 feet until the rope comes tight. Total distance of the fall (200 feet) divided by the length of the rope to the anchor (200 feet) equals a fall factor of 1.

An EN 1891 Type B–certified rope is between 8 and 9.9 millimeters in diameter and must be able to hold at least 18 kN (4,045 lbs.) and withstand five factor 1 falls with a weight of 80 kilograms (176 lbs.) on the end of the rope.

## Dynamic, Low-Stretch, or Static

The following criteria will help you assess which rope is best for your specific application.

A dynamic rope is required for situations where you'll be using the rope for leading. My preferred rope for toproping, rigging, hauling, and fixed-line applications is a low-stretch rope. I look for a rope with CE EN 1891 Type A certification, with a diameter of between 10 and 10.5 millimeters, to be compatible with various belaying and rappelling devices. I also check the rope's suppleness to ensure the rope will hold knots firmly and handle well. Sterling makes an excellent low-stretch polyamide (nylon) rope called the Safety Pro.

## Diameter and Sheath Percentage

Ropes sold for rock climbing commonly range from 9 to 11 millimeters, with the most popular diameter around 9.8 millimeters. Thinner ropes generally stretch more and cut more easily over sharp edges. A thicker diameter rope also affords more friction when used with rappelling devices.

Many manufacturers now provide information on the sheath's percentage of the total weight. A rope with a higher percentage of sheath (40 percent or more) will generally be more durable than one with a lower sheath percentage.

## Sharp Edge Resistance

The UIAA has developed a new, optional test for manufacturers to receive a "sharp edge resistant" certification. The test is very similar to the UIAA drop test, although instead of dropping the rope over a rounded bar simulating a carabiner, a sharp edge is used. This is a pass or fail test, and although not a true indicator of durability, it's a good measure of the rope's ability to resist slicing over sharp rock edges. As mentioned earlier, some of the only documented cases of modern climbing ropes breaking in the field have been when the rope was cut over a sharp edge.

## Static Elongation

This is a measure of how much the rope stretches under a weight of 80 kilograms (176 lbs.), telling you how much your rope will stretch when you hang or rappel on the rope. For fixed line applications, I prefer a low-stretch rope with a static elongation of around 3 to 4 percent. Most dynamic climbing ropes have a static elongation of about 8 or 9 percent.

## Dry or Non-Dry

When nylon gets wet, it absorbs water, which weakens the fibers. Nylon ropes can lose much of their strength when wet (usually at least 30 percent; some studies show more than 50 percent loss of strength), so manufacturers sell ropes with a "dry coating" to keep the rope from absorbing water and make it more abrasion resistant. If you're using a dynamic nylon rope in wet conditions, such as those encountered in mountaineering, you'll definitely want one with a dry coating.

If you're using a rope just for toproping, the dry coating will wear off quickly, so it's probably not worth the added cost, as dry ropes are generally more expensive.

## Rope Length

When I began climbing in the 1970s, the standard length for a dynamic climbing rope was 50 meters (165 feet). Today the standard is 60 meters (200 feet), and many climbers use 70-meter ropes (230 feet). These are the standard precut lengths you can buy from a climbing shop. Static and low-stretch ropes are commonly sold in precut lengths and are also sold directly from spools, cut to your desired length.

## Rope Care and Use

Avoid standing or stepping on your rope, which can grind sharp pebbles and grit through the sheath and into the core. Minimize your rope's exposure to UV light, which will weaken the fibers over time. Store your rope in a shaded, dry place.

If your rope gets dirty, you can wash it by hand in a tub or in a washing machine (preferably a front-loading washing machine, because a top-loading machine's agitator will abrade the rope) with hot water and a soap suitable for nylon. If washing your rope in a bathtub, make sure the tub is free from any chemicals that may damage the rope. I daisy-chain the full length of my rope before washing it in a machine to keep it from getting tangled. Let your rope dry by hanging it in a shaded area.

Be vigilant, and protect your rope from coming into contact with acids, bleaching or oxidizing agents, and alkalis. Acid is the arch enemy of nylon and can severely weaken nylon and polyester fibers. Be extremely careful not to expose your rope to battery acid or any type of acid that may be encountered in your garage or the trunk of your car. It is wise to store your rope in a rope bag.

It is not a good idea to borrow a rope, because you don't know its history. Don't lend out your rope, and keep track of its history and how long you've had it. Most manufacturers recommend keeping a rope for no longer than five to seven years, even with minimal use, and no longer than ten years, even if the rope has been stored and never used.

Inspect your rope by running your hand over the entire length of the sheath when coiling and uncoiling the rope. Visually inspect for excessively worn areas on the sheath, and feel for irregularities (voids, flat spots, etc.) in the core. Your rope should be retired (or cut to a shorter length) if you see the sheath is excessively worn or frayed, exposing the core, or if there are any anomalies in the core. Leader falls and fast rappels can burn the sheath of your rope, a result of heat generated by the friction from your rope running over a carabiner or through a rappel device. If the sheath feels glazed or melted, the rope should be retired.

## Marking the Middle of Your Rope

Many climbers use a black felt-tip marking pen to mark the midpoint of their rope. In 2002 the UIAA Safety Commission issued a warning based on testing done by the UIAA and by some rope manufactures that showed the ink from some marking pens decreased the strength (more specifically, the ropes ability to hold repeated falls in accordance with the EN 892 testing standard) by as much as 50 percent. While this may seem a shocking figure, the UIAA president pointed out that "such a marked rope can only break in practice when the two or three centimeters, which are marked, are placed over a sharp rock edge when the rope is loaded by a fall." While this is an extremely remote possibility—and other, more recent tests have revealed virtually no loss in rope strength—you may want to consider other ways to identify the midpoint on your rope, or at least use only marking pens sold or recommended by your rope's manufacturer. Tape is not a good option, as it can slide on the rope or, more likely, become gummy and stick in rappel and belay devices. A good option is to buy a "bi-pattern" rope, which is a rope that changes pattern at the middle, without a change in yarns or color. Another option is a bicolor rope, which has a color change at the midpoint of the rope. This requires the rope manufacturer to change yarns and use an "air splice" to join the yarns together. This is done by forcing the ends to entwine around each other using extremely high air pressure. The process creates a cosmetic blemish at the yarn change, which manufacturers claim is actually stronger than the continuous fibers because of the extra fibers at the splice. I've never been a fan, however. Cosmetically it looks question-able, and I've found it to be a wear point because the fibers bulge out a slight bit. If you don't have a mid-dle mark on your rope, simply start with both ends and flake the rope out until you reach the middle.

## Coiling and Uncoiling Your Rope

When you buy a new rope, take extra care the first time you uncoil it to prevent kinking. The best method is to simply unroll the rope from the coil, as if pulling it off a spool, holding the rope and rotating the coil until the entire rope is stacked on the ground, keeping the rope free from any twists. Once the rope is in a loose pile, inspect the rope by running it foot by foot through your hands from one end to the other, then coil it with the butterfly coil method.

## *Backpacker or Butterfly Coil*

The **backpacker coil** is also known as the **but-terfly coil**. This coiling method puts fewer kinks in your rope. It is also the fastest way to coil a rope, since you start with both ends and coil a doubled rope. I start by measuring two and a half arm lengths (both arms extended), then begin the butterfly. Fin-ish it off by tying the rope ends with a square knot around your waist. If I know I'll be using the rope the next time for toproping, I'll use this coiling method so that when I flake it out from the ends, I end at the middle of the rope.

*In situations where you'll need to scramble, the backpacker coil is an excellent way to carry your rope.*

## Butterfly Coil

## NEW ENGLAND COIL

This coiling method is ideal for lead climbing situations. The New England coil butterflies the rope, but as a single strand, making it easier to flake out and much less likely to tangle than the mountaineer's coil.

## *New England Coil*

## MOUNTAINEER'S COIL

Another standard coiling method is called the mountaineer's coil. This traditional method makes for a classic, round coil that can be easily carried over the shoulder or strapped onto the top of a pack. The big disadvantage of the mountaineer's coil is that it must be uncoiled as it was coiled, one loop at a time; otherwise it's easy to form a mess of slipknots that are time-consuming and frustrating to resolve. A neat mountaineer's coil is also difficult to achieve on a kinked rope.

# Slings and Webbing

In the 1960s and 1970s, 1-inch-wide tubular nylon webbing was the standard sling material, tied into a loop with a water knot or double fisherman's knot. Eventually, sewn slings with bartacked stitching came onto the market and were actually stronger than the same material tied with a knot. Sewn slings are not only stronger but also safer—you don't have to worry about the knot loosening and coming untied. For rigging rappel anchors, 1-inch tubular webbing is the most versatile.

## Flat Webbing

Flat webbing is woven solid, as opposed to tubular webbing, which is woven into a hose-like shape. It is stiffer and more abrasion resistant than softer tubular webbing, with a higher tensile breaking strength (Sterling 1-inch flat webbing is rated at 43.5 kN, or 9,800 lbs.), which makes it useful for high-strength applications. Its stiffness, however, makes it more difficult to knot and gives it poor handling characteristics, making it unpopular with climbers.

## Tubular Webbing

There are two types of tubular nylon webbing: mil-spec and climb-spec.

Since webbing was originally manufactured for military applications, mil-spec means the webbing meets the standards demanded by the military. Mil-spec has a coarser, rougher-textured weave, with a more pronounced ribbing across the width of the webbing. Climb-spec is a finer, higher-quality weave, without the noticeable ribbing and with a more tightly woven edge. Climb-spec usually tests slightly stronger than mil-spec webbing, and is generally more abrasion resistant and more impervious to tearing or slicing over a sharp edge, but both are suitable for rigging rappel anchors and are roughly the same price.

The Bluewater company, known for manufacturing high-quality webbing, says its climb-spec

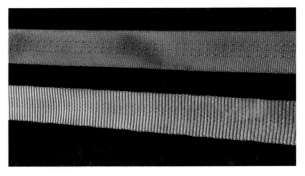

*Top: Bluewater 1-inch climb-spec nylon webbing, rated at 18 kN tensile strength (4,047 lbs.). Bottom: REI 1-inch mil-spec nylon webbing, rated at 17.8 kN tensile strength (4,002 lbs.).*

tubular nylon webbing "outperforms normal mil-spec webbing in strength, flexibility, knotability, and durability. There is minimum exposure to individual fibers as a result of high thread count and fine weave pattern." Bluewater's 1-inch climb-spec webbing has been tested to more than 6,000 pounds loop strength when tied with a water knot.

Sterling's version of climb-spec webbing is called Tech Tape, with a "smoother, denser weave and higher tensile strength" than their mil-spec webbing and a 4,300-pound tensile strength. Sterling's mil-spec webbing is rated to a minimum breaking strength of 4,000 pounds tensile strength and 6,129 pounds in a bartacked sewn loop.

Pre-sewn nylon slings are typically sold in 11/16-inch (18mm) width, bartacked into 24-inch or 48-inch loops with a rating of 22 kN (4,946 lbs.) loop strength.

Climbing shops sell both mil-spec and climb-spec 1-inch tubular nylon webbing from spools, cut to any length you wish. Be aware that these spools of webbing contain taped splices where the webbing ends have been joined together with masking tape. It seems impossible for it to happen, but I know of two cases where spliced webbing was sold to customers who then used it with only the

***Nylon Webbing Comparison. Top to bottom: 1-inch tubular nylon webbing tied with water knot (Sterling Tech Tape, rated at 4,300 pounds tensile strength); 18mm Metolius Nylon Sling, rated at 22 kN loop strength (4,946 lbs.); 18mm Black Diamond Runner, rated at 22 kN loop strength; 11/16-inch Sterling tubular webbing, tied with a water knot (rated at 3,000 lbs. tensile strength).***

masking tape joining the webbing together, in one case with devastating results.

One advantage of cut-to-length webbing is that it can be untied and retied around a tree, passed through a tunnel, or threaded through bolt hangers for a rappel anchor. I generally only carry 1-inch webbing when I know I'll be rigging rappel anchors and leaving it behind.

The Bluewater company recommends the maximum lifespan of its nylon webbing to be no more than five years and recommends retiring a nylon sling if it has been subjected to temperatures above 176°F, is scorched or glazed from a rope being pulled across it, shows signs of UV degradation from being left out in the elements (faded color and/or stiffness), or has been exposed to acid or bleach. Like nylon rope, nylon webbing can lose an appreciable amount of strength when wet or frozen. And remember, acid is the enemy of nylon.

According to Metolius: "Acids are exceptionally bad for cam slings and other nylon climbing products. Even fumes from a car battery can reduce the strength of your slings by as much as 90 percent."

## Knots for Webbing

Nylon webbing is an inherently slick material and should be tied with care. There have been many accidents where poorly tied knots in nylon webbing have failed. The two recommended knots for tying nylon webbing into a loop are the water knot (also known as the ring bend) and the double fisherman's knot (also known as the grapevine knot). The water knot should be neatly tied, with the finished tails a minimum of 3 inches in length. It is important to tighten the water knot carefully and firmly, as it tends to loosen when not tightened properly in a sling that is being used over time. A double fisherman's knot is hard to tie neatly with webbing and requires a much longer piece of material, but it is very secure and will not loosen. A disadvantage is that it is difficult if not impossible to untie once it has been heavily loaded. (See page 262 for knot tying directions.)

Why would you even use nylon webbing tied with a knot as opposed to a sewn runner? A sewn nylon runner is just as strong and more secure than the same material tied with a knot, since you don't have to worry about the knot loosening or coming untied. The answer is for use in applications like rappel anchors when tying slings around a tree or through bolt hangers. It is also sometimes useful to untie the knot, thread the webbing through something (like a tunnel), and retie it.

## Tensile Strength versus Loop Strength

Strength ratings are often given as *tensile strength* and *loop strength*. Tensile strength is tested by a straight pull on a single strand of the material with no knots, done by wrapping the material around a smooth bar (4-inch diameter gives the most accurate test) on both ends and pulling until it breaks. Loop strength is the material tested in a loop configuration, either tied with a knot (in the case of webbing, usually the water knot) or sewn with bartacked stitching. In general, webbing loop strength when tied with a water knot is about 80 percent of twice the tensile breaking strength, and bartacked sewn webbing loop strength is generally about 15 percent stronger than the same material tied with a water knot, depending on the quality and number of bartacks.

## Spectra and Dyneema Slings

Spectra slings, introduced in the late 1980s, were lighter, less bulky, and stronger than nylon. Dyneema is a more recent innovation, typically sold in various-length loops sewn with bartacked stitching in 10-millieter width. Dyneema and Spectra both have almost the identical chemical makeup of high-molecular-weight polyethylene, which, pound for pound, is stronger than wire cable. Most experts say that the manufacturer of Dyneema consistently produces more high-quality fibers than the manufacturer of Spectra material, and most of the slings on the market today are made from Dyneema.

Both Spectra and Dyneema slings are constructed from parallel fibers—very strong but with high lubricity, which means the material itself is inherently slick. That is the reason you can only buy it in sewn loops—it does not hold knots well. *Do not cut a Spectra or Dyneema sling and retie it with a water knot!*

Both Spectra and Dyneema have a lower melting point than nylon (around 300°F for Dyneema/Spectra compared to nylon's melting point of around 480°F). The lower melting point, along with the inherent slipperiness, make Spectra and Dyneema slings a poor choice for tying friction hitches like the prusik, klemheist, or autoblock compared to 5mm or 6mm nylon cord.

In a pinch, if you need to use a sling to tie a friction hitch, use a nylon one over a Dyneema or Spectra sling, as nylon will grip better. The newer, thinner (10mm width) Dyneema slings will work for friction hitches; they do have some nylon in their construction, but if they start to slide on a rope when under load, the friction will generate heat, which could potentially weaken the sling.

Both Spectra and Dyneema fibers do not retain dye and cannot be colored, so the fiber is distinctive in that it is always white. Manufacturers add a blend of nylon to Spectra and Dyneema, usually in a distinctive border pattern, and my guess is that in the future we'll see more nylon in the mix. The Metolius company recently came out with 13mm width slings that are a blend of 36 percent Dyneema and 64 percent nylon.

When using Spectra or Dyneema slings, think of them like a wire cable—they have no stretch, even with nylon blended into the weave. Avoid tying knots with them—it can be almost impossible to untie even a simple overhand knot in the newer, thinner Dyneema after it has been seriously weighted. Wild Country warns that the material loses a hefty percentage of its strength (around 50 percent) when tied in a simple overhand knot or girth-hitch—a problem that nylon does not have. The best way to use a Spectra or Dyneema sling is clipped to carabiners. If using them in a sling-to-sling configuration, either basket one sling over another or use a properly tied girth-hitch.

When buying slings, 1-inch or $^{11}/_{16}$-inch-width tubular nylon webbing will be the most versatile material for rigging rappel anchors, as it can be cut to a desired length and tied with a water knot. Double-length (48-inch) sewn nylon slings are also handy for tethering into anchors and extending your rappel device away from your harness. Any sling you purchase for climbing should have a minimum strength rating of around 14 kN (3,147 lbs.).

Recent studies show that dirty slings are weaker than clean ones. The Mammut company suggests that "to maintain the quality and safety of your slings, you need to clean them regularly." Mammut recommends that you "clean soiled slings in

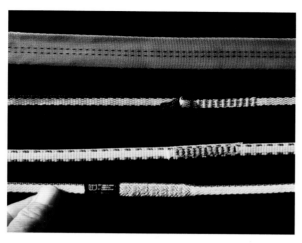

Dyneema Sling Comparison. Top to bottom: 1-inch tubular nylon webbing (for comparison); Wild Country 10mm Dyneema sling (22 kN, or 4,946 lbs.); Black Diamond 10mm Dynex Runner (22 kN); Mammut 8mm Dyneema Contact Sling (22 kN).

Girth-hitching two Dyneema slings together can decrease their strength by 50 percent; for most situations this is not a concern, since the loop strength is 5,000 pounds to begin with.

hand-hot water with a small amount of mild detergent or in a "delicates" machine cycle up to 30°C (86°F). Rinse in clear water. Leave to dry in shade."

## Cord and Cordelettes

A good all-purpose cordelette is 7mm diameter nylon cord, about an 18- to 20-foot length tied into a giant loop with a double fisherman's knot. I prefer a length that allows me to double the cordelette within the span of my outstretched arms. My favorite brand is Sterling, whose 7mm diameter nylon cord is rated at 12.4 kN (2,788 lbs.) and tests over 5,000 pounds when tied into a loop with a double fisherman's knot.

Cordelettes made with a Spectra or Dyneema core and nylon sheath have incredibly high strength and low stretch. Pound for pound, Spectra and Dyneema are stronger than steel (and are the material used in body armor for the military), but both Spectra and Dyneema lose an appreciable amount of strength when tied with knots. Because these cords are so light and strong, with less bulk to carry, they have become popular, especially for rock climbing. Bluewater markets the 5.5mm diameter Titan Cord, with a Dyneema core and nylon sheath, rated at 13.7 kN (3,080 lbs.). They say its "combination of high strength, low elongation and light weight provides superior characteristics over other combinations. Dyneema does not lose significant strength with repetitive flexing and offers a huge increase in abrasion and cut resistance over other materials. Bluewater Titan Cord can be cut and sealed with a hot knife. We recommend a triple fisherman's knot for tying 5.5 Titan into loops."

In recent years high-tech cords utilizing aramid fibers (namely Technora) for the core, with a nylon sheath, have become popular. Aramid fiber has extraordinary tensile strength (stronger than Spectra or Dyneema), with low stretch and an extremely high melting point (900°F), making it difficult to cut and melt. I've found that the best way to cut it is with wire cable cutters. Then I milk the nylon sheath over the end and seal it by melting the nylon with a lighter. The Sterling 6mm PowerCord has a Technora core and nylon sheath, with a single strand breaking strength of around 19 kN (4,271 lbs.); the 5mm Tech Cord, sold by Maxim/New England Ropes, with a 100 percent Technora core and polyester sheath, rates at a whopping 5,000 pounds tensile strength.

However, at the 2000 International Technical Rescue Symposium, Tom Moyer presented a paper titled "Comparative Testing of High Strength Cord" that revealed some startling deficiencies in Technora and other high-tech cords. Testing showed that with repeated flexing, aramid fibers break down much more quickly (losing strength) than good old-fashioned nylon. In his study, a flex cycle test was performed on various cordelettes. The cord sample was passed through a hole in a steel fixture, flexed 90 degrees over an edge, and loaded with a 40-pound weight. The steel fixture was rotated back and forth 180 degrees for 1,000 bending cycles, then the cord's tensile strength was tested (single-strand pull test) at the section that had been flexed. The Technora sample showed a remarkable loss of nearly 60 percent of its strength, while Sterling 7mm nylon cord and 1-inch tubular nylon webbing showed no strength loss at all. Bluewater Titan Cord (Spectra core/nylon sheath), showed a few hundred pounds of strength loss, but that was nowhere near the drastic loss of Technora. Further research

*Cord Comparison. Top to bottom: Bluewater 5mm Titan Cord tied with triple fisherman's knot (Dyneema core/nylon sheath; tensile strength 13.7 kN, or 3,080 lbs.); Sterling 6mm PowerCord tied with triple fisherman's knot (Technora core/nylon sheath; tensile strength 19 kN, or 4,271 lbs.); Sterling 7mm nylon Cordelette tied with double fisherman's knot (nylon core/nylon sheath; tensile strength 12.4 kN, or 2,788 lbs.).*

is warranted. The big advantages of these high-tech cords are their low weight, high strength, and low bulk, which are advantageous for multipitch rock climbing.

If you use these high-tech cords, you should tie the cordelette with a triple fisherman's knot and consider replacing them more often with high use. Keep in mind that the price tag on the high-tech cords is roughly twice as much as nylon. The bottom line is this: For an all-purpose cordelette, you can't go wrong with old-school nylon—a 7mm diameter nylon cord is a good choice.

To tie friction hitches like the prusik, klemheist, and autoblock, you'll want to use 5mm or 6mm diameter nylon cord (nylon core, nylon sheath). When buying this accessory cord, buy the softest, most pliable cord you can find. A stiff cord won't grip as well when used for friction hitches. Also, be aware of the difference between 5mm nylon accessory cord (typically rated at 5.2 kN, or 1,169 lbs.) and 5mm high-tenacity cord like Bluewater Titan Cord (rated at 13.7 kN, or 3,080 lbs.). You obviously would not want to use 5mm nylon accessory cord for your cordelette!

## Carabiners

Carabiners come in a variety of shapes and designs: oval, D-shaped, pear-shaped, wire-gate, bent-gate, and locking. Bent-gate carabiners are used primarily for sport climbing (attached to the rope-clipping end of a quickdraw).

A basic carabiner is of aluminum alloy, with a spring-loaded gate on one side. The spine of the carabiner is the solid bar stock opposite the gate. The small protrusion on one end of the gate is called the nose, and this visually tells you which way the gate opens. The basic design has a small pin on the gate that latches into a groove on the nose end. The preferable "keylock" design eliminates the pin, and the gate and bar come together in a machined notch. A wire-gate carabiner simply has a

*Carabiners come in a dazzling array of designs for various applications. Top row (left to right): asymmetrical D, regular D, oval, wire-gate D, bent-gate D. Bottom: pear-shaped locking.*

*Two oval carabiners with the gates properly opposed and reversed.*

wire under tension serving as the gate, which provides a wider opening because of its slim mass and eliminates "gate flutter," the vibration of a solid gate during a fall or peak loading of the carabiner.

For toproping, oval carabiners are useful for connecting the climbing rope to the toprope anchor master point. Because of their symmetry, the gates can be opposed and reversed, and the carabiner configuration still retains its oval shape.

Two opposed and reversed carabiners can also be used in lieu of a locking carabiner at any critical junction in the anchor system, in situations where you've run out of locking carabiners and need extra security at a key point.

D-shaped carabiners have the strongest configuration because when the carabiner is loaded on the major (long) axis, the weight naturally is loaded closest to the spine. For this reason, a locking D is a good choice for a belay/rappel carabiner. A locking pear-shaped carabiner is useful for many applications because of its wide aperture on one side, and it is a good carabiner to use with a Munter hitch. It is also a great carabiner to pair up for use at the toprope anchor master point. When you oppose and reverse two pear-shaped locking carabiners, the symmetry is maintained (unlike an asymmetrical D shape), and the climbing rope runs smoothly through the carabiners.

*Three oval carabiners opposed and reversed at a toprope anchor master point.*

*Two pear-shaped locking carabiners with the gates opposed and reversed at a toprope anchor master point.*

*Locking carabiners (left to right): Petzl William Triac, Petzl William Ball Lock, Black Diamond Twistlock, Black Diamond Screwgate.*

The most common locking carabiner is the screwgate. The screwgate locking carabiner is just that, a mechanism with a collar that screws shut over the nose of the carabiner. I like the Petzl designs that show a red stripe (red means danger!) when the gate is unlocked. Obviously, with a screwgate locking carabiner, you must remember to lock it. In fact, it's an important habit to always check your locking carabiners to make sure they *are* locked. Give them a close visual inspection; also press on the gate (squeeze test) as an additional safety precaution.

If you are a bit absent-minded, or catch yourself occasionally not locking your screwgate carabiner, you might want to buy an autolock or twistlock carabiner. The twistlock design has a spring-loaded gate that locks automatically, and there are several autolocking designs on the market that have even safer mechanisms that must be manipulated (like pushing the gate upward, then twisting the gate to lock it; or pressing a button, then twisting open the gate), but some climbers

find these difficult to use. Interestingly, for industrial workers in the Vertical Rope Access environment (rappelling and rope ascending on the faces of dams, buildings, and bridges), OSHA standards

*If you're forgetful about locking your carabiners, instructor Chris Baumann offers this tip: Paint a red stripe at the base of the locking collar in the unlocked position.*

*Bad! Never load a carabiner in three directions as shown here.*

require autolocking carabiners, as does the tree-trimming industry.

An important thing to remember with carabiners is that a carabiner is only about one-third as strong if it's loaded with the gate open. It's essential, therefore, to keep a few things in mind when using a carabiner:

- Always load the carabiner in the proper direction—on the major, or long, axis.
- Do not cross-load a carabiner (on the minor axis) or load it in three directions (called triaxial loading).
- Do not load a carabiner over an edge of rock—this can open the gate when the carabiner is loaded, and two-thirds of the carabiner's strength will be lost.

Retire a carabiner if it shows a groove from excessive rope wear, or if it has been dropped a lengthy distance down a rock face. If the gate is sticky, washing it with soap and water and using some graphite lubricant will usually take care of the problem.

In the professional realm, the industry standard for attaching the climbing rope to the toprope anchor master point is either two locking or three oval carabiners with the gates opposed and reversed. I've always preferred three ovals because of the symmetry and wide base they present for the climbing rope. If using two locking carabiners, pick a pair of pear-shaped (not D-shaped) lockers so the pairing is symmetrical when one is opposed and reversed. I've used three steel ovals for thousands of client days without incident. Simply oppose and reverse the outside carabiners to the middle one. The wide radius created by the width of the three carabiners, plus the added weight of steel versus aluminum, provides a more stable platform for the

*Three steel ovals with the gates opposed and reversed at a toprope anchor master point.*

***Kesley Lund leads Right Between the Eyes (5.7), Joshua Tree.***
PHOTO BY GREG EPPERSON

rope and tends not to flip sideways as often as two locking carabiners—a situation that can pin the rope against the rock while lowering if the climber's (weighted) strand is on the outside, away from the rock.

If you do a lot of toproping, you'll see that aluminum carabiners wear rather quickly, developing noticeable grooves. The worn-off aluminum particles also get on the rope and the belayer's hands. When this happens, you should retire them. Steel is far more durable and wears much more slowly than aluminum. One caution when using steel carabiners: If you drop them from any distance (say 20 feet or more), you should consider retiring them, as steel's metallurgical structure makes it more prone to micro fractures.

# CHAPTER 4

# Anchoring

## Rock Assessment

The first thing to think about when placing protection and building anchor systems is the integrity and structure of the rock itself. Catastrophic anchor failures have occurred, not because the gear placements were bad, or the rigging was flawed, but because the rock itself was unsound. Determining good rock structure and knowing what to watch out for are fundamental requirements to building safe anchors.

When placing gear, the ideal crack is what guides call "a crack in the planet," a deep fissure that runs perpendicular (at a right angle) to the plane of the rock face, cleaving a massive, solid face of granite.

In general you'll want to avoid two things: detached blocks and flakes. A detached block is just that—a chunk of rock that is not attached to the main rock structure but is either sitting on top of the cliff, like a boulder, or is part of the main rock face but completely fractured with cracks on all sides.

To assess a block, start by looking at its size. How big is it? Is it the size of your refrigerator, your car, or your house? Putting a piece of gear in the crack beneath a smaller block is a very bad idea. When the piece is weighted, it has an outward

*Use good judgment if anchoring to detached blocks. Avoid small ones and those resting on an inclined slab. I've adopted a rule from Yosemite Search and Rescue protocol: For a detached granite block to be used as a sole, monolithic anchor, it must be at least as big as a full-size refrigerator, situated lengthwise on a flat surface.*

*This block is not as big as a fridge but is being incorporated into a larger anchor system. Its position is low and locked in by surrounding blocks, making it secure for this application.*

*This large horn of rock is what I call "attached to the planet" rather than a detached block resting "on top of the planet." This is what you're looking for with natural rock features. It's being incorporated into a larger anchor system. The rigging rope is tied around the horn using a bowline with a bight.*

prying effect on the block. Even large blocks can shift easily, as I've encountered when boulder-hopping around car-size blocks, only to have one shift under my body weight. Look at how the block is situated. Is it perched down low, where it cannot slide out? Does it rest on a flat surface, or is it resting on an inclined slab? Generally, be very skeptical of using detached blocks as part of your anchor system, especially smaller blocks.

Flakes should also be avoided. A flake is formed by a crack in the rock that runs parallel to the main rock face. It can be wafer thin or several feet thick.

A flake is inherently weak, since any gear placement, when loaded, will exert an outward prying effect on the structure of the flake, which can fracture if not strong enough to bear the force. In a naturally weak rock, like sandstone, a thin flake of rock can be extremely weak.

Exfoliation Confrontation, a climb at Joshua Tree National Park, has a memorable crux where you reach underneath and undercling a flake of rock. Exfoliation is a natural process of granite formations and is the key in the formation of domes. Flakes of granite are layered, like layers of an onion, and the outer layer peels off from time to time due to weathering and gravity, exposing a new layer beneath.

One of the largest examples of exfoliation I've ever seen occurred in Yosemite Valley on a hot July day in 1996 at the Glacier Point Apron. An

*This camming device has been placed behind a thin flake of rock. If the cam is loaded, it will pry outward, potentially breaking the flake. How much force would be required to break the flake is unknown—but in this case, probably not much!*

a wide swath. A tourist, in line at the Happy Isles snack bar over a quarter mile away, was killed when hit by a piece of shrapnel from the blast.

enormous flake, roughly the size of a football field and about 4 feet thick, detached from a point high on the cliff, shearing off in one gigantic piece. After a 2,000-foot free fall, the impact resulted in a massive explosion, creating a 300 mile per hour shock wave of wind that felled a thousand pine trees in

*I came across this "rappel anchor" at Tahquitz Rock in Southern California. You don't have to be a geologist to figure out that this flake is ready to exfoliate. You wouldn't catch me rappelling off this dud. Almost every case of catastrophic anchor failure is due to poor rock structure.*

When building anchors, look at any flake with skepticism. How thick is it, and how well attached to the main rock structure or cliff face? Test its soundness by thumping on it with the palm of your hand. Does it vibrate? Is there a hollow sound? When analyzing rock structure, act like a geologist and scrutinize the rock and its various formations very carefully.

*A solid rock bollard attached to the main cliff structure. Although only a sole monolithic anchor point, the rigging is redundant in that the cordellete is doubled and tied with a figure eight loop.*

## Macro to Micro Rock Assessment

When assessing rock structure, evaluate from macro to micro. Macro is the big picture. Look at the main rock face. Is there a massive, solid rock structure? Is there a crack in the planet? Or are the cracks an intricate matrix where no massive piece of completely solid rock exists. Are you dealing with blocks or flakes? Can you avoid using them? These are questions you need to ask. Never blindly place gear in cracks without first scrutinizing the big picture: the overall structure and integrity of the rock itself.

Microstructure is what's inside the crack you'll be using. Is the surface of the rock rotten, grainy, dirty, or flaky? Are there hollow spots or hollow flakes inside the crack itself? Microstructure can affect the integrity of your placements as much as the overall macrostructure.

*This three-piece anchor looks great, except for one thing: bad macro structure. A force on the pieces could move the entire block, since it's cracked on all sides. Remember, the number-one cause of catastrophic anchor failure is bad macro structure.*

This detached flake is a great example of bad rock structure.

The camming device placement looks great—nice and tight in a parallel-sided crack. But how good is the rock quality? Close inspection reveals a microstructure problem on the crack's left wall, rendering the placement less than ideal.

Bad microstructure: The right side of this nut rests on a fragile flake.

## Natural Anchors

Natural anchors utilize the natural features you'll find at the crag environment, such as trees, and the configuration of the rock itself. Trees are plentiful in some areas, rare in others, such as in a desert environment. How do you assess the reliability and strength of a tree?

In 2015 John Morton, a search and rescue technician with the Snohomish County Search and Rescue and Everett Mountain Rescue in Washington State, published an exhaustive study he compiled of tree strength in the Pacific Northwest, sampling twelve different tree species. What he concluded was that trees that are routinely subjected to high winds are stronger.

Trees with a minimum diameter of 7 inches (a circumference of 22 inches) in areas commonly subjected to winds from 35 to 55 mph tested between 10 kN and 25 kN at 2 feet up from their

base. For 7-inch-diameter trees routinely subjected to higher winds (60 to 90 mph), the results were higher: 30kN to 60 kN.

To trust a single tree as a monolithic sole anchor, here's a good rule of thumb: The tree should be a minimum 9 inches in diameter (28-inch circumference), which is roughly the size of your helmet, and also meet the following criteria:

- The tree is living and structurally sound.
- The trunk and base are vertically aligned.
- The tree is rooted in soil with no voids (not in sand or gravel).
- The trunk is symmetrical at its base.

Because of the drier climate, trees at climbing sites in the southwestern United States are generally more reliable anchors than trees in the Pacific Northwest or on East Coast, where the climate is wetter and more humid. When setting up a toprope anchor, use

*OK. A properly girth-hitched nylon sling.*

*Good. A double-length (48-inch) nylon sling tied with an overhand knot makes the sling itself redundant.*

*Good. A figure eight follow-through knot used to tie the anchor rope directly to the tree.*

two separate trees in the anchor system if possible; if only one tree is available, back it up with another gear placement or two if it's less than a monolithic tree.

The rock itself can be used for anchoring. Look for large spikes or horns of rock attached to the main rock structure to tie off as part of your anchor. A tunnel in a solid rock structure is called a thread, and is utilized by threading a sling or cord, or tying a rope, through the tunnel. Limestone is a rock type with many threads, whereas threads are a rarity in granite.

Use detached blocks with caution. They should be well situated, unmovable, and not top heavy. Avoid using blocks resting on a slanting surface or a slab. I like to tie off the block around its entire mass, rather than using the pinch where the block touches another rock surface or where two blocks touch each other. This way, even if the block shifts slightly, I still am anchored to the mass of the block. When tying off blocks, watch for sharp edges that may fray or cut your rigging rope, and use padding or an edge protector when needed.

A friend of mine put up a new route at Joshua Tree—a 40-foot-high sport climb with five bolts—up the face of a massive block that was a facet of a larger cliff. One day I got a phone call: "Tony's route fell down!" I didn't believe it until I walked out there and saw it with my own eyes. The gigantic block was top heavy and had simply toppled over; the side where Tony's route had been was now straight down in the dirt, leaving behind a void in the cliff the size of a small house. I got down on my hands and knees and peered underneath. I could see one of the bolt hangers! Bouldering legend Chris Sharma visited the site shortly thereafter, climbing what is now one of Joshua Tree's most difficult boulder problems—up the newly exposed overhanging face of one side of the block.

In some instances a single, bombproof natural anchor (guides refer to this as a "monolith") is safely used for a rappel or toprope anchor—like a 3-foot-diameter ponderosa pine tree, or a knob of rock the size of your refrigerator that's part of the main rock structure. Just make sure your sling or rope around

*A "thread" is a sling or cord threaded through a tunnel, rare in granite but common in limestone. Here a Bluewater Titan cordelette (3,080 lbs. tensile strength) is doubled, looped through the thread, then tied off with an overhand knot, creating a very strong four-loop master point. It all boils down to the structural integrity of the rock arch, which appears to have a small crack at its narrowest point. This thread is in granite, reliable as long as the direction of pull is down. I'd consider this same thread in sandstone to be unreliable.*

the anchor is redundant. For example, when rigging a rappel anchor around a massive tree, use two separate slings with two rappel rings to gain redundancy in your anchor system, at least in the rigging. When

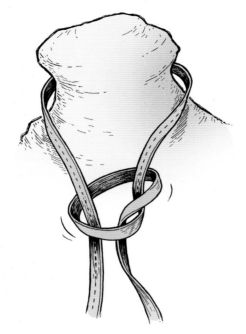

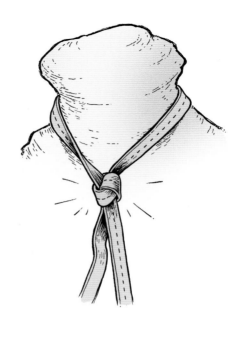

*A slip hitch used to tie off a knob of rock.*

*How to tie a slip hitch. The slip hitch can be tightened by pulling on one strand, making it more secure than a girth-hitch for tying off knobs of rock.*

rigging a belay or toprope anchor, loop two strands of the cordelette around the tree, then tie a figure eight knot for a two-loop master point. Clip in with two carabiners, opposed and reversed, and you have redundancy in your anchor rigging (although technically, a single tree is nonredundant). Always use caution and sound judgment when using a nonredundant natural anchor.

*Double-length nylon sling, girth-hitched on a horn. If used for protection, the action of the rope might loosen the sling—better to use a slip hitch or choke the sling back on itself.*

*Choking the sling back on itself weakens it by 30 to 40 percent, but increases the chances of the sling staying there.*

*Sling girth-hitched on a fist-size chockstone. As long as the pull is straight down, this stone is wedged like a giant hex, and is probably as strong as any nut placement. A pull up and out, however, might easily dislodge it.*

*A monolithic tree anchor. This massive live pine tree at Tahquitz Rock in Southern California is 60 feet tall and well rooted at its base. The rigging is redundant, since the cordelette has been looped around the tree and tied off with a figure eight loop.*

# Nuts

## *The Evolution of Chockcraft*

A chockstone is simply a rock wedged in a crack. Naturally occurring chockstones can be as small as a pebble or as big as a house. The notion of using a chockstone for an anchor dates back to the origins

*A selection of chocks from the 1970s. Nuts have evolved over the years but are still based on the same original basic designs.*

*A selection of modern-day nuts.*

of the sport. In the late 1800s in the British Isles, rock climbers began using natural chockstones for anchors by slinging a cord around them and attaching their rope to the sling with a carabiner. The use of artificial chockstones—called chocks or, more commonly, nuts—began in the early 1960s at a North Wales cliff at a crag named Clogwyn Du'r Arddu. The hike up to the crag followed a railroad track, and some ambling climber picked up a nut along the way and pocketed it. Up on the cliff he threaded a small cord through the nut before wedging it in a constriction in a thin crack. Thus the subtle art of chockcraft was born.

In American rock climbing, pitons were used almost exclusively for protection and anchors until the 1970s. In Europe, pitons were made of soft iron, and once hammered into a crack they were nearly impossible to remove and reuse. Legendary American climber John Salathé, a wrought-iron worker by trade, developed the first hard steel pitons, forged from an old Ford Model A axle, which he used for his famous ascents in Yosemite Valley during the 1940s. These high carbon steel pitons could be driven and then removed and reused, over and over again.

Yvon Chouinard refined and innovated the design of chrome moly steel pitons from 1957 to 1965, improving on Salathé's designs with the introduction of knifeblade, horizontal (called the Lost Arrow), and angle pitons. These pitons revolutionized big wall climbing in Yosemite during the "Golden Age" of the 1960s, when hundreds of placements were required for the ultimate big wall climbs in Yosemite, like El Capitan. Once placed, they could be removed by the second, leaving the climbing route in the same condition for the next climbing team.

Climbing standards in Yosemite led the world at the time. But it came with a price. On popular climbs in Yosemite, the repeated pounding and removal of hard steel pitons began to permanently damage the cracks, leaving ugly "pin scars" every few feet up crack systems. Cracks were getting "beat out," and something had to be done. The National Park Service actually closed down a few climbs in Yosemite because of piton damage.

When the great American climber Royal Robbins made a trip to England in the 1960s, he saw how effective nuts could be, and he imported the idea back to Yosemite. His 1967 ascent of The Nutcracker, one of Yosemite's most popular climbs, was done entirely with nuts—Royal's way of showing that nuts were a viable alternative to the destructive pitons. Climbing the route today, you'll notice there still are piton scars on the route, a testament to how slow American climbers were to embrace the new and gentler technology of chockcraft—a big change from bashing hard steel pitons into cracks with heavy blows from a hammer.

The change was finally precipitated by the fact that many cracks were simply being destroyed. Even granite is relatively soft when compared to cold hard steel. But it wasn't until Yvon Chouinard introduced chocks to American rock climbers in his 1972 equipment catalog, and Doug Robinson espoused the virtues of nuts in his seminal treatise, *The Whole Natural Art of Protection*, that the American climbing community firmly embraced the idea of "clean climbing"—a new ethic where climbing anchors were placed and removed without scarring or damaging the rock.

Today there are thin-crack climbs in Yosemite where, for hundreds of feet, every finger jam is in an ancient piton scar, although now instead of using pitons, nuts can be slotted into the V-shaped bottom of the old pin scars.

Artificial chocks now come in a dazzling array of shapes and sizes, the largest ones capable of holding more than 3,000 pounds and the tiniest micro-nuts designed to hold body weight only. First introduced by Chouinard Equipment in 1971, the hexentric, commonly called a hex, is a unique, six-sided nut with four distinct attitudes of placement. It was followed by the Stopper in 1972, with

*Piton scars on a Yosemite crack.*

its simple but effective tapered trapezoidal shape. Although many new designs have been introduced since then, they are basically variations on a theme to these classic and timeless designs, which are as viable today as they were more than forty years ago.

The ingenious Tricam, invented by Jeff Lowe in 1980, is essentially a single cam that can be used either passively or actively. Since it has a tapered

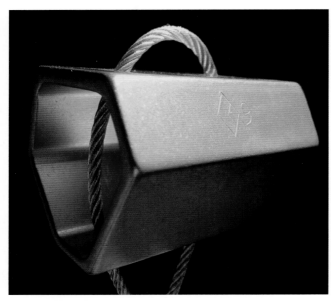

*The classic designs of the hex (left) and the Stopper (right) have changed little since their inception in the early 1970s.*

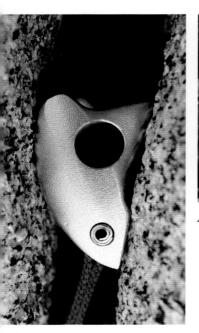

*A well-placed Tricam in camming (active) mode.*

*A well-placed Tricam in passive mode.*

*This Tricam, placed in the camming mode, has no room for the camming action to take place. If I had to grade this placement, I'd give it a D.*

design, with a point on one end, it can be wedged like a nut (a passive placement) or used like a cam (an active placement), where a mechanical action (i.e., camming) takes place. The camming action occurs when the sling is loaded on the back, or spine, of the cam, between two rails that contact the rock on one side of the crack, creating a force that pivots like a fulcrum onto the pointed end on the other side of the crack. The design is useful for many horizontal crack situations, but its main draw-back is that it's somewhat difficult to remove with one hand once it has been well set or weighted.

When placing a nut, or any other piece of gear for that matter, again the first thing to consider is the overall integrity of the rock itself. I can't over-emphasize the importance of rock assessment. Nuts have very low holding power in soft sandstone, or rotten or flaky rock. Avoid placing nuts in cracks

*Stopper in a bottleneck placement. There is simply no way that in a downward pull, the nut could be pulled through the bottleneck. Something would have to give: either the rock itself or the nut or wire cable.*

*Very good. This Stopper placement is in good, solid rock and has flush surface contact on both sides of the nut. I'd grade this one an A-.*

*Good surface contact on both sides of this endwise placement, although the crack is slightly flared. Grade: B-.*

*Bad. The left side of this nut lacks surface contact with the rock. Grade: D-.*

*Fail. Poor surface contact, particularly on the right side; there's insufficient narrowing of the crack below the placement. Might hold body weight, but not a leader fall.*

*OK. This stopper is in a good bottleneck but is not set deeply enough inside the crack, making it susceptible to failure in any outward pull, since it lacks surface contact on its left side. Grade: C.*

*Good. The left side of this nut is nearly 100 percent flush, and the curve of the nut on its right side fits the curve of the crack. Grade: A.*

*Excellent. This nut has good surface contact on both sides, plus the lip on the right side of the crack protects against any outward force. As far as endwise placements go, on a scale of 1 to 10, this one's a 10.*

*Hugh Banner invented the offset nut in the 1970s, creating a shape that is tapered in two directions.*

*Opposing nuts. Slider nuts, like the ball nut, are based on this concept. I'd use this technique if I had nothing else to fit the crack, but it could work in a pinch (pun intended).*

*This DMM alloy offset fits nearly perfectly into this mildly flaring crack.*

*The Black Diamond Micro Stopper. This design, where the cable is soldered directly into the nut, fits well in shallow cracks due to its narrower profile.*

*This number 3 Micro Stopper has excellent surface contact. Its breaking strength is rated at 5 kN (1,123 lbs.), roughly half that of a large stopper of 10 kN (2,248 lbs.)*

*A number 6 Micro Stopper has a breaking strength of 8 kN (1,789 lbs.); although in a bottleneck, this placement lacks surface contact on its right side and, because of the stiff wire, is susceptible to being plucked out by any outward force. Here, the next smaller size would fit better. When I'm leading, I carry groups of small nuts on an oval carabiner, about a half-dozen of similar size per biner, and use them like a set of keys. If one doesn't fit, I'll go to the next size, keeping them all on the biner. Once I find my placement, I'll unclip the biner and put a quickdraw on the placement.*

*Two nuts in a horizontal crack, rigged in opposition with clove hitches.*

under or around detached blocks, or in cracks behind loose flakes. Look for "straight-in" cracks in massive rock structure, where the crack runs perpendicular to the plane of the rock face.

Once a good crack system is found, look for obvious constrictions in the crack itself. A "bottleneck" placement is found where the crack tapers drastically and the proper size nut is fitted in the narrowing constriction.

With a basic tapered nut, like the Stopper, the preferred placement is in the narrow configuration, since this setting has the most surface contact and stability. The wider endwise configuration is an option for narrow slots and shallow cracks, but it ultimately has less surface contact and generally less stability.

The typical nut placement is in a vertical crack, but horizontal cracks will work if there is a narrowing at the lip of the crack and you can slide a nut in from the side, then pull it into the constriction.

The real art of chockcraft comes into play with the subtler placements. Look for any slight variations in the walls of the crack. When placing a nut, aim for maximum surface contact between the metal faces of the chock and the walls of the crack.

When the walls of the crack are virtually parallel, using the camming action of a Tricam or hex is the best option for a nut placement, although this is territory that specific camming devices were designed for. Unless you can see an obvious V-shaped taper in the crack, chances are you won't be able to get a reliable nut placement—it's that simple.

*Excellent. This hex placement has near-perfect flushness on both faces of the nut in a solid straight-in crack. Loading the nut's cable will kick in the camming action of the hex.*

*Bomber. This perfectly flush endwise placement couldn't be any better.*

*I'd grade this one a D-. It lacks surface contact on its left side, and the crack is a bit flared.*

*C+. Relatively flush on both sides, but the rock microstructure is grainy, with large crystals, and the right wall of the crack flares out a bit.*

*A nice, flush fit. My concern is the rock structure, and the possibility of the rock itself fracturing.*

Of paramount concern when placing a nut is the direction of pull. In what direction will the chock be loaded? Most placements can withstand a pull in only *one* direction. While the nut may be able to withstand a load of 2,000 pounds in that one direction, the slightest tug in the opposite direction might jerk the nut right out of its placement. When incorporating a nut placement into an overall anchor system, look at the ultimate direction your anchor system will be loaded, and equalize your placement in a line toward the master point.

Setting a nut properly is also important. Many novice climbers make a great nut placement but fail to set it properly, which makes the nut susceptible to levering out of its placement if pulled from a different angle than intended. Setting the piece is accomplished by simply applying several stout tugs in the direction the piece will be loaded, most easily accomplished by attaching a sling to the nut with a carabiner and yanking on the sling, firmly wedging the nut in its intended placement. While this definitely makes the nut more difficult to remove, it is an important concept that many novices miss.

Cleaning a nut can be as easy as yanking it in the opposite direction from the intended direction of pull, but be careful with recalcitrant nuts, which can suddenly pop out and hit you in the face or

teeth. Yanking a piece out can also send your hand bashing into the rock, scraping your knuckles. A better approach to removing a nut is to use the nut tool, giving the nut a tap opposite from the direction of loading. An easy way to loosen larger nuts is to tap the nut with a carabiner, metal to metal.

Becoming skilled at the art of chockcraft takes practice. I often urge experienced climbers who really want to learn the subtleties of chockcraft to spend a day at a trad area like Joshua Tree armed with only a selection of nuts, climbing some of the old classics that were put up before the advent of spring-loaded camming devices. Doing so will force them to focus intensely on the fine points of chockcraft.

If you're inexperienced at placing nuts, to gain confidence quickly, hire a guide for a day of anchoring practice so that you can be critiqued on your placements by a professional.

Every nut placement is different—some less than perfect, some bomber, some worthless. You should have enough knowledge to know what's good and what's not, and what constitutes a placement you can trust.

## Cams

In the mid-1970s a stout, muscular fellow by the name of Ray Jardine could often be seen peering through binoculars, gazing upward at the various nooks and crannies on the walls of Yosemite Valley. With his thick beard and glasses, he looked like a birder, but Ray wasn't looking for birds. The bulging forearms gave it away—Ray was a climber, and he was looking for the ultimate crack: one of those perfectly straight cracks that split Yosemite's steep walls like a surgeon's incision, shooting upward for 100 feet, uninterrupted.

Ray had invented a new technology—the spring-loaded camming device, or SLCD—that allowed him to place reliable protection in even perfectly parallel-sided cracks. When he found

*Spring-loaded Camming Devices (SLCDs).*

his ultimate crack climb, he swore his partners to secrecy and set out on a mission: to climb the most difficult crack ever climbed in Yosemite. He named it The Phoenix—a fingertip- to hand-size crack on a gently overhanging wall high above Cascade Falls in the lower valley. After dozens of attempts using his newfangled technology, he finally succeeded in climbing Yosemite's first 5.13. Ray called his miracle invention the "Friend," and soon the word was out. Some climbers called it "cheating"; others claimed it was "the greatest invention since the nylon rope."

Marketed by Wild Country, the Friend soon became an integral part of every rock climber's rack. Ray soon retired from climbing and, financed by his proceeds from licensing the

Friend, went on to sail around the world, hike the Pacific Crest Trail, row across the Atlantic, and ski to the South Pole.

The idea of the SLCD, or "camming device" for short, is simple in concept yet complex in design. Jardine's original design consisted of a unit with a rigid aluminum shaft connected by an axle to four independent aluminum spring-loaded cams (called "lobes"). The cams retracted via a trigger bar that slid up and down a slot in the shaft. The unit was fitted into a parallel-sided crack with the cams retracted; when weight was applied to a sling tied into a hole in the bottom of the shaft, the cams were activated in response to the load. To keep the unit from being pulled out of the crack, a corresponding force held it in place. The downward

*The original Wild Country Friend was one of the greatest innovations in rock climbing.*

*The Metolius Power Cam has color-coded dots that help you assess your placement.*

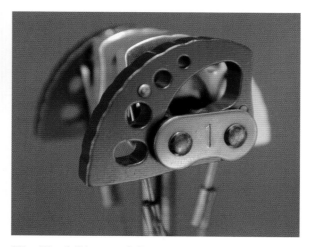

*The Black Diamond Camalot was the first double-axle design.*

force in the direction of the shaft was transferred outward at the cams, which generated an outward force against the walls of the crack.

The disadvantage of Ray's design was that a rigid shaft could not flex or bend in the direction of pull, an especially troubling problem for placements in horizontal cracks.

*The Metolius offset TCU (three-cam unit) works well in slightly flaring cracks.*

improvements since the invention of the Friend was the first double-axle design, the Camalot, introduced by Black Diamond Equipment, which allows for a much greater range of cam placement. Now, in addition to units with four cam lobes, there are TCUs (three-cam units) and offset cams (for flared cracks).

### Placing an SLCD

When placing an SLCD, the first thing to consider is rock quality. SLCDs can fail if the rock is soft, brittle, or loose. They can easily pull out if placed behind a small, loose block or thin flake of rock. In an ideal placement in solid granite, a Black Diamond Camalot can hold as much as 14 kN (3,147 lbs.). Never rely on a camming device to hold in very soft sandstone, or in rotten or flaky rock. Cam manufacturer Metolius advises: "Rock fails in two basic ways: either a relatively large piece breaks off or the surface layer is crushed under the pressure of the cam lobe, allowing the cam to 'track out.' You

Today there is a huge array of SLCDs on the market, and most of these designs have flexible wire cable shafts instead of rigid ones. One of the biggest

*Bad. Any force applied to this Black Diamond Camalot will be converted to an outward force that can pry out and potentially break the flake of rock it's placed behind.*

must assess the integrity of the rock and choose the soundest possible location for your placements. Look for fractures in and around the walls of a potential placement that could denote weakness, as well as pebbles, crystals, or micro-flakes that could snap off. Be extremely suspicious of placements behind flakes or blocks."

Since they rely on friction to a certain extent, camming devices are not as strong in exceptionally slick or polished rock, or rock that is wet or icy.

Again, avoid placements behind detached blocks and loose flakes—the outward expansion of the cams can generate a tremendous force that can pry the rock loose. Look for straight-in cracks in solid rock. A straight-in crack is one that runs perpendicular to the face of the rock, bisecting the rock at a right angle.

When placing a camming device, look for a section of the crack where the walls are uniformly parallel, or where they form a subtle pocket. Avoid widening cracks, where the crack is wider above the cams; because of its spring-loaded design, the

*Camalot placed for protection on a lead climb. The crack and the placement look good, but how strong is the flake? In general, avoid flakes and seek straight-in cracks that bisect the plane of the rock face at a 90-degree angle.*

*Bad. Even though the cams on this Black Diamond Camalot are within the acceptable range (right around 50 percent retracted), the widening crack above the cams will allow them to easily "walk" into the wider section. This can occur even with minimal loading and unloading of the device, such as from the action of a lead rope or hanging and lowering from a toprope anchor, potentially leading to complete failure if the cams open all the way. Avoid this situation— the cams can potentially walk to an open and unstable position. Grade: D.*

camming device will have a natural tendency to wiggle upward as the cam is activated. This phenomenon is known as "walking." This walking movement is most exaggerated when the piece is repeatedly weighted and unweighted, as in toproping. In a crack where the walls are uniformly parallel, or where the crack narrows slightly above the

cams, if there is any walking, the cams will not open any wider and will stay within acceptable retraction range. As a test, grab the sling and yank and pull on it to see what walking, if any, occurs. This is an exaggerated test; when you actually use the piece, the force will be more constant. Any piece will "walk" if you yank back and forth on it with

*Excellent. In my mind, the perfect placement. We have solid, massive rock—a crack in the planet—and the cams retracted uniformly at about 80 percent. This is what I strive for with every Camalot placement: nice and tight, where the bottom tips on the lobes all come into line. Grade: A+.*

*Bomber placement. This Camalot is retracted at 50 percent. When placing Camalots, strive for 50 percent and tighter. Fifty percent retraction is when the bases of the lobes on the cams are at a 45-degree angle relative to the vertical axis (the direction on the stem), or when the bases of the cams form a 90-degree angle relative to each other. Grade: A.*

**Good. This Metolius Power Cam displays optimal green "range finder" dots in a solid, parallel-sided crack. Grade: A.**

**This Metolius Power Cam has colored dots in small drilled holes on the edge of the cams to assist you in assessing your placement. Green is the recommended range. Yellow means caution; you're slightly out of the optimal range. Red means danger; you're making a potentially bad placement.**

**Poor. Although the range of retraction is acceptable, this Metolius Power Cam could easily walk up into the wider pod in the crack above the cams, rendering the placement unstable. Also, the outside right cam has poor surface contact and is too close to the edge of the crack. Grade: D-.**

enough vigor. The key point is that this is something to be aware of and watch for.

Another key to a good placement is the range of retraction on the cams. Black Diamond recommends that the Camalot be placed in the lower to mid-expansion range (50 to 90 percent retraction is ideal). Wild Country advises the following for its single-axle designs: "It is vitally important that all the cams make contact with the sides of the rock,

Metolius recommends that in a horizontal crack, the outside cams should be placed on the bottom of the crack for maximum stability.

Very poor. The cams are barely retracted and nowhere near the recommended range. The piece can easily walk, and it might fail completely. Grade: F.

Too tight. This Camalot is around 90 percent retracted. Any tighter, and it may be very difficult to remove. There is also some loss of holding power in the last 10 percent (90 to 100 percent retracted) on a Camalot.

A larger size cam would be better, but this Metolius Power Cam is in a pocket in the crack that lends some stability to the placement, even though it is borderline on the red "range finder" dots, signifying a marginal placement. Grade: C-.

preferably in the middle half of their expansion range (i.e., the cams should be one-quarter to three-quarters open)." Metolius recommends selecting "the largest size cam that will fit without getting stuck. Cams should not be placed near the wide end of their expansion range. When a unit is loaded, it expands as the slack is removed from the system and the cams and rock compress. A nearly tipped-out cam won't have enough expansion left to accommodate this process. A loose cam is also more prone to walking and has little range left to adjust."

**Bad. The crack is way too flared for this Metolius Power Cam, and the cam on the right side has very poor surface contact with the rock. Grade: F.**

**This Camalot is in a slightly flaring crack, with the inside cams retracted tighter than the outside ones, although each set of cams (inside and outside) are within a suitable range and all the cams have flush contact with the rock. Grade: C-.**

**Good. This Metolius cam is in the tighter aspect of its range. Green means good to go. Grade: A.**

*Bad. The cams are too open, rendering the placement unstable. Shoot for at least halfway tight on the cams. Grade: F.*

*The same crack with two different placements. In the left-hand photo, the left outside cam has poor contact and is too close to the edge of the crack. By flipping the cam around (right photo), the gold cam now has flush surface contact with the rock. Since the inside and outside sets of cams are offset, flipping the cam one way or the other can often afford a better placement, particularly in shallow cracks in corners.*

To illustrate what constitutes an acceptable range of retraction for the cams of a camming device, let's look at the Black Diamond Camalot in greater detail.

What is 50 to 90 percent retracted for a double-axle camming device like the Camalot? When you're looking at the Camalot without pulling on the trigger, it's at 0 percent retraction. Squeezing the trigger mechanism so that the cams are as tight as possible is 100 percent retracted. In a very tight placement, at 100 percent retracted, the Camalot will likely be very difficult to remove, and you risk losing an expensive piece of gear. In the last 10 percent of the tightest aspect of the range (90 to 100 percent retracted), the Camalot also loses some of its holding power—another reason not to go too tight on a placement. The starting point for a good placement is at 50 percent retraction, which is when you pull the cams at least halfway tight. Looking at the base of the cams, 50 percent retraction is when the base of each cam is at a 45-degree angle relative to the vertical axis of the Camalot. If the cams are symmetrically retracted, they will be at a 90-degree angle relative to each other. A common mistake that novices make is to place a Camalot near the outer limit of its range (0 to 50 percent retraction). This can prove to be a very unstable placement if the unit moves at all in the crack, which can easily happen if the Camalot is placed in a crack that widens above the cams and the piece is repeatedly weighted and unweighted. Again, the optimal Camalot placement is when the cams are at least halfway tight (50 percent retracted). From the beginning position, pull the trigger mechanism until the range on the cams is half the starting size, then go only smaller and tighter from

*In addition to parallel-sided cracks, Camalots can also work well in pods or pockets, as shown here. Just make sure the cams are in the recommended range.*

the placement, because the cam will be less stable, hence more prone to walking, and it will have less expansion range left to accommodate walking to a wider position. If the cam you choose aligns in the yellow zone, the next larger size will align perfectly in the green zone. Use that cam instead, if it's still on your rack. Never use a placement in the red zone unless it's the only placement available."

Study the literature that comes with any camming device you purchase and learn what the manufacturer recommends for the acceptable range of

*This Camalot has problems. It violates a rule stated in the Black Diamond literature under BAD PLACEMENTS: "Never place a unit so that the cams are offset (e.g., with two cams extended and with two cams retracted. It may not hold a fall." Also, the left outer cam is dangerously close to the edge of the crack. Grade: F.*

there. Scrutinize your placement after the camming device has been placed in a crack to make sure the cams are in the acceptable range.

Metolius cams have a unique color coding that assists you in assessment. The company gives this advice: "Verify that you have chosen the best size by making sure that the green Range Finder dots are lined up where the cam lobes touch the walls of the placement. Yellow dot alignment is okay too, but you must exercise more caution with

The innovative design of the Link Cam,
manufactured by Omega Pacific, covers a size
range of up to four standard cams. When leading
trad climbs, I often carry this gold size (number
3) on the back of my harness, in case I've used
up all my cams of a particular size and need
that size for a crucial anchor placement.

Bad. The problem here is not the placement
itself, but rather bad microstructure. The left
wall of the crack consists of rotten rock, ready
to exfoliate if the cam is loaded with any great
force, like in a leader fall. Grade: D-.

retraction and the various placement criteria. Most
manufacturers also have informative PDF files on
camming device guidelines that you can download
from the company's website.

Using a rigid-stem camming device
in a horizontal placement risks
breaking the metal stem. This can
be remedied by the "gunks tie-off."

*The "gunks tie-off"—named for the Shawangunks in New York, a trad area famous for steep face climbs protected by mainly horizontal cracks—is a pre-tied loop of high-tensile cord through the hole in the stem closest to the cam head.*

*The best option for a horizontal placement with cams is a flexible-stemmed unit that can withstand a downward force. A leader fall may bend the stem and render it damaged, but it will save the day.*

## Fixed Anchors

### Pitons

A piton is a metal spike that is hammered into a crack for an anchor. The blade of the piton is the part hammered into the crack, leaving the protruding eye into which you can clip a carabiner. Piton anchors are something of a rarity these days, but occasionally you'll come across fixed pitons (also called pins) at the top of a crag. Follow these steps before using any fixed pin:

First, assess the rock structure and look at the crack where the piton resides. Is it behind a block or flake, or is it in a straight-in crack with good structure? A good piton should be driven in all the way to the eye, and it should not wiggle when you clip into it with a sling and pull on it to test it. The piton itself should not be excessively corroded or cracked. (Look closely at the eye of the piton, as this is usually where the piton will be cracked.) To effectively test a fixed pin, you really need a hammer. Give the piton a light tap—it should have a high-pitched ring to it, and the hammer should spring off the piton. If you don't have a hammer, the best test is to clip a sling into it and give it a vigorous yank in the direction you'll be loading it. You can also tap it with a carabiner or small rock. Over time, pitons suffer from the vagaries of thermal expansion and contraction, particularly

*Pitons (left to right): Lost Arrow horizontal, Angle, Leeper Z, knifeblade.*

*Knifeblade piton (top) and RURP.*

*Pound it in the rest of the way.*

*To place a pin, insert it into the crack by hand. Ideally, it should go in about two-thirds of its length before pounding.*

*An angle piton driven all the way into the rock in a straight-in crack, and ideal pin placement.*

in winter; water expands when it freezes, prying and loosening the piton. Often a piton can be easily plucked out with your fingers after only a few seasons. If utilizing fixed pitons for protection or as part of your anchor system, use them with skepticism—and if possible, back them up.

## Bolts

The most common fixed anchor is a two-bolt anchor. Some knowledge of the history, characteristics, and specifications of bolts used for rock climbing will improve your ability to assess the reliability of bolt anchors.

In the 1960s and 1970s, bolts were placed by hand drilling—an arduous process where a drill bit was inserted into a drill holder and then a hammer was used to pound on the holder to painstakingly drill into the rock. Once the hole was deep enough, a bolt, with a hanger attached, was hammered into the hole. The most common bolt during that era was the ubiquitous ¼-inch contraction bolt, the Rawl Drive, manufactured by the Rawl Company and designed for the construction industry for anchoring in masonry or concrete. A contraction bolt has a split shaft that is wider than the diameter of the hole. When pounded into the hole, the two bowed shaft pieces are forced to straighten slightly, contracting under tension in the hole. This works fine for hard granite; but in soft rock like sandstone, the split shaft doesn't really contract all that much, and there is little tension to keep it in the hole, resulting in very weak pullout strength (i.e., pulling straight out on the bolt).

Another problem with ¼-inch bolts is that they came in various lengths, some as short as ¾ inch. Once placed in the rock, there was no way for future climbers to determine the length of the bolt merely by inspection.

There are two basic styles of ¼-inch Rawl Drive bolts: buttonhead and threaded. The buttonhead design has a mushroom-like head and is pounded into the hole with the hanger pre-attached. The threaded Rawl Drive has threads with a nut on the end to hold the hanger in place—a weaker configuration, since the threads can weaken the shear strength of the shaft if the hanger is at the level of the threads. More significantly, the threaded design has a serious flaw: Pulling straight out on the bolt hanger will only be as strong as the holding power of the nut on the threads—a dangerous problem if the nut is at the very end of the threads.

The shear strength on a brand-new ¼-inch Rawl Drive bolt is roughly 2,000 pounds, but the problem with contraction bolts is not shear strength but pullout strength, which varies drastically depending on the quality and hardness of the rock. In very soft sandstone, the pullout strength of a ¼-inch contraction bolt is extremely low, rendering the bolt unsafe.

The buttonhead Rawl Drive bolts also were sold in ⁵⁄₁₆-inch diameters, far more reliable as long as they were placed in good, hard, fine-grained granite. With a shear and pullout strength in excess of 4,000 pounds, the ⁵⁄₁₆-inch buttonhead was for many years the bolt of choice for first ascensionists who were hand-drilling bolts. The ⁵⁄₁₆-inch buttonhead Rawl Drive has been discontinued, but the ⅜-inch buttonhead is still on the market, with a shear strength of 7,000 pounds and a pullout strength of more than 4,000 pounds in the best granite. The problem with buttonhead Rawl Drive bolts is that they're made of carbon steel, which corrodes over time. What we once thought as bomber in the 1990s are now considered suspect, and at least one ⁵⁄₁₆-inch buttonhead failure (due to corrosion) has led to a climbing fatality.

Probably the most disconcerting problem associated with bolts from the ¼-inch era is not the bolts themselves but the hangers. During that time, hangers made for rock climbing were manufactured primarily by the SMC company. Thankfully, these hangers are easily identified—the "SMC" brand is stamped on them. There were two series of hangers—one good and one very bad. The bad hangers were nicknamed the SMC "death hanger," since some of them failed under body weight after only

*The infamous ¼-inch threaded Rawl Drive contraction bolt, complete with the SMC "death hanger." This ticking time bomb was removed and replaced from a route on Suicide Rock, California.*

*Buttonhead Rawl Drive contraction bolts (left to right): ³⁄₈-, ⁵⁄₁₆-, and ¼-inch sizes.*

a few seasons of exposure to the elements. These hangers are identifiable by a distinctive corrosive discoloration—a yellowish or bronze tint—whereas the "good" SMC hangers, made from stainless steel, show no signs of corrosion or rust and still appear silvery bright, even after twenty-five years. Another subtle but noticeable difference is in the thickness of the hangers: The "bad" hangers are roughly the thickness of a dime; the "good" ones, as thick

as a quarter. Another way to distinguish between them is to look closely at the SMC stamp on the hanger itself. On the "good" hangers "SMC" is stamped vertically; on the "bad" ones "SMC" runs horizontally.

Another dangerous relic from the 1970s is the Leeper hanger. More than 9,000 of these hangers were manufactured by Ed Leeper of Colorado; they were subsequently recalled because of stress corrosion problems with the metal, which rusted badly since it was not made of stainless steel. These hangers are easily identifiable because of their strange geometric shape and rusty condition.

*Learn the difference between these two hangers, one good, one very bad. They were manufactured by the SMC company and stamped "SMC" on the hanger. The one on the left is the infamous SMC "death hanger"— slightly thinner and, since it was made of carbon steel, corroded with a yellowish, bronze, or rust tint. The "good" SMC hanger on the right is made of stainless steel, and shows no sign of corrosion even after thirty years on the rock. Another identifying feature is that on the "bad" hanger the letters "SMC" are stamped horizontally, while on the "good" hanger, "SMC" is stamped vertically.*

*A ⁵⁄₁₆-inch buttonhead Rawl contraction bolt with "good" SMC hanger. In a good placement in solid granite, when new these bolts were rated at over 4,000 pounds shear strength. But since they're made of carbon steel, corrosion over time has become a problem, and they're now considered suspect.*

*A relic from the 1970s, this ¼-inch Rawl Drive buttonhead still looks good after twenty-five years, as does the "good" SMC hanger, with no signs of corrosion. Brand-new, these bolts have a shear strength of 2,000 pounds, roughly that of a medium wired stopper, but since the bolt is made of carbon steel not stainless steel, corrosion over time degrades them. Having replaced many of these, I can tell you that they're ticking time bombs. Often when I'll pry one out to replace it, the resistance is about the same as pulling a nail out of plywood, especially in soft rock, where the bolt's split shaft had minimal contraction.*

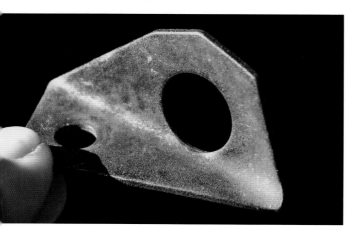

*The recalled Leeper hanger can easily be identified by its unique shape and rusty condition.*

Sport climbing was ushered into the United States in the 1980s, and climbers began to place bolts on rappel using cordless rotary hammer power drills. Since these bolts would now have to absorb numerous falls, climbers began to look for the strongest bolts available. The standard became ⅜-inch diameter for good, solid rock (like granite) and ½-inch diameter for softer rock (like sandstone)—standards that are still prevalent today.

Although there are numerous types of bolts used in rock climbing today, the gold standard has long been the "five-piece Rawl" expansion bolt (now sold as the Powers Power Bolt). This expansion bolt has a shaft with a hex head on one end and threads on the other end (the end that goes in the hole), with a cone-shaped piece screwed onto the threads. The shaft has a two-part split sleeve, and as the hex head is tightened, the cone climbs up the threads and under the sleeves, which presses the sleeves outward, "expanding" the bolt in the hole.

*Bad corrosion on a ⅜-inch-diameter threaded Rawl Drive bolt, with a badly corroded Leeper hanger to match.*

*The ⅜-inch threaded expansion bolt is another commonly seen bolt. Check to make sure the nut is tightly screwed down to secure the hanger.*

*A "spinner" is a bolt placement where the hanger moves freely, and you can spin it around the bolt in circle. Here, the hole wasn't drilled deeply enough, so when this 5/16-inch button head was pounded in, it hit the back of the hole before the buttonhead came up flush against the hanger.*

The more you tighten it, the wider the sleeve gets. The performance and strength of the bolt rely to a great extent on two things: the tolerance (diameter) of the hole and the strength of the rock itself. In good rock, the ⅜-inch Power Bolt is rated at over 7,000 pounds shear strength, with a pullout strength of roughly 5,000 pounds.

Now that many bolts have been out there for more than twenty-five years, we're finding out some things about how long a bolt will last. Many of the carbon steel bolts more than twenty-five years old are seriously corroded. This corrosion happens more quickly in mountain environments than in desert environments, but the bottom line is this: *A stainless steel bolt matched with a stainless steel hanger is the way to go.* Mixing metals (carbon steel and stainless steel) can accelerate deterioration because of galvanic corrosion (a reaction between different metals) and is no longer recommended.

Since these bolts are really designed for the construction business, the Powers Fastener company lists strength ratings based on the density of

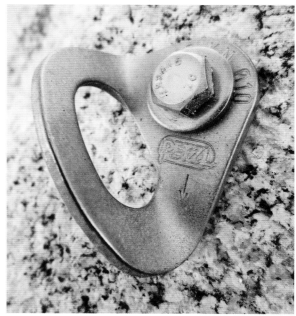

*The ⅜-inch-diameter stainless Powers "Power Bolt" expansion bolt matched with a stainless steel hanger is considered the current minimum standard. In good granite these bolts rate at around 7,000 pounds shear strength and 5,000 pounds pullout strength. Most climbers who replace old bolts now use ½-inch-diameter stainless steel Power Bolts (10,000 lbs. shear strength). If you're installing bolts, use a stainless steel bolt matched with stainless steel hanger to avoid any corrosion problems or reactions between mixed metals.*

the concrete they are placed in. Concrete is given a psi (pounds per square inch) rating. For example, "2,000 psi concrete" means it would take a weight of 2,000 pounds to crush a square inch of concrete. Hard, dense granite is analogous to 6,000 psi concrete; soft sandstone is more like 1,000 psi concrete.

Once a bolt has been installed, it's impossible to see what's going on beneath the surface (such as the length of the bolt); all you'll see is the head of the bolt, making identification of the type of bolt more difficult.

If you'd like to educate yourself, peruse "mechanical anchors" on the Powers company website (www.powers.com); you'll get an excellent tutorial on the various types of bolts and how strong they are in differing rock types.

Even if you're not an expert in mechanical engineering or in identifying bolt design and type, you should know what to watch for when inspecting a bolt anchor. An obvious red flag is rust. SMC "death hangers," Leeper hangers, homemade aluminum hangers, and any bolt or hanger with obvious signs of corrosion should never be trusted. Look closely and identify the diameter of the bolt. A ⅜-inch-diameter bolt has become the minimum standard, along with a stainless steel hanger. A bolt with threads and a nut holding the hanger in place is generally not as strong as the hex head types.

The rock should not show cracks emanating from the bolt placement—a more common problem with contraction bolts than expansion bolts.

In a good placement, the hanger should be flush against the rock and should not budge or be deformed in any way. A "spinner" is a bolt that protrudes enough so that the hanger can be easily spun around 360 degrees. This generally means the hole was not drilled deeply enough when the bolt was installed, and the bolt contacted the bottom of the hole before the hanger could be drawn flush against the rock.

If the bolt wiggles slightly when you pull on it or the hanger is loose, and the bolt has a hex

head or a nut on threads, tightening the bolt with a wrench may help; but most likely the bolt has a problem that can't be fixed. If while trying to tighten the bolt, you feel no increasing resistance and it won't tighten any further, the bolt has serious problems. This usually means the tolerance (diameter) of the hole is too big for the bolt or the rock is too soft.

As someone who has replaced many bolts over the years, I can tell you that any ¼-inch bolt should be considered suspect, particularly

*A well-engineered rappel anchor. Both bolts are ⅜-inch stainless Powers bolts with stainless steel Petzl hangers, along with a stainless steel chain, quick link, and ring. Everything was painted before installation to match the color of the rock.*

*All these old bolts at Joshua Tree were replaced with brand-new stainless steel hardware, courtesy of the ASCA.*

in less-than-perfect rock. I've plucked out many ¼-inch contraction bolts that came out with about the same resistance as a nail being pulled out of plywood. To replace a ¼-inch bolt, the best method is to pry it out of its hole, redrill the same hole to a ½-inch diameter, and install a ½-inch-diameter stainless steel Powers Power Bolt (10,000 lbs. shear strength) with a stainless steel hanger. I like to paint the hanger (before I install it) the same color as the rock so that the bolt is visually unobtrusive. It's a good feeling to replace a ticking time bomb with a solid anchor that will last a lifetime.

The American Safe Climbing Association (ASCA) has been very active in donating the necessary (and expensive) hardware to climbers, like myself, who take on the task of upgrading unsafe bolt anchors with modern stainless steel bolts and hangers. If you'd like to support and donate to the ASCA, you can contact them at www.safeclimbing.org.

*Racking up.*

## Standard Rack

Here is an example of the standard rack I usually carry. It will allow you to climb most routes in trad climbing areas. Buying more large nuts (like hexes) will save you money if you're on a budget, but camming devices will prove more versatile. Few experienced climbers carry a full range of hexes these days.

- 2 sets of wired nuts from 0.2 to 2 inches (e.g., Black Diamond Stoppers, sizes 2–12)
- 1 set of micro nuts (e.g., Black Diamond Steel Nuts sizes 00, 0, 1, 2, 3, 4, 5)
- 1 set of hexes or tricams from 1 to 2.5 inches (e.g., Black Diamond Hexes, sizes 5–8; Camp [Lowe] Tricams, sizes 2–4)
- 1 nut tool
- 1 set of small camming devices 0.3 to 0.75 inch (e.g., Metolius Master Cams sizes 00, 0, 1, 2, 3)
- 2 sets of camming devices from 0.4 to 3 inches (e.g., Black Diamond Camalot C3s sizes 0.3, 0.4, 0.5, 0.75, 1, 2, 3)
- One 4-inch camming device (e.g., Black Diamond #4 Camalot)
- 6 quickdraws with carabiners
- 6 single-length (24-inch) slings
- 2 double-length (48-inch) slings
- 2 cordelettes (18 to 20 feet of 7mm nylon cord)
- 25 to 30 carabiners
- 4 to 6 locking carabiners

# Anchor Systems

## The RENE Principal

The RENE principal is a simple, easy to remember acronym used for evaluating anchor systems. RENE stands for Redundancy, Equalization, and No Extension.

Redundancy means there is no place in the anchor system where you are relying on any single piece of equipment, be it a strand of cord, sling, or carabiner—in other words, there is always a backup. For bolt anchors the minimum would be two bolts, preferably ⅜-inch diameter. For gear anchors utilizing nuts and camming devices, a good minimum number (and the industry standard for professional guides) is three pieces of gear. Regarding rock structure, if the integrity of the rock is at all in question, using two different rock structures (e.g., two different crack systems) would add redundancy.

Equalization means that when the load is applied to the master point on the anchor system, the weight is evenly divided onto all the various components in the anchor. An anchor can be pre-equalized, which means the system is tied off to accept a force in one specific direction (most often the case in toproping and top belaying), or self-equalizing, meaning the anchor is rigged to adjust to loading within a range of direction changes.

No Extension means that if any one piece in the anchor fails, no significant amount of slack will develop before the load can be transferred to the remaining pieces. This is a key concept to remember when rigging toprope anchors that are extended over the edge, as the anchors are often a significant distance away from the master point.

*Two bolts pre-equalized with a double-length (48-inch) nylon sling tied with an overhand knot for a toprope setup. The two pear-shaped locking carabiners are opposed and reversed. This simple setup is redundant, equalized in one direction, and rigged for minimal extension. A nylon sling is a better choice than Dyneema for this application, since it has a modicum of stretch and the knot will be easier to untie. If using a Dyneema sling for this purpose, consider using a figure eight instead of an overhand to make it easier to untie after it's weighted.*

A good rule of thumb is to limit any extension in your anchor system to no more than half the length of a single (24-inch) sling.

## Principals of Equalization

### Pre-Equalized: The Cordelette System

The cordelette system is a pre-equalized system, meaning that once you tie off the cordelette in the anticipated direction of loading, if the load shifts slightly in any direction, all the load goes onto one placement (albeit with minimal extension), unlike a self-equalizing system that adjusts with changes in the direction of the loading. For many anchor systems, you can in most cases readily determine the direction your anchor system will be loaded in, so complex self-equalizing rigs are not required. The cordelette system is essentially a system of backups. If one piece fails, the load transfers instantly to the remaining pieces with minimal shock loading, since the rigging limits extension.

The beauty of the pre-equalized cordelette system is that it is easy to remember and simple to rig. The cordelette is fairly versatile in that it can be used to rig two, three, or four placements. The most common fixed anchor you'll encounter is a two-bolt anchor. An easy and bomber rig is to start by

*Four-piece anchor pre-equalized with a 7mm diameter nylon cordelette.*

*Four-piece toprope anchor pre-equalized with 6mm Sterling PowerCord cordelette.*

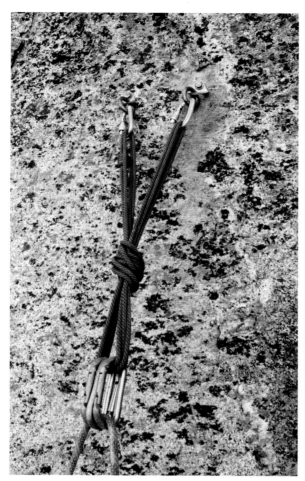

*Simple two-bolt toprope anchor rigged with a doubled 18-foot 7mm nylon Sterling cordelette. The cordelette is doubled to start with, producing four strands at the master point loop, and the climbing rope is clipped into three oval carabiners opposed and reversed. The bolts have Fixe Ring Hangers. The welded rings are rated at 10,000 pounds breaking strength.*

*Demonstration of pre-equalized cordelette with three anchor placements, tied with a 7mm nylon cordelette. A clove hitch has been tied to the top left piece to keep the double fisherman's knot away from the end loops. This is a simple and effective rig as long as the direction of load is predetermined, which is most often the case when toproping.*

doubling the cordelette, then clipping the doubled strand into both bolts with locking carabiners. Pull down between the bolts, gather all the strands together, and tie a figure eight on a bight. This gives you four strands of cord at the master point.

To rig three or four placements, clip the cordelette into all the placements, then pull down between the pieces and gather all the loops together. I like to clip a carabiner into all the gathered loops and pull in the anticipated loading

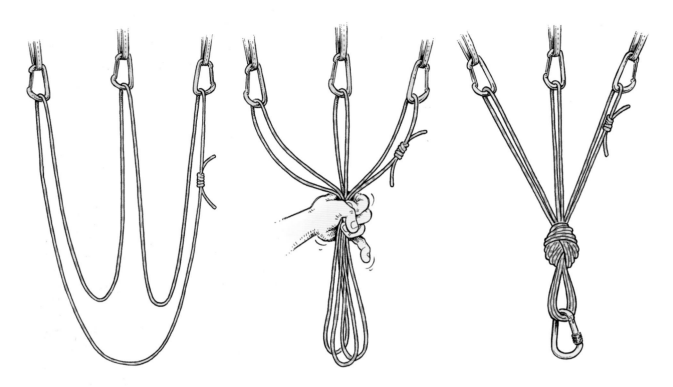

*An 18- to 20-foot-long cordelette is usually long enough to equalize three or four anchor points, as long as they are not spaced too far apart. Use a sling or two if necessary to get all the carabiners you'll be clipping into within a workable range. Clip a single strand of the cordelette into each carabiner, then pull down between the pieces and gather the loops (with three pieces you'll have three loops). Clipping a carabiner into the loops before you tie the knot will make it easier to equalize all the strands. Tie a figure eight knot to create your master point, which should be roughly 3 to 4 inches in diameter. If you don't have enough cord to tie a figure eight, an overhand knot takes up less cord.*

direction, then tie a figure eight knot with the carabiner attached to help even out all the strands. If you find yourself coming up a bit short on enough length to tie off all the loops with a figure eight, an overhand knot will take up less cord; even though it's a slightly weaker knot, this is not a factor, since you'll have at least three or four loops at your master point. Another trick is to take a regular length (24-inch) sling and clip it into the piece that's farthest away from you—this will give you more length to work with on the cordelette.

*The drawback of the cordelette system (left) is that if the direction of the anticipated load changes, one piece in the anchor takes all the load (right). Think of the cordelette system as a system of backups: If the one piece that is loaded fails, the load goes onto the next piece, with relatively minimal extension in the system. For toproping anchors and top belaying, since the load on the anchor system is relatively low, the cordelette system has the advantage of being easy to use and simple to rig, negating any potential for major shock loading.*

*Three-piece anchor rigged with a 7mm nylon cordelette. Since nylon cord stretches, the very short bottom arm will absorb most of the force in this setup. If you're using a high-tensile cord (Dyneema or Technora) this stretch is negated, since the material is basically static. Guide Chris Baumann offers this tip when rigging a nylon cordelette with a long arm: "Lean in to the shortest arm before you tie the knot, creating a tiny bit of slack in the shorter arms." In this case, before tying the knot, if you had "leaned" a little to the right, the short arm would have a bit of slack, allowing the top arms to load and stretch before the shorter arm loaded.*

## Adjusting the Cordelette

My colleague Chris Baumann is a rock climbing instructor who guides at Joshua Tree and Donner Summit, California. He offers these tips on how to fine-tune cordelette equalization:

"After tying your cordelette into a master point (with a figure eight loop) you may have experienced, or probably will experience, an instance when you misjudge your angle of pull, creating slack on one or two arms of the cordelette. Whether you are hanging from the anchor, ready to belay up your second, or have just set your master point carabiners to hang a toprope, if you notice that the equalization is a bit off, there are some quick and easy fixes without having to take apart your master point. When this happens to me, I use a sequence of hitches and knots to achieve the perfect angle of pull quickly. In the following sequence, each one of the hitches and knots takes up progressively more slack.

"Start with just an extra coil through the carabiner; if that doesn't take enough slack, remove the coil and try adding a Munter hitch, then a clove hitch, then a figure eight.

"If the connection knot on the cordelette is set too close to a carabiner, you won't be able to use the hitches. The figure eight can be tied anywhere in the strand."

Here a 7mm nylon cordelette has been untied and used in its full length. Many professional guides tie their cordelettes with a knot that can be easily untied so that, if necessary, they can use the full length as shown here. A good knot to use to tie your cordelette into its original loop is a flat overhand (make sure the tails are at least 8 inches long, or back it up with a second overhand tied right on top of the first one) or a figure eight bend, tied with the tails at least 3 inches long. The figure eight bend is a much stronger knot, but it's more difficult to untie.

*Three-piece cordelette anchor. Note how the cams have been positioned so that the stems are not bent over the lip of the crack.*

When untied, the cordelette can equalize three more widely-spaced pieces, where the standard, fixed-loop cordelette would be too short. To rig three points, tie a figure eight loop on each end, clip these into the two outside pieces, then clip a strand to the middle piece. Pull down the cord between the pieces and you'll end up with a loop to the middle piece and a single strand to each outside piece. Tie a figure eight loop and you'll have a three-loop master point.

## Self-Equalizing Systems

### THE SLIDING X

The sliding X (aka magic X) is a simple way to equalize two anchor points with a sling, creating a mini-anchor system that adjusts as the load shifts in direction. In scrutinizing the overall anchor system, if I use a sliding X between two pieces, I count this as only one placement as far as redundancy is concerned, because it is only one sling. However, by

*When rigging a sliding X, make sure you clip into the loop you've created by twisting the sling.*

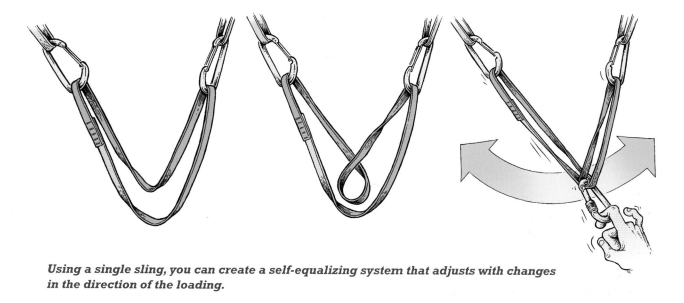

*Using a single sling, you can create a self-equalizing system that adjusts with changes in the direction of the loading.*

equalizing two placements that can adjust to slight shifts in direction, you create one more inherently bomber piece.

If using the sliding X with a long sling (like a sewn, 48-inch double–length sling), you can minimize extension by tying overhand knots just above the clip-in point. This allows the system to adjust, but limits any extension if one piece fails.

*A simple two-bolt anchor rigged for toproping with a sliding X using two separate slings and three oval carabiners at the master point for a redundant, self-equalizing system. With a two-bolt anchor, I always use locking carabiners on the bolt hangers. The drawback of this rig is that if one bolt were to fail, the system would extend to the length of the slings. As a general rule, limit the maximum extension in your anchor system to half the length of a single (24-inch) sling, which is what you have here.*

*A tricky belay anchor on Mechanic's Route, Tahquitz Rock, California. When I got to this spot, I realized I'd left my cordelette at the previous belay, so I had to improvise. The top two pieces are equalized with a sliding X, with an overhand knot tied to limit any extension to the top piece. The double-length red nylon sling is tied with a figure eight to create redundancy at the master point.*

*Two pieces equalized with a sliding X. An overhand knot is tied on the long arm of the sling to limit extension. If the top piece fails, the sling moves only a few inches. This rig is not redundant, since the master point is a single loop of twisted sling.*

*A two-cam anchor on Tahquitz Rock, equalized with a sliding X using two separate slings. While making three separate placements is a dogmatic goal for gear anchors, consider one of the most common anchors on face climbs: two bolts. Here we have perfect rock structure— immaculate, fine-grained granite—and two perfect Camalot placements. Would I trust this anchor? Absolutely. I belayed off it. Each Camalot has a breaking strength of 14 kN (over 3,000 lbs.), each sling is rated at 22 kN (nearly 5,000 lbs.), and two opposed and reversed carabiners are stronger than that. Know your equipment, its breaking strengths, and how it all adds up. A good rule of thumb is for your anchor to be no weaker than 25 kN (5,620 lbs.).*

*Two-bolt toprope anchor rigged with a sliding X and extension-limiting knots. By using a double-length (48-inch) nylon sling tied with two overhand knots, the sling itself becomes redundant at the master point, since it has two loops of webbing.*

*Since there is no knot on the locking carabiner side of the sling, this setup lacks redundancy at the master point, since you're relying on a single, twisted loop of the sling.*

To set up a simple self-equalizing anchor system from two bolts, you can use two single-length slings together with a sliding X, creating a redundant rig with minimal extension.

*Stacked Xs. In this three-piece anchor, redundancy has been achieved by tying two extension-limiting knots on the purple sling.*

Stacked Xs. By tying two overhand knots on both the red and yellow double-length nylon slings, this three-piece anchor has redundancy and minimal extension throughout the system.

This toprope anchor is self-equalizing but lacks redundancy in three critical elements: in the single, rewoven 1-inch tubular nylon sling; the single yellow cordelette; and the single locking biner that connects them. While plenty strong, the issue here is not one of strength, but of redundancy. Lack of redundancy is a problem for unmonitored toprope anchors like this one, particularly if it's being heavily used, since the soft nylon cordellete will get abraded over the edge and no one will see it happening. Also, if one of the three pieces were to fail, you'd get some major movement in the red sling, resulting in shock loading the two remaining pieces.

## THE QUAD: EVOLUTION OF THE CORDELETTE

Since John Long and I introduced the quad in the third edition of *Climbing Anchors,* back in 2006, the quad system has gained popularity as a rigging system for multipitch anchors, particularly with professional guides. The quad is also a great system for equalizing two-bolt toprope anchors. It gives you near-perfect equalization with minimal extension and great strength.

To rig the quad on a two-bolt anchor, start by doubling your cordelette, then grab the middle with your fist. Tie an overhand knot on each side of your fist, and you're ready to rig. Clip the double-strand loops into the bolts with locking carabiners, then clip only three of the four strands at the master

*A two-bolt anchor rigged with a 7mm cordelette and the quad system. The cordelette is clipped directly to the bolt hangers with locking carabiners, bypassing the cheap hardware store lap links (which are only rated at around 1,000 lbs.).*

*Detail of quad rig master point rigged for toproping with three oval carabiners opposed and reversed.*

**Quad rig using Sterling 6mm PowerCord and three steel oval carabiners for a toprope setup.**

**Detail of quad rig with two locking carabiners opposed and reversed.**

point, leaving one loop outside your master point carabiners. This ensures that if one bolt fails, you are clipped into a pocket on the master point.

*By splitting the four strands, two and two, the quad offers two separate, redundant master points, great for belaying from single or multipitch anchors. To use the quad on a multipitch anchor, split the end loops two and two, giving you two separate but redundant master points. The quad can easily be rigged from two or three anchor points.*

*Rigging a three-point anchor with the quad. First, double the cordelette (left). Clip a single loop into two points, pull the cordelette down in the direction of anticipated loading, even the loops, then tie an overhand knot (lower left). Tie a similar overhand knot and clip to the third piece (lower right). Ideally, the third piece should be your strongest placement. Now you have two redundant master points.*

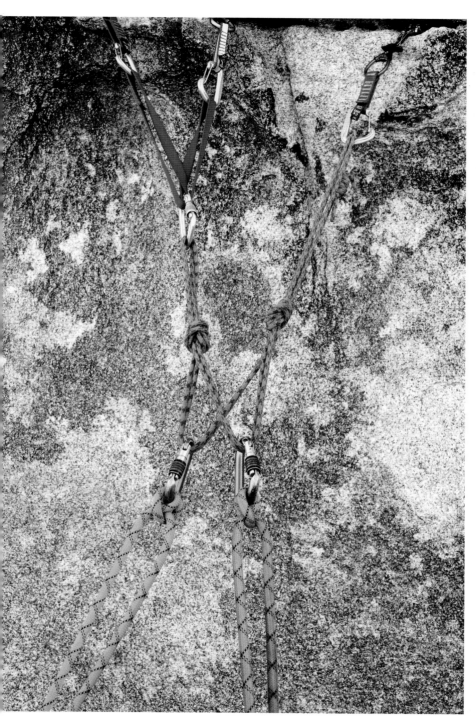

*Three-piece anchor using a combination of quad and sliding X rigging to create a self-equalizing anchor system.*

# Vectors

A vector is a quantity that incorporates both direction and magnitude. Picture a high liner balancing out on the middle of a taut line. If he weighs 200 pounds, the load at each end where the line is attached will be roughly 1,000 pounds. Why is this? When two anchor points are equalized, as the angle of the wire, sling, cord, or rope approaches 180 degrees, the forces at the anchor points increase drastically. When the angle is narrow, the load is distributed at around 50 percent to each anchor.

Keep this in mind when you build anchor systems. If the angle between two anchor points reaches 120 degrees, you'll load each anchor at 100 percent. Strive to keep all the angles under 60 degrees so that you'll be splitting the load roughly 50/50. A good rule of thumb is to always keep the angles under 90 degrees. Also, avoid rigging a sling between two anchors in a triangular configuration (called the American Triangle), which, even at 90 degrees, places 1.3 times the force at each anchor point. An American Triangle rigged at 120 degrees would almost double the load at each anchor point!

## American Triangle

Load per anchor with 100 lbs. of force

| Bottom Angle | V Rigging | Triangle Rigging |
|---|---|---|
| 30 degrees | 52 lbs. | 82 lbs. |
| 60 degrees | 58 lbs. | 100 lbs. |
| 90 degrees | 71 lbs. | 131 lbs. |
| 120 degrees | 100 lbs. | 193 lbs. |
| 150 degrees | 193 lbs. | 380 lbs. |

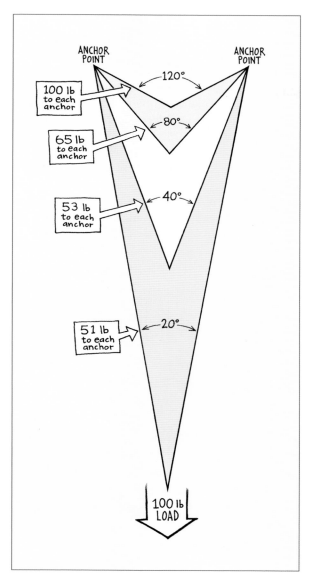

This diagram illustrates how a 100-pound load is distributed between two anchor points at various angles. Keep the angle between two anchors as narrow as possible, striving to keep it under 60 degrees. At 120 degrees the load is 100 percent at each anchor! Think of 0 to 60 degrees as ideal, 60 to 90 degrees a caution zone, and over 90 degrees a danger zone.

The American Triangle rigged at a rappel anchor. Avoid rigging with a triangle configuration—it adds unnecessary forces to your anchor points. Stick to a V configuration to limit the force to as low as possible.

## The Joshua Tree System

Joshua Tree National Park is a vast area, with hundreds of crags to choose from. The setups can be time-consuming and gear intensive because most anchors require gear placements set well back from the cliff edge, and bolted anchors are a rarity. Out of necessity we developed a system to rig toprope anchors that is both efficient and redundant, using a length of low-stretch rope. I call it the Joshua Tree System, and I can vouch for its efficiency—it's the system we've used for more than thirty years in my climbing school on countless toprope setups.

For your rigging rope, I'd recommend either 10mm or 10.5mm diameter. For most situations a 60-foot length will suffice. My favorite rigging rope is the Sterling Safety Pro, which is EN 1891 certified, with a stretch of about 4 percent in a toprope fall situation. This rope handles well and has good abrasion resistance. It can also be used for fixed lines, tethering, rappelling, and toproping. You don't want to use a dynamic rope for toprope rigging, since its stretch will make it seesaw back and forth over edges, and you don't want to use a low-stretch rope for leading.

To rig the Joshua Tree System, visualize a V configuration, with two separate anchors at the top of the V and your master point at the bottom, or point, of the V. The master point is tied with a BHK ("big honking knot"), which is essentially an overhand knot tied on a doubled bight, which gives you two-loop redundancy at the master point.

In the Joshua Tree System, we call the rigging rope an "extension" rope, or "extendo" rope. The two separate strands of rope that run from the master point to anchors A and B are the "legs" of the extension rope.

Ideally, the angle of the V should be less than 60 degrees—and at least less than 90 degrees. Once you have determined where the climb is and where you want your master point, picture the V in your mind and begin to set your anchors. If using natural anchors, it could be as simple as two trees. If you climb at areas with many trees at the clifftop, you're

in luck; the Joshua Tree System will simplify your rigging. All you need is the rigging rope itself—no slings or cordelettes required. Tie one end of your rigging rope around one tree with a simple bowline. Run the rope over the edge, and tie a BHK. I usually weight a bight of rope with a few carabiners and let it dangle about 4 feet over the edge, knowing that when I pull it back up and tie the BHK, the master point will be about 4 feet higher, which is the length of doubled bight taken up by tying the BHK. Then tie around the second tree with a bowline with a bight, and you're done.

With gear anchors the combinations are endless, but a good minimum is at least three gear placements. Most of my setups tend to end up with two gear placements on each end of the V. If you learn

*Using a tether for safety while rigging a toprope. One end of a double-length nylon sling is attached to the rigging rope with a klemheist knot; the other end of the sling is attached to the harness belay loop with a locking carabiner.*

## Tying the BHK ("Big Honking Knot")

*Start by taking a 4-foot-long bight and doubling it.*

*Tie an overhand knot on all four strands.*

*Thread the two loops back through the loop you've created,*

*or incorporate the loop into the master point carabiners.*

to tie double loop knots, you can eliminate the need for slings and cordelettes in most situations.

For safety as you approach the cliff edge, protect yourself by tethering with a double length (48-inch) $^{11}/_{16}$-inch nylon sling. Pick the leg of the V you feel is stronger or the one that's redundant (two pieces) and tether to that strand by tying a klemheist knot around it and attaching the other end of the sling to your harness belay loop with a locking carabiner. A nylon sling is preferable to a Spectra or Dyneema one, since nylon grips better on the friction hitch and has a bit of stretch, whereas Spectra or Dyneema is slicker, static (like a wire cable), and has no stretch. Now you can slide the klemheist knot up and down the

*Tether detail. If you're working at the cliff's edge, protect yourself. This climber has rigged his BHK master point, all the while protected with a personal tether—a double-length nylon sling. He's secured one end to his harness to a locking biner; the other end is attached to the rigging rope via a klemheist knot.*

rigging rope to safeguard yourself as you work near the edge. Tie a BHK (see photos) so that your master point dangles just over the lip of the cliff edge, positioned directly above your chosen

*Overview of the Joshua Tree System. The left "leg" of the extension rope is attached with a double loop bowline to two cams; the right leg is clove hitched to single, bomber cam. A BHK is tied for the master point, with three opposed and reversed oval carabiners ready for the climbing rope.*

*Close-up of the master point on the Joshua Tree System using a BHK and three steel oval carabiners with the gates opposed and reversed.*

climb. Attach your climbing rope with carabiners (either two opposed and reversed locking or three opposed and reversed ovals) and run the rope back to anchor B, attaching it with a clove hitch to a locking carabiner. This will allow you to adjust the tension and fine-tune the equalization. Use edge protectors at the lip to protect your rope from abrasion and cutting if sharp edges are present.

*Another version of the Joshua Tree System. Here, both legs have two cams equalized with sliding Xs— an elaborate rig, but one that fully adjusts to any shift, however minor, in the direction of pull. In most setups I prefer to use double-loop knots; it's more efficient, and since I know the direction my anchor will be loaded in, I'm not worried about drastic vector changes.*

*The Joshua Tree System rigged with two double-loop figure eights.*

If you learn to tie double loop knots like the double-loop figure eight and double-loop bowline, along with the in-line figure eight, you'll be able to eliminate many slings and cordelettes from your anchor system and become more efficient in your rigging. For example, when using the Joshua Tree System, I often start with two bomber pieces at the end of one leg on my extension rope, then equalize them with a double loop knot, thus eliminating the need for slings or cordelettes. As I move toward the edge and perhaps find more anchor placements, I use the in-line eight to equalize these pieces to the system. The double loop knots and in-line eight are mandatory for those of you who wish to become master riggers!

# Unmonitored Anchor Systems

Make sure the extension rope is not resting over sharp edges at the lip of the cliff. This setup is an "unmonitored" anchor system, which means that once rigged, you'll be at the base and not able to watch what is happening at the anchor—like the extension rope abrading over an edge. Take special care to prevent this by padding the edge (a pack or rope bag will work) or, better yet, using commercially made edge protectors.

*Toprope all day long with your extension rope rubbing on a sharp edge, and you'll end up with a seriously abraded rope like this one.*

*A commercially made edge protector, like this one sold by Petzl, is a wise investment. Attach it to your rigging rope with a friction hitch.*

## Making the Transition from Rigging to Rappelling

If you decide to rappel to the base, you will need to transition from your extension rope to your rappel rope. Slide the klemheist knot on your personal tether down one leg of the extension rope (pick what you consider to be the stronger leg) until you approach the edge. Before you get to the edge, pull up your doubled rappel rope, rig your rappel device, and back it up with an autoblock. Slide the klemheist knot down until it's just on top of the BHK. Make the transition over the edge, using the extension rope for balance, and until you've weighted your rappel system. Double-check everything before removing your personal tether, then proceed to rappel.

*Instructor Erin Guinn making a safe transition from rigging to rappelling. She's used a 48-inch nylon sling for her tether, attached to the rigging rope with a klemheist knot. She's backed up her rappel device with an autoblock knot clipped to her harness leg loop with a locking carabiner.*

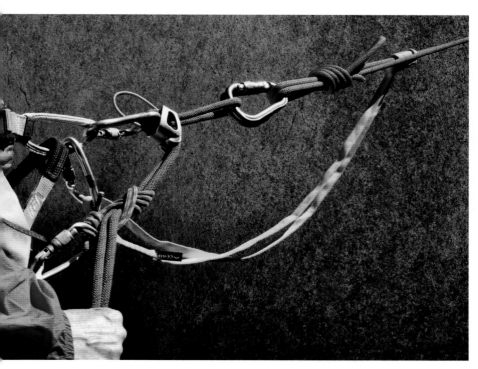

*Transition rig detail. If you know you'll be rappelling, don't make your BHK loop too long, since you'll need to get around it without your tether coming tight. Before you unclip and remove your tether, weight your rappel system and double-check everything. Make sure your autoblock is engaged and not up against your rappel device, which would keep it from grabbing the rope properly.*

## Anchor System Assessment for Gear Anchors

To assess the anchor system, I use a macro-to-micro progression. Don't lose sight of the big picture and get focused on the minutia. Number one is the structural integrity of the rock itself. Without solid rock, no matter how great the individual placements are, a catastrophic failure is possible due to failure of the rock structure. The ideal is the "crack in the planet"—a crack in massive rock that bisects the plane of the rock face at a right angle. Loose blocks, flakes, and cracked rock should all be considered suspect. Be critical in assessing rock structure—it's literally the foundation your anchor is built upon.

Next, look at the overall anchor rigging. Is it redundant? Is it well equalized, with no extension? A good rule of thumb is to limit the extension in any anchor system to no more than half the length of a single (22-inch) sling. To pass muster, the anchor system must satisfy the RENE principal in general.

Finally, scrutinize each individual placement, starting with the microstructure of the rock. Are there loose flakes, hollow spots, or any rotten or disintegrating rock within the crack? Then look closely at each individual placement. If it's a nut, does it satisfy the SOS. principal? If it's a camming device, is it in the manufacturer's recommended range of retraction?

# Sport Climbing

## History

A "sport climb," by strict definition, is a climb that consists entirely of fixed hardware for protection and for the anchor. To lead a sport climb, you'll only need quickdraws, slings, and carabiners. Usually the fixed hardware consists of reliable bolts, although in rare cases they're supplemented by a fixed piton or two. The modern standard has evolved to a minimum of ⅜-inch-diameter stainless steel for bolts, although most bolt replacers now use ½-inch diameter as the evolving standard.

In general, most sport climbs don't have dangerously runout sections, but there are exceptions. On harder climbs this can be a section where you simply can't let go long enough to clip a bolt, or a section of easier climbing relative to the grade of the crux.

The term "sport climb" wasn't heard in the United States until the 1980s. Before that, through the 1970s and into the early 1980s, a "ground-up" ethic prevailed at many traditional climbing areas in the United States, like Yosemite, Tahquitz and Suicide Rocks, and Joshua Tree, California, and Eldorado Canyon, Colorado.

First ascents were done without preview, and bolts were drilled on the lead, often from precarious stances. As far back as 1972, visionary climber Doug Robinson wrote: "But every climb is not for every climber; the ultimate climbs are not democratic. The fortunate climbs protect themselves by being unprotectable and remain a challenge that can be solved only by boldness and commitment backed solidly by technique."

But as techniques progressed, climbers were drawn to steeper and blanker faces, where it was impossible to let go with both hands to hand-drill and place a bolt.

The use of hooks for aid made it possible to drill bolts on the lead, ground up, on these steeper routes. The zenith of the ground-up era was undoubtedly John Bachar's lead of the Bachar-Yerian route (5.11c R) in Yosemite in the summer of 1981, which follows a vertical water streak studded with knobs leading up the intimidating 400-foot west face of Tuolumne Meadow's Medlicott Dome. Bachar risked 100-foot falls venturing into unknown terrain. To this day the route has become a test piece for elite face climbers wishing to test both physical and psychological limits. But there haven't been many takers—in almost forty years the route has seen only a couple dozen ascents.

In Europe, sport climbing was well established in France by the 1980s, principally due to the nature of the rock: overhanging limestone riddled with finger pockets but devoid of crack systems. For free climbing to progress, top-down rappel bolted

*Terri Condon leads Tension Tamer (5.13a), Bear Crag, California.*

**PHOTO BY GREG EPPERSON**

***John Bachar at Joshua Tree, 1985.***

obvious what we had to do. If something as outrageous as Chain Reaction went free, then almost everything would go. All the elements were there—featured rock, rappel bolting, cleaning, hangdogging, lots of free time, sufficient technical skills, and no opposition. The final point was key. I wasn't pursuing my style to revolt against the established norms in climbing. All I was trying to do was tick another route off my list. And I was using the most efficient process that I could devise to do that. I might not have been a rebel, but I didn't give a damn about doing things exactly how they'd been done before. I truly believed that I had found a better way to push limits of difficulty." Smith Rock State Park quickly became a US sport climbing mecca, and today the park boasts more than 1,800 sport routes.

Soon, sport climbs were sprouting up everywhere, but in the 1980s and early 1990s at traditional climbing areas like Yosemite and Joshua Tree, top-down rappel-bolted sport climbs weren't widely accepted. An era that can only be termed "bolt wars" ensued as staunch traditionalists chopped rappel-placed bolts as fast as they were placed.

In 1985, after returning from a climbing trip to France, where he witnessed the evolution of French sport climbing, a young and talented upstart by the name of Christian Griffith established the first sport climb in Eldorado Canyon, Colorado, Paris Girls (5.13a), which was summarily chopped. The bolts were reinstalled, and Griffith went on to establish Eldorado's most difficult face routes at the time—Desdichado (5.13c), up a spectacular overhang, and Lakme (5.13b), up a stunning arête on Eldorado's Redgarden Wall. While Eldorado Canyon, with its majority of traditional climbs, never became a sport climbing center, other Colorado areas like Boulder Canyon, Shelf Road, Clear Creek Canyon, and Rifle Mountain Park would become major sport climbing areas.

In 1986 visiting French climber Jean-Baptiste Tribout established the first climb in America to be

routes seemed the next logical progression of the sport, and French free climbers soon eclipsed Americans constrained by traditional ground-up ethics.

Alan Watts is widely credited with establishing the first US sport climbs at Smith Rocks, Oregon. In 1983 Watts climbed Watts Tot's (5.12b) up a vertical, nearly featureless face, and Chain Reaction (5.12c) up a spectacular, overhanging arête, ushering in an era that would change American rock climbing forever.

In his Smith Rock State Park guidebook Watts writes about Chain Reaction: "With that one ascent all the pieces fell into place, and it became graded 5.14 with his redpoint of To Bolt or Not to Be (5.14a) at Smith Rocks. This served as a wake-up call for American rock climbers that the future for increasing standards of difficulty would be through sport climbing.

While the bolt wars raged at traditional bastions like Joshua Tree and Yosemite Valley, isolated areas without traditional history were simultaneously being developed into popular sport climbing areas—places like Owens River Gorge and Clark Mountain in California, the Calico Hills of the Red Rocks in Nevada, Kentucky's Red River Gorge, and the Rumney Cliffs of New Hampshire.

By the mid-1990s climbing gyms began to sprout up in almost every major urban center in America. A new generation of climbers, who had learned on artificial walls, ventured outside, naturally drawn to sport climbing. This new generation largely eschewed scary runout traditional climbs and adopted a healthy appetite for well-protected, fun sport climbs. The bolt wars ended, and sport climbing was here to stay. The next controversy, which has continued to this day, is the retro-bolting of older traditional routes, adding bolts to make the routes safer for the masses. It will be up to the next generation to define the future of the sport, but it's my hope that retro-bolting the Bachar-Yerian route and routes like it will never happen.

# Sport Climbing Safety

## Common Sport Climbing Accidents

With closely spaced bolts, bolted anchors, and no dangerous runouts, what can go wrong? But accidents do happen on sport climbs, on a shockingly regular basis. One of the most common accidents is a lowering accident, caused simply by the rope not being long enough to lower the climber to the ground, and no knot on the end of the rope to close the system. Another common mishap is a leader fall with the rope between the legs while climbing to the right or left of a protection bolt,

which flips the falling leader upside-down rather violently, resulting in head injuries. Incorrectly clipping the quickdraw can lead to the rope unclipping itself during a leader fall. Let's review the fundamentals of sport climbing and how to prevent these scenarios.

## Leading Sport Climbs

### SAFETY CHECKS

The first thing to do is to close the system. This means dealing with both ends of the rope. You can close the system by having both climbers tie into each end of the rope or, if the belayer isn't tying in, simply tying a stopper knot in the belayer's end. Seems simple, but not closing the system leads to at least one tragic accident seemingly every year at some sport crag in America. One of America's most famous climbers was dropped some 20 feet to the ground in a lowering accident without a closed system; luckily, he fully recovered from his injuries and went on to do great climbs. Not every anchor at a sport crag is set at 100 feet or less; some anchors will be more than half your rope length, requiring a longer single rope (70 meters, or 230 feet) or two ropes to get down. In a single-pitch environment, you should *always close the system*. It's a good safety habit.

If you haven't developed the habit of partner safety checks, now is a good time to start. More than one expert climber has tied in while distracted, completed the climb, leaned back from the anchor to be lowered, and fallen to the ground as his or her rope tie-in knot failed. This happened due to lack of a safety check; these climbers never developed the habit of checking as part of their program. As a climbing instructor, it's so ingrained in my protocol that it has become part of my climbing routine.

I use the ABC acronym: Anchor, Belayer, Climber. This works for both leading and toproping scenarios. First check the ground anchor (if it exists), usually connected to the belayer via the rope and a clove hitch. Then check the belayer. Check the harness, knot, belay device. Then check the climber's harness and knot tie-in. If using a Grigri to belay, Petzl recommends checking the Grigri by a quick stout pull on the non-brake strand to make sure the device properly locks off. The anchor, belayer, and first point the lead climber will clip into should all be in a line. Now you're ready to climb.

On a route with a difficult start right off the ground, consider asking your partner to spot you as you climb up to the first bolt. You should be well-versed on properly rigging your quickdraws and how to clip them. The rope should run from the inside out through the carabiner (i.e., from the rock out to you). For me it's easiest to clip my rope into the carabiner with the hand opposite the gate's position. For example, with my right hand, I find it easiest to clip the carabiner with the gate facing left. I rack all the quickdraws on my right side for right-handed clips (quickdraws with gates facing left), and vice versa for my left side (left-handed clips), since on difficult sport routes you'll only have one hand to clip. Practice clipping—both hands with gates facing both right and left—until you're proficient. The worst time to fall is when you're just about to clip, since you'll have a lot of rope slack in your hand.

If you're climbing directly above the bolt, which side you position the gate on the rope bearing end of the quickdraw is inconsequential; if you're

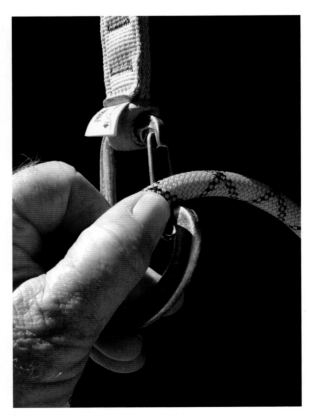

*If the gate is facing right, it will be easiest to clip with your left hand by capturing the carabiner with your middle finger and holding the rope with your thumb and forefinger.*

 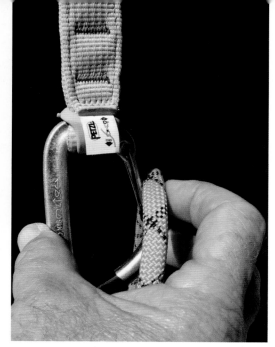

*If the gate is facing right and you have to clip it with your right hand, grab the base of the carabiner with your thumb and middle finger, and clip the rope using the forefinger.*

*Correct quickdraw orientation. The rope runs from the inside out. The climber is moving right, and the gate is facing left.*

*Incorrect orientation. The rope runs from the outside in.*

Peter Croft leading My Laundry (5.9) at Joshua Tree. He's moving to the right of the quickdraw, so the carabiner gate faces left. The rope is on the outside of his left leg, not between his legs.

*Dangerous quickdraw orientation. The rope runs from the outside in and the gate is facing right, the same direction the climber is moving, If the climber falls, the rope can potentially cross over the gate and unclip.*

directly above the bolt, you'll want to position the rope between your legs. If you veer off slightly to the right or left, you'll want to pay attention to two things (this is important!):

1. The position of the rope relative to your legs.

2. Which way the carabiner gate on the rope bearing end of the quickdraw is facing.

If you're moving to the right of the bolt, position the rope in front of your left leg, not between your legs. The gate of the carabiner that your rope is clipped into should be facing left (opposite the direction you're climbing).

If you're moving left from the bolt, position the rope in front of and on the outside of your right leg. The carabiner gate should be facing right.

## Falling

Falling is a part of sport climbing. And there is a technique to falling. First, don't push off or out from the rock when you fall—when the rope comes tight, any outward momentum you've created will be converted to inward momentum and send you crashing into the wall. Also, pushing off with your legs creates more force and momentum for your fall. If you find yourself swinging toward the wall, brace yourself with both arms extended outward and both legs in a rappel/lowering stance. In big airy falls, I've found that grabbing the rope with both hands just above my knot helps maintain a stable posture and keeps me from flipping sideways.

If you're in a position where you might fall, and your belayer can't see you, get his or her attention by saying "Watch me!" A response of "I'm with you" goes a long way to help muster the confidence to go for it. If you do come off, yell "Falling," especially if you're out of sight of the belayer.

On low-angle slab sport routes, a fall can be more like a slide. On swinging, low-angle falls, a quick running/paddling motion with your feet can keep you from getting scraped up.

## Transitions: Lowering and Rappelling

Before embarking on the lead, go over a game plan with your belayer and discuss what you'll do at the anchor. If the anchor has gated cold shuts or mussy hooks, it's as simple as clipping in and lowering off. If using quickdraws, make sure the rope-bearing carabiner gates are opposed and reversed; or, better yet, use locking carabiners with the gates opposed and reversed. By using slings or a cordelette, you can easily rig a more reliable two-bolt anchor setup (see chapter 5).

Before lowering, after clipping in, communicate with your belayer; if possible, look down and establish visual contact to make sure he or she is paying attention and is in the proper brake position.

Miscommunication at this critical juncture has led to numerous lowering accidents. One fatal accident occurred in a toproping situation where the belayer assumed the climber was not going to be lowered. The climber yelled "I'm OK," which the belayer mistook as "Off belay." Unfortunately, when the climber leaned back to be lowered, the

*Mussy hooks are designed for clipping in and lowering off.*

belayer had already taken the rope out of the belay device.

Go over your climbing signals with your partner, and use a standardized set of signals. We've always used the following unambiguous signals in my climbing school, and in thirty years we've never had an incident of miscommunication.

- Tension (or "Take")
- Tension On (or "Got You")
- Lower Me (or "Ready to Lower")
- Lowering
- Stop (or "Hold")

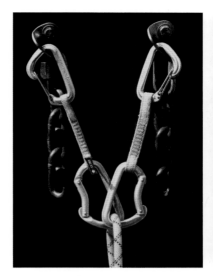

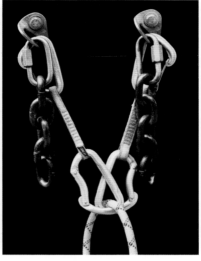

**OK. Two quickdraws rigged for toproping with the gates opposed and reversed. Not ideal, since whatever chains, rings, or hardware store doodads exist can press on the gates once the draws are weighted and potentially open one.**

**Better. The draws are clipped behind the chains and quick links so that when they're weighted, they won't be pressing on the hardware.**

**Even better. All locking carabiners on the draws for security, safeguarding against any unforeseen gate opening. The oval lockers at the master point are opposed and reversed.**

**Here the bottom locking ovals are in a better configuration for the rope to run through smoothly, although the top lockers are connected to some rusty quick links of unknown vintage.**

**This setup allows your group to toprope off the locking carabiners without wearing down the chains; then the last person can either lower down or rappel.**

## Lowering through Chains/Rings

If you're transitioning from a lead or toprope to lowering from chains/rings, you'll need to thread your rope through the chains or rings. There are two methods.

### METHOD 1: THREADING A BIGHT AND LOWERING ON A LOCKING CARABINER.

This method assumes the chains/rings are wide enough to thread two strands (a bight) of rope. The advantage of this method is that you are on belay throughout the process.

**Step 1.** Attach yourself to the anchor with a personal tether, quickdraws, or sling.

**Step 2.** Thread a bight of rope through the chains/rings and tie a figure eight on a bight.

**Step 3.** Attach this to your harness belay loop with a locking carabiner.

**Step 4.** Untie your figure eight follow-through tie-in knot, pull the rope end through the anchor, and let it dangle at your side.

**Step 5.** Call for tension, get a response from your belayer, then proceed to be lowered.

## METHOD 2: TRANSITION FROM LEADING OR TOPROPING TO LOWERING.

**Step 1.** Attach yourself to the anchor with a personal tether, into the anchor master point if possible. If the anchor points are separated, you can use two separate slings.

**Step 2.** Pull down about 8 feet of slack from your quickdraw or toprope master-point and tie a figure eight loop. Clip this with a locking carabiner into your harness belay loop.

**Step 3.** Untie from the rope, thread it through the rings/chains, then retie in with a figure eight follow-through to your harness.

**Step 4.** Unclip your locking carabiner with the figure eight loop from your belay loop, clean the quickdraws/toprope rigging, communicate with your belayer (call for "tension" or "take"), unclip your personal tether, and proceed to be lowered.

## Transition from Toproping to Rappelling

**Step 1.** Attach yourself to the anchor's master point with a personal tether and a locking carabiner. Call "Off Belay" to your belayer.

**Step 2.** Pull up a few feet of rope, tie a figure eight on a bight (or overhand loop), and attach it to your harness with a carabiner.

**Step 3.** Untie your figure eight follow-through tie-in knot, and thread the rope end through the anchor.

**Step 4.** Tie a stopper knot in the end of the rope.

**Step 5.** Unclip the rope from your carabiner, and pull enough rope through the anchor to complete your rappel. If you're not able to see the end of the rope you've threaded touching down on the ground (or get verification from your partner that the end is down) go to the middle mark of the rope. If you don't have a middle mark or bi-pattern rope, you can always measure from both ends to find the middle. My preference has always been to climb on bi-pattern ropes so that it's easy to find the middle. If you can't see it, check with your partner to see what's going on with the other end of the rope. Are they still tied in? Or is there a stopper knot?

**Step 6.** Rig your rappel device on your personal tether, and back it up with an autoblock attached to your harness belay loop with a locking carabiner.

**Step 7.** Clean the toprope rigging and you're ready to rappel.

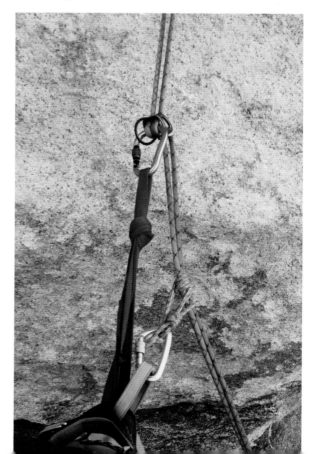

## Belaying Sport Climbs

Sport climbing falls can often be jarring for the leader, especially when the rope is zigzagging through many quick draws, as the friction in the system reduces overall rope stretch. On steeper routes, a "soft catch" will also keep the leader from slamming into the wall so violently.

To provide a soft catch as a belayer, you'll need to develop a more dynamic belaying technique. In the old days a dynamic belay meant letting the rope slip a little bit instead of locking off.

With autolocking devices like a Grigri, where the cam locks solidly in a fall, you'll have to use your stance, body position, and body movement to provide a dynamic belay. Timing is the key. Anticipate the fall by bending your knees slightly. The moment the rope comes tight, simultaneously hop into the air. Every fall is different, and at higher fall factors, the impact may propel you upward—be ready to brace yourself with your legs against the wall.

The dynamic belay is not appropriate for all situations. A common misconception is that a ground anchor is never required in sport climbing. Be aware

*Method 1 of feeding slack to the leader with a Grigri. The advantage of this method is that your brake hand stays on the rope and you never grab the device or open the cam. Keep both hands on the rope and feed the rope into the device as you pay out with the rope with the non-brake hand above it. The key is to feed slow to fast, without a sudden jerk. A good analogy is your car seatbelt: If you pull fast and hard, it will lock; but if you start slow and pull smoothly, and don't yank it, it won't lock.*

that a common sport climbing accident is a belayer accident, where the belayer is pulled so violently that the person loses control of his or her stance and gets slammed into the wall or pulled up into the first quickdraw, often resulting in hand injuries.

*Method 2 of feeding rope to a leader with a Grigri. The advantage of this method is that you can feed slack quickly without the device locking up, although it takes some practice to use the proper grip. The disadvantage is that if you're holding the Grigri and pressing down on the handle during a fall, the Grigri's locking mechanism won't engage. So it's important to keep a grip on the rope with three fingers of your brake hand and only press down on the Grigri's handle with your thumb. Don't grab the entire Grigri itself with your hand.*

The ground anchor is a good idea in many situations: in uneven terrain where the belayer can get pulled off their perch, when the leader outweighs the belayer by 50 pounds or more, where there is a high fall factor, and when there is a real danger of a falling leader hitting a ledge or hitting the ground. The worst accident I've personally had in more than forty years of rock climbing was a belaying accident. I was belaying without a ground anchor, and I was pulled off my stance, across a gap, and into an arcing swing into the cliff. In another incident,

*Lowering with a Grigri. If using a rope bag, make sure the system is closed with a knot in the end of the rope.*

*If the climber far outweighs you, a ground anchor is useful, even on flat ground. If you're belaying a leader with a ground anchor, allow about 3 feet of slack to your connection; you'll be able to provide a softer catch if you're pulled that short distance if the leader falls, providing a more dynamic belay but not losing control. When you're lowering, come tight against the anchor to help brace yourself and bolster your stance.*

while leading on a new sport route at Joshua Tree, 5 feet above the second bolt, a hold broke as I was mantling up to a ledge. Before I started, I made sure my belayer had a ground anchor, since I outweighed him by 60 pounds. At the end of my fall, my feet were 2 feet above a boulder. It was a close call. Without the ground anchor, I probably would have broken my legs, or worse.

The best way to attach yourself to a ground anchor is with the rope. The rope, since it's dynamic, will add some modicum of stretch to the system compared to anchoring straight in with a nylon sling, which has little stretch or, in the case of a Dyneema sling, no stretch. Tie into the rope as you normally would, then clove hitch to a locking carabiner attached to the ground anchor, which can be anything from a natural anchor (like a sling or cord around a tree or a block of rock) to a single piece of protection set for an upward force. Every situation is different, and in some instances, where a leader can potentially hit the ground or a ledge, you'll want to be tight to your ground anchor. Where the leader has room to fall, allow about 3 feet of slack to the ground anchor, which will give you the opportunity to provide a dynamic belay but also maintain control and not get slammed into the cliff.

*Merrill Bitter leads Chain Reaction (5.12b), Smith Rock, Oregon.*
PHOTO BY GREG EPPERSON

*Bird Lew on Snowshed Wall,
Donner Summit, California.*

PHOTO BY GREG EPPERSON

# CHAPTER 7

# Trad Climbing

## Static versus Dynamic

In 1987 I worked on the movie *Star Trek V: The Final Frontier* as a climbing double for Captain Kirk (William Shatner). In the opening sequence of the film, Captain Kirk, on "shore leave" in Yosemite Valley, decides to free solo the Nose Route of El Capitan.

The director informed me that for the free solo scenes (which included the Boot Flake pitch on the Nose Route, a 5.10c hand crack 1,700 feet off the ground), I'd be belayed via an ⅛-inch wire cable, since we had to hide it from camera. This was before modern CGI (computer-generated imagery) that made it easy to paint a rope out of the picture, and stuntmen routinely did falls rigged on ⅛-inch steel cable with elaborate shock-absorbing systems. To assure my safety I was to learn the ropes, so to speak, of cable rigging. A meeting was arranged with Kenny Bates, the top Hollywood cable fall stuntman at the time, at Stoney Point, a local bouldering area just outside Los Angeles. It was like we were from two different schools: me the dynamic climbing rope world, and him the static cable stunt world. Kenny taught me how to properly swage the cable ends into loops and how to use the various thimbles and shackles, but I wasn't convinced of the safety of a cable belay for climbing.

When I got to Yosemite, I teamed up with John Dill, head of Yosemite Search and Rescue, to do some tests. I rigged a 20-foot length of ⅛-inch cable (rated at 2,000 lbs. tensile breaking strength) attached to a concrete block that weighed 200 pounds, using a stout oak branch as my anchor. I noticed a smirk on John's face when he realized what I had in mind. I raised the block a few feet, then dropped it. The cable snapped like kite string. Then I raised the block a mere foot and dropped it. It snapped like kite string. Then I introduced a 9mm nylon climbing rope into the system, attached to the cable. I dropped the block dozens of times, up to 10-foot drops, and the cable never broke. The dynamic rope was the key, even with a static belay (the rope being tied off to an anchor).

Kenny went on to perform a 400-foot fall for one scene in *Star Trek V* on his descender rig, which was essentially a giant fishing reel spooled with ⅛-inch cable, using an air fan and disc brake to slow it down at the very end. When it was time to get hoisted up to perform the stunt, his hands were shaking so badly he could barely clip in.

Impact forces depend largely on how the energy of the fall is absorbed over time. If you tie into a 100-foot bungy cord (which stretches 100 percent) and jump off a bridge, it will stretch 100 feet and take several seconds for the bungy to absorb the energy of the fall; therefore, the impact force at the anchor is relatively low.

Take the same fall on a 10-foot length of cable and it will snap every time, even though the static tensile breaking strength is 2,000 pounds. Why? Because there is no stretch, so the cable absorbs the energy of the fall in less than a millisecond, creating a high-impact force since the force is not dissipated over time.

The DMM company produced a series of videos illustrating this principal, showing drop testing on Dyneema versus nylon slings. The Dyneema

Calculating the fall factor.

slings broke in many of the tests because Dyneema, much like a wire cable, is static. The nylon slings fared better, since nylon slings have a bit of stretch, but nothing close to a dynamic rope. The bottom line is this: The dynamic rope is your shock absorber, and anything else you can do to lower the impact force on your protection and anchors is just icing on the cake.

## The Fall Factor

The fall factor is the total distance of the fall, divided by the length of the rope out from the belay. If the leader is 100 feet above and falls 10 feet, that's a fall factor of 0.1, an easy catch for the belayer. Anything approaching fall factor 1 is a tough catch, with some lifting force to the belayer, so a ground anchor would be recommended.

The highest fall factor is 2 and can occur on a multipitch climb if the leader is above the belay, with no protection, and falls. Another way to create a fall factor 2 is to tether into an anchor or piece with a sling or PAS and fall from above the anchor.

## Fall Forces

In most climbing textbooks there's an emphasis on anchor systems—redundant, equalized, with minimal extension. But unless there's a leader fall directly onto the belay anchor on a multipitch route (the dreaded factor 2 fall), the anchor has only to absorb minimal forces, a little more than body weight if belaying a follower with a direct belay. Don't lose sight of the big picture: The greatest forces in rock climbing are routinely placed on a single piece of gear, during leader falls.

This is because the force is multiplied by the pulley effect, which is essentially double the force of the falling leader minus the friction factor created at the carabiner. Most estimates put this at 1.66 times the impact force at the end of the rope. It works like this: Picture a toprope situation. A

200-pound climber falls and hangs on the rope. The belayer, holding the other side of the rope, must hold 200 pounds. The piece must absorb the force on both sides—the 200-pound climber hanging on one end and the belayer holding the 200 pounds on the other end. Thus the anchor is loaded to 400 pounds. It's a little more complicated than that, since the friction factor (0.66) means that in reality the belayer feels as though he or she only needs to hold roughly 66 percent of the climber's 200 pounds to hold the fall. And any slack in the rope will create a higher force when the climber falls.

## Worst-Case Scenarios

In the 1990s Petzl estimated that with a dynamic rope, rigged with a direct belay off the anchor, and a fall factor of 2, the highest impact force that a falling climber can generate is about 9 kN. This impact force would be the same in a 20-foot fall factor 2 and a 40-foot fall factor 2, because with more rope in the system, there is more rope stretch to absorb the energy.

Petzl estimated that the maximum force a falling leader can generate is actually fall factor 1.9 when the rope is clipped into protection, through a carabiner just above the belay, because of the pulley effect that multiplies the force. In this extreme situation, the falling climber generates 9 kN of force on his or her end of the rope and the belayer must absorb 6 kN of force at the belay device (remember the friction factor is 66 percent). So the piece of protection the leader has fallen on has to absorb a total of 15kN (9kN + 6kN), which is the maximum force achievable in the worst-case situation, give or take a kilonewton, based on the falling climber's weight and the dynamic elongation of the rope.

But these lab tests were done with a rigid metal mass (80 kg, or 179 lbs.) being dropped, not a human climber. In recent years new tests were done using a real live climber, and the results were drastically different. With a real human body absorbing the impact instead of a metal weight, the forces

*Hanging belay at Red Rocks, Nevada. Here Mike Moretti pays out the leader's rope, clipped to the right-hand bolt of a two-bolt anchor with a locking carabiner, thus eliminating a factor 2 fall potential. He's attached himself to the master point with a clove hitch and braced himself for an upward force if the leader were to fall on this traverse up and right from the anchor. He's adjusted his stance so that he's created some distance between his belay device and the first point the leader's rope is clipped into. His rope is well managed—butterfly-looped across his tie-in strand.*

Belay on a multipitch climb at Tahquitz Rock, California. Here the leader is ready to go, and the belayer has put him on belay. When he unclips his clove hitch, he'll clip his rope to the top piece, which already has a quickdraw waiting for his rope. The leader's rope is butterfly-looped and ready to pay out without any tangles. Once the leader is up on the pitch, if he were to fall, the upward pull on the belayer would soften the impact, and the right-hand piece in the anchor, which is placed for an upward force, would keep the leader from getting pulled too far.

were roughly 56 percent less in all the drop tests. In the fall factor 1.9 scenario, with a real human, 56 percent less force on the falling climber would be more like 3kN, the force at the anchor 5 kN, and the force at the redirected piece 8kN. So with a real human, the force during a fall factor 2, using this percentage, would be more like 5kN. But, again, it's not quite that simple. Other variables, like the type of belay device used and how far the rope slips, also come into play. For example, Petzl has theorized that the difference between using a manual braking device (Reverso) instead of a Grigri reduces the impact force by a whopping 30 percent due to how quickly and solidly the Grigri locks off compared to the Reverso, which slips a little bit.

## Fall Factor 2

On a multipitch climb, if you're leading 20 feet above the belay and fall, you'll sail past the belay and fall at least 40 feet before rope stretch kicks in. This is the dreaded fall factor 2.

The first line of defense is simply not to fall in the first place. Many leader fall accidents occur when a leader simply won't give up and casts off into unknown moves without being in control. Practicing downclimbing on moderate boulder problems will help you develop a foundation for mental control in these situations. Knowing when to back off and exercising good judgment is your best line of defense. Hubris will get you hurt.

Doug Robinson, in his article "The Whole Natural Art of Protection," sums it up well: "Learning to climb down is valuable for retreating from a clean and bold place that gets too airy. And having the humility to back off rather than continue . . . a thing well begun is not lost. The experience cannot be taken away."

There is some debate on how to deal with a fall factor 2 situation on a multipitch climb. Should you clip the lead rope into the anchor's master point or the topmost piece in the anchor? There is no simple answer due to the variables, the most obvious one being how trustworthy is the belay anchor?

One solution is to not create a fall factor 2 situation in the first place. If you're forewarned that the route has a fall factor 2 situation, as long as there is enough rope at your disposal, and assuming the anchor is reliable, the leader can clip the anchor's master point, continue into the next pitch up to the first good gear placement, then lower back down to the belay, thus eliminating the possibility of a fall factor 2. The only drawback I can think of to this solution is that if the climbing is delicate and tenuous, the rope drag built up at the end of the pitch may be a problem.

Another solution, if the anchor is reliable, is for the belayer to lower some distance (say 20 feet) below the anchor and belay from there. The leader can then clip into the anchor's master point, no longer looking at a fall factor 2, since more rope is in the system from the belay device. And if enough force is generated in the leader's fall to yank the belayer upward, that will only soften the impact force—a good thing, as long as the belayer doesn't lose control and there's no ledge for the falling leader to hit. One option here would be for the belayer to lower down to the first good upward directional piece and clip into that as an additional safeguard, especially if the leader outweighs them by more than 50 pounds.

If all the placements in the anchor are bomber, the leader can clip the topmost piece of the anchor, creating a gap of a few feet between that clip and the belayer's device. The problem in this scenario is that, again, the force is multiplied at that clipped point due to the pulley factor (a force of x 2 minus the friction factor = 1.66 x); the belayer will get pulled violently into that piece and get slammed into the wall.

Another solution, with a solid anchor, is a direct belay, which is normally not recommended for lead belaying. In recent years there has been new thinking on this technique, as a direct belay eliminates the multiplied force and the slamming of the belayer, but it is not recommended with an assisted braking device (e.g., Grigri) due to the next stance and protection placement; clip a manual braking device (MBD) like an ATC into the rope at this point, and tie a catastrophe knot on the brake strand below it. Then you'll be ready to switch from the Munter to the MBD after the leader's clipped his or her first piece of protection.

If the anchor can't be trusted, you're treading on thin ice, and the best solution is to belay directly off your harness (to limit the impact force on the belay anchor) with an MBD and back it up with a catastrophe knot on the brake hand side. Brace yourself in the best stance you can muster, and do your best to absorb the energy of the fall with your legs and

*Rigging for a fall factor 2 using a quad with a Munter hitch direct belay. This is a tough catch, so it's advisable to estimate the length of the leader's runout to the first good piece, back it up by clipping the rope to an MBD (like an ATC) that distance down the rope, and then back that up with a catastrophe knot on the brake strand side. In a worst-case scenario, if the leader falls and the belayer loses control, the backups will come into play.*

*The maximum friction you can generate with a Munter hitch belay is when the two rope strands are parallel.*

device's solid lock-off that transfers more impact force onto the anchor. A direct belay with a Munter hitch solves this problem but is a hard catch for the belayer (gloves recommended!). If using a Munter hitch direct belay, create a backup system by conservatively estimating the distance to the leader's

*Two-bolt anchor on a multipitch climb rigged with a quad. Here the leader will shortly embark on a short traverse to the right before any protection can be had. He's clipped his rope directly to the master point, so if he falls, the belayer should brace for a pull straight in to the wall.*

## What Is a Kilonewton? (kN)

A newton was named for, you guessed it, Sir Isaac Newton in recognition for his groundbreaking work: Newton's second law of motion. A newton measures mass in motion.

One newton is the force required to accelerate 1 kilogram of mass at the rate of 1 meter per second squared, or roughly the force of gravity acting on a small mass on planet Earth. One kilonewton is equal to 1,000 newtons.

To wrap my head around this concept, I like to think of it in terms of pounds and how much load a piece can sustain. One kN is equal to 100 kilograms of load, or 224 pounds of force. So a sling that's rated to 22 kN could theoretically hold 2,200 kilograms (4,946 lbs.). It's not that simple, however, since a kN rating signifies the maximum impact force the sling can withstand, which is a force of gravity rating (force = mass × acceleration), but it's easier for me to grasp the concept that, yes, I could hang a car from that sling.

torso. If you completely lose control, the catastrophe knot will jam into the belay device—averting disaster as long as the anchor does not fail.

In fact, in all these scenarios, a catastrophe knot (one that will jam in your belay device) can serve as your final line of defense if you lose control of the belay.

## The Zipper Effect

I witnessed the full ramifications of the zipper effect on a climb called The Pirate at Suicide Rock, California. It's an ultrathin crack, rated 5.12d as a free climb but commonly led as a practice aid route using tiny wired stoppers. The belayer was positioned at the base of the climb, 10 feet out from the

CLOSE UP
TAPER NO LONGER DEPENDABLE

DIRECTION
OF
PULL

DIRECTION CHANGES

a.

b.

*The leader's goal is for the rope to run in a relatively straight line by judicious use of quickdraws and slings, eliminating a conflagration of varying directions of pull on all the pieces in the system. Double-rope technique, popular in Europe, makes it easy to rectify the problem on most pitches, but this technique is more complicated, especially for the belayer, and has never really caught on in America.*

wall, as the leader methodically aided up the crack. Halfway up the pitch, a piece pulled out and the leader fell. The first nut placement rotated upward and popped out, as did the next one, the next one after that, and all the nuts after that except the one the leader had fallen on, which just happened to be a #3 wired stopper—the zipper effect.

When leading trad pitches, the first placement is a critical one, especially if the belayer is some distance out from the base of the pitch or, on a multi-pitch climb, if the first placement is off to one side. Once another placement is made, and the system is weighted in a fall, the direction of pull on that first piece will bisect the angle of the rope.

For this first critical piece, an omnidirectional placement is indicated. It's the key to the leading system for the entire pitch, as it locks the rope into the cliff. The best choice is a camming device, set to withstand any outward or upward force. A tricam in the active mode, two nuts rigged in opposition, or a nut buried in a constriction set for an outward force will work as second best.

As the leader proceeds up the pitch, any subsequent angles created by the rope zigzagging through the pieces will have similar forces applied, bisecting any angle created in the rope system below the placement the leader falls on or weights.

## Falling

When leading trad pitches, remember this fundamental: Don't climb with the rope between your legs, unless you're directly above a piece. If you're moving right, run the rope outside your left leg, and vice versa. If you're off to one side above a piece and fall with the rope between your legs, the position of the rope will flip you upside down. This results in a lot of head injuries for falling leaders.

Don't push out from the wall unless you're trying to avoid an obstacle, like a small ledge, since when the rope comes tight you'll swing back in to the wall harder with the pendulum effect you've created. Don't try to grab the rope below the piece

on the way down—if you do latch onto it, you'll only get a rope burn.

Fall like a cat; try to absorb the impact of the fall with your legs in a wide stance, and flex your knees to absorb some of the force. Remember to communicate with your belayer, especially if he or she can't see you. "Watch me!" is the signal to let your belayer know you're at a tough spot. Falls can happen without warning, like when a foothold breaks, but yelling "Falling!" will let your belayer prepare for the jolt if the person can't see you. A short fall happens so quickly, it's over before you realize you've even fallen. If you can register that "Hey, I'm falling here," and sense your body flying through the air, it's a big one.

### Rope Stretch and Protecting the Follower

In recent years, ropes have gotten thinner, with more stretch. The EN 892 dynamic rope certification standard allows up to 40 percent dynamic elongation in the drop testing, and most ropes on the market these days stretch an average of about 35 percent in a leader fall. At the same time, the trend has been toward longer ropes (e.g., 70 meters) to complete longer pitches. So if you're leading with 200 feet of rope out and zero rope drag, and fall from 20 feet above your last piece, you'll sail 40 feet before the rope stretch even kicks in—then you'll fall an additional 70 feet before you stop!

If the rope is zigzagging through pieces, the rope stretch will be less, since the friction through the carabiners limits the rope's ability to stretch throughout its entire length, but it can still be substantial.

One thing that many climbers don't account for is rope stretch while belaying the second. As a guide, I'm hyper-aware of this because it's about the only way someone can get hurt falling on a toprope (the other way is from a swing). Most dynamic ropes will stretch about 10 percent in a fall while seconding or toproping (more with a heavier climber and with any slack in the rope). With 100 feet of rope

*Here the leader has made a major error: not protecting for the follower, who has just removed the last piece of pro, which protected the top moves on the face above the crack for the leader; now the follower is facing a major pendulum if he were to fall. The leader could have chosen to belay directly above where the follower is now positioned, where there is a good ledge with good cracks, or could have placed a good directional piece before moving right over to this two-bolt anchor.*

out, that's 10 feet; and if your second falls just above a ledge, he or she might hit it. As a belayer, keep this in mind—tighten the rope under a bit of tension when someone is right off the ground or just above a ledge when you have a lot of rope out and the person is facing tough moves.

As leaders, we sometimes get so focused on protecting our next move that we forget to place protection for the follower. While leading a traverse, placing a piece right before a hard move is great for the leader, but when the follower unclips it, he or she will be facing a huge swing if the next piece is far away. If no protection is available for the follower, one solution is to lower down from higher up on the pitch and unclip a few pieces so that the rope runs straighter.

Peter Croft leading My Laundry (5.9) at Joshua Tree. Note where Peter has placed a piece of gear at the start of the horizontal crack leading right—not for him, since it's easy climbing, but for the follower, who faces a tricky move after cleaning the second quickdraw.

Peter Croft leading Sidewinder (5.10c) at Joshua Tree. Note the use of long runners to reduce rope drag, and how the rope runs outside his right leg, not between his legs. He's decided to climb a bit higher before he places his next piece, to better protect his follower.

## Multipitch Efficiency

As a guide, I like to keep it simple. And 90 percent of the time when I'm guiding multipitch, I'll place three bomber pieces, pre-equalize them with a cordelette, and I'm done. My goal for the master point is to rig it at waist level to eye level. I'll belay my client with my Grigri clipped into the master point. I've never been a fan of plaquette devices, mainly because I usually don't guide long routes,

so I don't belay two clients at the same time, and I don't like the extra workout on the shoulders from pulling the rope through the device. Most guides I

*Three-piece multipitch anchor pre-equalized with a cordelette. The bottom cam is set for an upward pull.*

*Four-piece multipitch anchor pre-equalized with a cordelette. The bottom two cams are rigged in opposition with clove hitches, making this anchor multidirectional—good for downward, outward, and upward pulls.*

know started with plaquette devices but ultimately switched to Grigris when the second, lighter generation came on the market. Who needs an extra workout belaying? To me it's always been worth the extra weight for the ease of pulling the rope through the device, plus the Grigri is more useful for all the various potential rescue and assistance

scenarios, the most common being a short 3-to-1 haul to help a client get past a tough spot he or she can't free climb. It's also simpler to lower someone with a Grigri than with a plaquette device; just make sure to redirect the brake strand. If I'm guiding two clients, I'll clip myself to the shelf, then belay each client separately and clip both clients to the main master point.

In recent years the biggest innovation for multipitch belay anchor rigging has been the evolution of the quad rigging technique, now the favored technique of many professional guides. By splitting the four strands (two and two) you'll have two separate master points to clip into. This is especially useful for direct belays, hanging stances, and multipitch rappelling scenarios.

*This cordelette rig affords two master points, each having three loops. If I'm guiding two clients, I'll clip myself into the shelf (top carabiner) and belay off the main master point (bottom carabiner). I'll have both followers clip in at the main master point. To correctly use the shelf, your carabiner must be clipped into all the loops on the arms of the cordelette, whether it's two, three, or four, depending on the rigging.*

*Two-bolt anchor rigged with a quad using a direct belay with a Grigri.*

*Two-bolt anchor rigged with standard cordellete method using a direct belay with a Grigri.*

*A three-bolt belay at Tahquitz Rock, California, rigged with the standard cordelette method. I'm clipped into the main master point with a clove hitch, and I'm using my Grigri for a direct belay clipped to another locking carabiner on the shelf (all three loops of the arms of the cordelette). Clipping carabiner to carabiner is fine as long as they are locking carabiners, especially in a monitored situation.*

*2. Loop one carabiner through the other . . .*

*3. . . . and even up the three loops.*

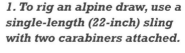

*1. To rig an alpine draw, use a single-length (22-inch) sling with two carabiners attached.*

*4. Clip them back into the carabiner, and you have it. You can use the alpine draw in its shortened quickdraw length; or when you need to deploy its full length, clip into a piece, unclip the other carabiner from all three loops, then clip it back into any of the three loops. Pull down and you'll have the full-length sling. The big advantage of the alpine draw is that you can do this all with one hand—far easier than trying to use a sling that's around your neck and over your shoulder when you're on a steep climb where it's hard to let go.*

*Climbers at Verdon Gorge, France.*

## Multipitch Rope Management

The Navy SEALs have a saying: "Slow is smooth and smooth is fast." The key to rope handling for multipitch is taking the time to do it right the first time so that you don't have to do it again. Detangling ropes can really slow you down, so taking the time to properly flake the rope at every stance will save you time in the long run. As a guide, a worst-case scenario for rope management is having a client have to deal with a tangled rope while I'm leading. If you're the belayer and must deal with a tangled rope, start by tying a catastrophe knot on your brake hand side.

Erik Kramer-Webb is an AMGA Certified Rock Instructor and one of California's most experienced guides; his state-of-the art training through the AMGA has given him unique insights into becoming more efficient at multipitch rope management. First, Erik recommends:

"If there's a belay ledge, stacking the rope on the rock is preferable to making loops over your tie-in. It's less work on your arms and will give more of your focus to providing a great belay. Make a tight 'pancake stack' about 2 feet in diameter, patting it down occasionally with your hand or foot to keep it as compact as possible. If you are not swapping leads, then 'flip the pancake' by carefully flipping the stack over so that the leader's end is back on top.

"On hanging stances, it is best not to let the rope hang down. Butterfly the rope back and forth across your tie-in strand to the anchor. If swapping leads, butterfly the loops long to short, starting at about foot level. If one climber is leading both pitches, use the 'butterfly flip' technique. Butterfly the loops short to long. Make the first loop 9 inches, the second loop 10 inches, etc., making each additional loop an inch longer. When your partner is at the anchor, flip the loops on top of his tie-in and it's good to go for belaying the next lead.

"Where cracks, flakes, horns, bushes, loose rock, or other rope-snagging features are present, don't let the loops hang down below your feet. Be wary of long loops getting blown around on a windy day and getting stuck."

*Gear changeover. Here each climber is clipped to a quad master point.*

*Three-point quad anchor. The belayer is using a Petzl Reverso in the autoblocking mode for a direct belay of the second.*

## Strategies for a Party of Three

Here is where it's easy to get tangles. The culprit is usually the strand of rope that comes from the back side of your clove hitch. Instead of letting this strand hang down, tuck it into your harness.

"When climbing with two ropes as a team of three, the ropes can get crossed much more easily, which will slow your party down as you keep re-flaking the ropes in order to untangle the crossed strands," says Erik. "Keep one rope on the left and the other on the right. As the followers arrive at the stance, clip the tie-in locker on the left side of the master point for the left rope, and the tie-in locker for the right-side rope on the right side of the master point. If the next pitch goes right, stack the lead rope on the right, and keep the second rope on the left side of the ledge. When the second starts climbing, he ideally won't have to step over or under the other rope before he can follow the pitch."

Erik adds: "Unlike a two-person team, in a team of three it is more efficient to have your best climber lead all the pitches. Swapping leads in a party of three creates more rope complexity."

If time is not a factor, belaying each climber one at a time is the traditional method, the least complicated, and the slowest. If you're proficient in

*You can belay two climbers at the same time with an autoblocking device like the ATC Guide (left) or a plaquette device like the Kong Gigi (right).*

using autoblocking or plaquette devices (e.g., Black Diamond ATC Guide, Petzl Reverso, Kong Gigi), then belaying both the second and third climbers at the same time on separate ropes is most efficient in terms of speed—the leader makes one big stack with both ropes. Another option is to belay the second climber, then fix a line for the third climber, who can self-belay using progress capture devices (see chapter 9).

To speed up three-person team belay change-overs, Erik recommends that the followers clean the gear using a gear sling. "The follower hands the gear sling to the leader, who reracks while the second and third climber can re-flake the ropes."

*Shelly Dunbar leads Levitation 29 (5.11c), Red Rock, Nevada.* PHOTO BY GREG EPPERSON

*Cleaning an aid pitch on the*
*Shield Route, El Capitan.*

# Aid Climbing

In 1970, when I was eleven, my initial inspiration to become a big wall climber came from Warren Harding's slide show at Pat's Ski and Sport Shop in Southern California. He'd just climbed the Wall of Early Morning Light on El Cap with Dean Caldwell, in one push; it took them twenty-seven days.

I saved up my money from my job as a paper boy and began buying pitons, a few at a time, until I had assembled a complete rack, from rurps to a 4-inch Bong. I'd lay out all the pitons in order from small to large and just stare at them. I guess you could say I started out with an equipment fetish.

After that I purchased a Forest single-point suspension hammock and hung it from the pull-up bar that spanned my bedroom doorjamb. Reclining in the hammock, I closed my eyes and imagined myself high on El Cap in some airy bivy, with clouds drifting by and the ground a couple thousand feet below. My reverie was suddenly and rudely interrupted, however, when the pull-up bar ripped from the doorjamb and hit me square in the forehead, knocking me out. Luckily, I was only a foot off the floor.

That summer, the final inspiration came from actually laying hands on El Cap during a family vacation, after the short hike to the base with my dad and my three brothers. I climbed a little way up the smooth granite and gazed upward. At that moment I made a pact with myself and El Cap.

"Get down from there; if you fall you're gonna break your leg!" my dad yelled up at me.

Back in the car, cruising the valley loop in our station wagon, I made a proclamation: "Someday I'm gonna climb El Capitan."

*Climbers on the Shield Headwall, El Capitan.*

**Werner Braun in El Cap meadow, 1983.**

"Son, nobody can climb that rock; it's too sheer," my dad replied.

But I'd already read my copy of Steve Roper's *Climbers Guide to Yosemite Valley* a dozen times, cover to cover, like it was my Bible and climbing my religion. I knew El Cap was first climbed a year before I was born, in 1958, and I could recount the details like a passage from scripture.

"Dad, it's already been climbed a bunch of times. The first ascent of the Nose Route was in November 1958, by Warren Harding, Wayne Merry, and George Whitmore."

My dad just glowered at me in the rearview mirror and said nothing as we drove toward Camp Curry. Ten years later, just before my twenty-first birthday, I climbed the Nose Route.

## The Yosemite Method of Leading

Yvon Chouinard introduced the Yosemite Method of leading an aid pitch in his 1972 equipment catalog, calling it "the most efficient sequence of artificial climbing." This technique utilizes two etriers (pronounced A-tree-As), also known as aiders, which are commercially made ladders made of nylon webbing, usually with five "rungs" plus a "hero loop," an additional shorter top sling that allows a super high step to facilitate long reaches.

*Charlie Peterson in etriers on the Nose Route, El Capitan.*

While there are numerous variations based on specific situations, the basic Yosemite Method sequence goes like this:

1. Make the placement.

2. Clip in a free carabiner (ovals work best).

3. Clip in an etrier.

4. Step into the etrier. If the placement is doubtful, test it by bouncing with more than your body weight. After it passes this test, but if the placement appears marginal, reduce any sudden jerky movements and shift your weight slowly and smoothly between your etriers.

5. Reach down and collect the previous etrier; reduce rope drag if necessary by adding a quickdraw or sling to the previous placement.

6. Step up and clip your rope into the free carabiner of the placement when you're about waist level with the placement.

For extreme aid climbing, where it's a challenge to construct a placement good enough to hold your body weight, clipping in with a daisy chain to test the new placement makes more sense. This way you can bounce-test the placement without moving so far up to it; if it pops, it's attached to your daisy chain. For extreme aid you'll definitely want to wear a helmet, and not look up while you're testing it; if you do, the piece will probably hit you in the face if it fails. Ouch!

A caution here about aid climbing with daisy chains. Use them only for testing your placements and hanging off placements to rest. Don't leave a

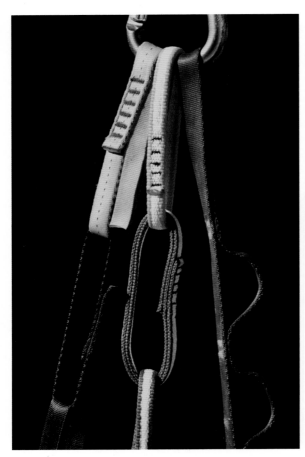

*Tether comparison. Left to right: Sterling nylon Chain Reactor, Metolius Dyneema PAS, Black Diamond nylon daisy chain.*

known as carabiner shift. I experienced this first-hand while aid climbing on a big wall in Yosemite. I was 1,000 feet up the North Face of Quarter Dome (just up Tenaya Canyon from Half Dome). I had thoroughly tested my copperhead placement, but as I was standing on it, I heard a loud click—the sound of the weighted etrier carabiner displacing the other etrier's carabiner. Simultaneous with this miniscule shock loading, the copperhead pulled and sent me hurtling down the wall. Ovals,

*Warning! If using a traditional daisy chain with bartacked pockets, do not clip a carabiner into two loops. This creates an extremely weak connection (3 kN, or 674 lbs.).*

daisy chain clipped in and climb above it to the next placement. If your higher placement fails, you're looking at a factor 2 fall onto the daisy chain clipped to the lower piece. This scenario has led to broken cams—and broken backs.

If you're going to use a daisy chain, I recommend a nylon one over a Dyneema one, simply because nylon has a bit of stretch, whereas Dyneema is essentially static.

For your free carabiner, an oval carabiner definitely works best; it prevents a phenomenon since they have a wider radius than D-shaped biners, are less prone to carabiner shift and can easily accept two etrier carabiners without them shifting for position.

For slightly less than vertical to slightly overhanging aid climbing, two etriers, each on a separate carabiner, work fine. I've always rigged my etriers with smaller D-shaped carabiners and clipped them with the wider end up and gate facing the rock. This violates the old "down and out" carabiner rule, but you'll find this makes them far easier to clip and unclip without scraping your knuckles.

For wildly overhanging headwalls, overhangs, and roofs, two sets of two etriers is the way to go, with each set of two rigged to a single biner. Here, daisy chains, clipped in short, facilitate resting. Pulling on the rope below the top carabiner also helps by creating a pulley effect on strenuous overhangs, as does using the "rest position," which is accomplished by bending one leg at the knee, tucking your foot under your butt, and sitting on it while in the etrier.

## The Yosemite Method of Big Wall Climbing

In 1963, during the second ascent of El Capitan's Dihedral Wall route, Royal Robbins began using techniques that would revolutionize big wall climbing in Yosemite—so efficient was the new Yosemite Method. This revolutionary innovation was the use of jumars for rope ascending, cleaning, and hauling. Previously, climbers had painstakingly toiled up fixed lines using prusik knots.

The Yosemite Method is still used by climbers today as the standard technique for big wall climbing. It goes like this: The leader leads the pitch—by free climbing, aid climbing, or mixed free and aid belayed on the lead line (a standard dynamic climbing rope)—and trails a second rope, the haul line, clipped to her harness and dangling free to the previous belay. The preferred haul line is a 10mm diameter low-stretch rope (CE EN 1891), which is more abrasion resistant than a dynamic rope. Once the leader establishes a belay anchor, she anchors the lead line to a master point. Once this rope is fixed, the second jumars the lead line to clean the pitch. This leaves the leader free to haul the bag on the haul line. If the bag gets stuck, the second can help out by freeing the bag if it is within reach.

## Jumaring

The original mechanical ascender was the Swiss-made Jumar. Today there is a wide variety of mechanical ascenders on the market, but since the Jumar was the original design, the name has become generic, and "jumaring" has become a generic term for ascending a rope with mechanical ascenders.

*The Petzl Ascension ascender.*

*Scott Cosgrove jumaring a fixed line high above Yosemite Valley, with El Capitan in the background. Both jumars are attached to his harness with slings, and he's chosen to place both etriers on his lower ascender.*

*Todd Gordon demonstrates basic rigging of mechanical ascenders for vertical and less-than-vertical terrain. Nylon daisy chains have been threaded through both harness tie-in points and attached to the ascenders with locking carabiners. The etriers are clipped with non-locking carabiners into the locking carabiners at the ascenders (biner to biner) for easy detachment of the etriers—allowing them to be disconnected without unlocking the attachment carabiner. This is handy for when the terrain becomes low angle and you no longer need the etriers, but still want a safe connection to the ascenders as you slide them up the rope. The daisy chain length to the top ascender (in this case his right-hand ascender) can be adjusted by which loop you use on the daisy chain. When using a daisy chain, never clip the carabiner into two pockets—it's a weak (3 kN, or 674 lbs.) and dangerous connection. For vertical and less-than-vertical jumaring, the top daisy's length should be adjusted so that when you're sitting in the harness, you can reach up and comfortably grab the jumar's handle.*

*Setup for overhanging jumaring on a fixed line. Here both etriers are clipped to the lower ascender, and the length of the daisy chain connection has been shortened.*

## The Yosemite Method of Jumaring

The Yosemite Method is based on safety and simplicity. Both ascenders are attached to the harness with slings, and both ascenders have etriers clipped to them. For the slings you can use daisy chains, a PAS, or regular slings. I recommend nylon over Dyneema or Spectra for any sling connection, since nylon has a bit of stretch; Dyneema and Spectra don't. The daisy chain or PAS allows you to adjust the distance easily by clipping into different loops. Whatever style of sling you use, attach it to your harness not with a carabiner but by girth-hitching it into both tie-in points on your harness (the same two points where you thread the rope to tie in). This method eliminates a carabiner connection, removing the possibility for inadvertent unclipping.

Attach each ascender to its sling with a locking carabiner. I like to attach my etriers with a non-locking carabiner clipped to the locking carabiner on my ascenders (biner to biner) so that I can quickly remove the etriers without unlocking the carabiner that attaches the jumars to my harness.

Mechanical ascenders can be bought as a pair, one designated "right hand" and the other "left hand," because the release lever is designed for the thumb side of the hand for quick and efficient removal and reattachment to the rope. I always lead with my left-hand ascender on top, even though I'm right-handed (probably because that's the way I learned), but go with whatever hand you feel most comfortable. I use my right leg in the etrier on the bottom ascender.

The key to efficient jumaring is the length of the slings and where you position your feet in the etriers. The top sling should be adjusted so that when you're hanging in your harness off the top ascender, you can reach up and comfortably grasp the handle of the ascender with your hand. The sling connection from the bottom ascender to your harness is not critical, since when you're hanging, you'll always be hanging off the top ascender. With the bottom ascender placed just below the top one,

bend your leg at a 90-degree angle and place it into a foot loop on your etrier. When you straighten out your leg and stand up, simultaneously slide the top ascender up as far as you can, then immediately lean back and sit in your harness. Use your leg strength, not your arm strength. Jumaring takes some practice, but once you get the hang of it, you can zip up a fixed line quickly.

When I teach someone jumaring for the first time, I give him only one etrier (for the bottom ascender) and break it down like this: "Stand on the bottom ascender and sit on the top ascender." Once you get this concept down, you'll be much more proficient and use far less arm strength while jumaring. The best angle to learn on is a fixed line on a wall or cliff that is slightly less than vertical. Adjusting the length of the slings connecting the ascenders to your harness will make the process more efficient. The rule is: The lower the angle, the longer the sling; the steeper the angle, the shorter the sling. Again, the sling connecting the top ascender to your harness is the critical length.

A good technique for free-hanging jumaring is to place both etriers on the bottom ascender and keep the sling to your top ascender very short. Start with both knees bent at 90 degrees in the etriers. When you straighten out both legs in unison, simultaneously and quickly slide the top ascender up and immediately hang in your harness; then repeat the process.

I consider two mechanical ascenders on the rope to be safe; one ascender, not safe. If you take one ascender off the rope, you should have a backup, such as clipping in short by tying a loop knot below the ascenders and clipping it to your harness belay loop with a locking carabiner, or tethering to an anchor with a sling if you're jumaring a fixed line and passing an anchor point. Remember, mechanical ascenders are designed for body weight only and are not intended to hold the force of a fall. Most mechanical ascenders will shear off the sheath of the rope at around 5 kN (1,124 lbs.) of force.

*Climbers on the Nose Route,
El Capitan.*

If you're jumaring a diagonal line, an additional safeguard is to clip your smallest carabiner around the rope and the base of the handle of the jumar to keep it from getting levered off the rope.

## Cleaning Aid Pitches

For climbs with short stretches of aid, if the follower doesn't have ascenders, she can clean the pitch by clipping etriers straight into the free carabiner on the placement, just as the leader did. To clean a piece, she clips above it to the next placement, then cleans the piece by reaching down from the lower rungs of her etrier while clipped to the piece above it.

For full-on aid climbs and big wall climbs, the second typically jumars the lead line to clean the pitch. The ascenders are backed up by (1) being tied into the end of the rope and (2) clipping in short: tying figure eight loops and clipping them to the harness belay loop with a locking carabiner at regular intervals (every 25 feet or so). How often you clip in short depends on several variables, such as the steepness of the wall and any potential obstacles you might hit—namely, ledges—if the ascenders were to fail. On an overhanging wall you're relatively safe, so you can increase the distance between clipping in short to save time.

Jumaring is relatively straightforward on a vertical rope, but it becomes more complicated when the rope zigzags through pieces or traverses sideways or horizontally out a roof. When the rope is under tension and forms an angle at the carabiner it's clipped through, you won't be able to unclip it with your body weight on the rope below it. If the angle isn't too drastic, sometimes you can maneuver your body sideways enough to eliminate the tension on the carabiner, allowing you to unclip it. Then you can adjust the height of the jumars and clean the piece from the optimal position.

If you can't unclip the rope, and the next piece isn't too far away diagonally, unclip your top ascender and reclip it above the piece, sliding it as high as you can up the rope. Transfer your weight to the etrier on the top ascender, and firmly grasp and pull down on the rope below the lower ascender. Then, with your other hand, release the cam on the ascender (without removing it from the rope), and let the rope slowly slide through your hand until you've lowered yourself sideways to where the rope is again vertically aligned. Then unclip the lower ascender and reclip it on the rope just below the top one. Now you can unclip your rope from the piece and clean it.

If the rope runs horizontally, like out a ceiling or roof, sometimes it's easier and less awkward to clip your etriers directly into the free carabiner of the placement as the leader did, sliding the ascenders along the unweighted lead line and clipping in short for safety. This is why it's advantageous to clip your etriers with a separate carabiner into the locking carabiner of your daisy chain, so they can be easily removed while your daisy chain is still attached to your ascender with the locking carabiner, with no need to unlock the gate. This necessitates the placements being close enough together to clip one while hanging off the previous one.

## Following Pendulums and Tension Traverses

Many big walls involve pendulums, where the leader lowers off a fixed pendulum point, then runs and swings sideways, usually to another crack system. Some of the most famous ones are on the Nose Route of El Capitan—the pendulum to the Stoveleg Crack involving a 40-foot sideways run across the wall, jumping over a dihedral, then sinking a hand jam into the Stoveleg Crack at the end of the swing. Higher, 1,700 feet up, is the King Swing from Boot Flake, on a section of the wall so steep and exposed that when you make the swing, your toes barely touch the wall.

During a tension traverse, the leader lowers off the fixed point then uses tension on the rope, in

*Banny Root following the pendulum into Stoveleg Crack, Nose Route, El Capitan.*

combination with using hand and foot holds, to work sideways across an otherwise unclimbable section.

In either scenario, the leader can lessen the difficulty of following the traverse on ascenders by placing the first piece after the pendulum as high as possible.

To follow a pendulum or tension traverse, here are the steps:

1. When you reach the pendulum point, clip in with a personal tether. In approaching the pendulum point, leave a couple feet of rope between the top ascender and the pendulum point, because when you clip into and hang off the pendulum point, you're un-weighting the rope, and your ascenders will move up a bit as the rope shortens (reverse rope stretch).

2. Unclip your top ascender and reclip it above the pendulum point, sliding as far up the rope as possible.

3. Tie a figure eight loop between your top ascender and the pendulum point, and clip it to the belay loop of your harness with a locking carabiner.

4. Pulley yourself tight to the pendulum point (leave a carabiner for expediency) by pulling yourself in with the rope and ascender below it.

5. Grasp the rope below the lower ascender, release the cam (without removing the ascender from the rope), and lower yourself until your rope again runs vertically above you. On big pendulums you'll want to use a Grigri or rappel device to lower with instead of the lower ascender.

6. Once you're back to where the rope runs vertically, make sure both ascenders are back on the rope, with the figure eight loop backup directly below them. Untie from the end of the rope, make sure there are no knots or twists in the rope, and pull it through the pendulum point. Retie the end of the rope back in. Carry on.

On a slight direction change, you can often just firmly grasp the rope below the lower jumar, pull down on the rope, and release the cam with your other hand, letting yourself move sideways a short distance.

*Left: Following on jumars.*

*Below left: Example of the rigging to follow a pendulum on jumars, in this case a pendulum to the left. The yellow sling is clipped to the pendulum point, necessary to unweight the jumars and tie the figure eight loop, which is attached to the belay loop with a locking carabiner.*

*Below right: Lowering out on the pendulum. If it's a short one, you can lower yourself with just your hands on the rope. For a big one, rig a belay device or an ABD like a Grigri.*

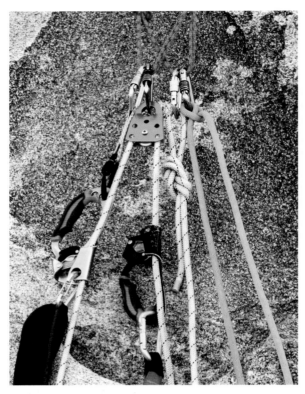

The Yosemite Method of hauling, invented by Royal Robbins. The upside-down jumar is the "detent" jumar, which acts like a ratchet to hang the load when you're not pulling. Hang some gear from this ascender to weight it down so that when you pull on the other ascender, the detent ascender doesn't ride up but stays put. The ascender on the right can be attached with a sling to your belay loop, which allows you to pull using your body weight, or you can clip an etrier into it and use your leg power to help pull. You'll want a good pulley and some gloves. In this setup, reaching down with your left hand and pulling up on the rope as you pull down on the right side ascender is what works best.

Here the pulley has been replaced with the Petzl Mini Traxion. No need for the detent ascender, since the Mini Traxion has a built-in ratchet that locks off.

## Bivouacking

There's no better way to get to know a cliff than to spend the night on it. It's been many years since I last bivouacked on a big wall, but I can remember it like it was yesterday. It was during the first ascent of a new aid route up the East Face of Higher Cathedral Rock in Yosemite.

The route was remarkable for its sheerness—not even a ledge wide enough to lie down on for 2,000 feet—so all the belays and bivouacs were hanging. The climbing had been grueling, every foot gained up the wall a struggle; the cracks shallow and poor, without a solid placement for pitch after pitch, save for the bolts we slugged in at the anchors.

As the sun slowly sank to the west, we realized we'd need to set up a hanging bivouac. We drilled a few bolts, spread out horizontally, to hang our single-point suspension portaledges.

My partner, Alan Bartlett, had been around the block a few times—with 4,000 Joshua Tree routes under his belt and first ascents all over the place—but he'd never done a hanging bivouac. Alan's buddy, Steve Gerberding, who'd climbed El Cap a hundred times (not an exaggeration!), loaned him a portaledge so well rigged that, within minutes, Alan was comfortably reclining on it drinking a warm beer, a smile on his face.

We snacked on salami, cheese, crackers, and nuts and spoke optimistically that the next day would bring better cracks. As the alpenglow slowly faded from the West Face of Sentinel Rock, I drifted into a deep sleep. I awoke sometime in the middle of the night, disoriented until I got my bearings: *No, this isn't my bedroom; I'm hanging off a wall in Yosemite!* I settled into this reality and took in the other-worldly scene. A full moon slowly rose above the valley rim, silhouetting the soaring Cathedral Spires. Hundreds of bats poured out of some crack high above, cavorting in the moonlight in great swirling torrents.

***Dave Katz looks down from the bivouac ledge. Zodiac Route, El Capitan.***

Dawn on a big wall in Yosemite Valley is a magical experience—the sunlight gradually illuminating the rock forms in a grand light show. To save weight, we had decided not to bring a stove, but since I was a coffee junkie I had brought chocolate-covered espresso beans for my caffeine fix.

Once we started climbing, our optimism for solid placements quickly faded, with another day of tedious, scary aid climbing, pitch after pitch, then another hanging bivouac. The next day was more

*Banny Root waking up after a night on El Cap Tower, Nose Route, El Capitan.*

of the same, and we grew tired and frustrated at our slow progress. Our physical and mental resources were dwindling, as was our water supply. With only a couple hundred feet to go, we were forced to bivouac again.

While packing for the climb, Alan said he would adhere to what Steve Roper recommended in his *Climber's Guide to Yosemite Valley*, published in 1971: "At least one and a half quarts of water per man per day should be taken in midsummer." Normally I allotted myself 1 gallon per day, which is good rule for wall climbing in the summer in Yosemite. But

water is a heavy. One gallon weighs about 8 pounds, so there's a balance between how much water you'll need and how much you can carry and haul up the

*Portaledges allow you to bivouac anywhere on a route and serve as resting platforms for ledge-less big wall free climbs. Here Scott Cosgrove relaxes on the North Face of Higher Cathedral Spire during an attempt at a first free ascent of the route.*

climb. The weather was nice and cool, so I reduced my ration too.

We'd separated our personal water supplies, and that night at the bivouac, I realized that my stash had dwindled to only a single quart, for that night and all the next day.

The last couple of pitches went slower than we'd anticipated, since we had to hand-drill several bolts, but by noon we topped out under a scorching sun, relieved to be off the wall, but out of water and surrounded by a couple hundred pounds of gear.

With all the hardware in the haul bag, it weighed about 175 pounds; and by the time I staggered down to the valley floor with that pig on my back, I'd never been so thirsty in all my life. In my car I had an ice chest with a stash of water that was still ice cold. Nothing I'd ever drank had ever tasted so good, or been as deeply satiating.

Alan's Toyota truck shell had deep bear claw scrapes down the side, and his back hatch was partially mangled from an attempt to pry it off. Underneath his car were dangling wires, like the bear had torn them apart just for spite. In the bed of his truck was a plainly visible igloo cooler. "You didn't have any food in there, did you?" I asked Alan. "Only chocolate doughnuts" was his response. Luckily, he was able to drive away.

Lessons learned: Don't leave food in your car; and don't bring less than a gallon of water per person, per day, on a summer big wall climb in Yosemite.

*On the Nose Route, El Capitan.*

*Robert Finley solos
Needle Eye, Needles,
South Dakota*

# CHAPTER 9

# Soloing

## Free Soloing

Early in my career as a climbing school manager, a client gave me some honest feedback. He told me that when his guide free soloed in front of him to set up and take down his toprope anchor, it gave him a sick feeling in the pit of his stomach. He was worried about what would happen if his guide fell.

I assured him that despite its dangerous appearance, free soloing by an experienced climber was indeed very safe, and that among the top free soloists, no one had ever fallen.

That was many years ago, and sadly, I can't say that now. Among those who have fallen to their death free soloing, several have been my friends. You could say they died doing what they loved, but they left this world too soon, without saying their proper good-byes.

When a friend called me on June 3, 2017, and asked, "Did you hear about Alex Honnold?" I got that same bad feeling in my gut. But I was relieved when he said, "He just free soloed El Cap." Honnold's free solo of the 3,000-foot Freerider route (5.13a) was the first route up El Cap's massive main facade to be climbed rope-less. Climbing pundits called it rock climbing's greatest achievement, some heralding it as the greatest singular achievement in sports, period. You can't really top that one. Alex commented after the climb that he was thinking about focusing on hard sport climbing.

While free soloing can ultimately be the most exhilarating and purest form of rock climbing, I wouldn't say it's the most relaxing. Unexpected things can happen; a seemingly solid hold breaks,

*Peter Croft solos Bearded Cabbage (5.10d), Joshua Tree, California.*

a bird flies out of a crack, a bee stings you on the ankle, a foot slips on lichen. And there is a fine line that you don't want to cross—that line between the pure joy of fun-in-the-sun rock climbing, moving smoothly and flowing up the climb with nothing but air beneath your feet, and the sudden shadow of fear that can sweep over you as quickly as a dark cloud eclipsing the sun. It's happened to me, when things got a little too bold and airy, the sky a little too close, my heart beating a little too fast.

The free soloist faces the possibility of the ultimate irony: falling and dying as a direct result of not wanting to fall and die, knowingly risking life for the pleasure of pure, unfettered freedom of movement in the vertical world.

If you're contemplating free soloing, do it for the right reason: for yourself, not to impress others. Start easy and work your way up the grades, on climbs you've done before. The great free soloists do the same routes over and over, like boulder problems, getting the climbs ruthlessly wired, becoming intimate with every hold. And allow yourself enough margin for error so that you're not approaching that fine line.

## Rope Soloing: Self-Belaying

Petzl is the leading manufacturer of progress capture devices (PCD), ascenders, and rope clamps. Although these devices were not designed specifically for rope soloing, in recent years the Petzl Mini Traxion has become very popular for self-belaying, particularly in Yosemite, where climbers routinely "mini trax," doing laps on long crack pitches or working the moves on their latest big wall free climb. With this popularity, Petzl has addressed the use of their PCD products for self-belaying.

Interestingly, Petzl begins their technical discussion with a remarkable caveat: "Solo climbing is not recommended: Climbing with a partner remains the best solution." That being said, rope soloing can give you the freedom to climb whenever you want,

*Rope solo rig using a Petzl Ascension ascender clipped to the belay loop and a Petzl Micro Traxion rigged with a chest harness. The Micro Traxion is attached via a quickdraw, connected to the two points on the harness with a metal quick link. Petzl recommends using oval locking carabiners to clip the devices for this application. In rigging any self-belay system, study the manufacturer's guidelines to make sure you're rigging the devices properly.*

without a partner, as long as you have access to the top of a cliff or have previously rigged a fixed line.

This is expert-level stuff, so if you venture into rope soloing, know the risks, do your homework,

*Detail of the Petzl Ascension properly clipped in for self-belaying. Note that the rope is clipped inside the carabiner. Always use two different progress capture devices when self-belaying on a single fixed rope, and make sure the bottom device won't ride up to inhibit the function of the top device.*

study the devices, and stick to what the manufacturers of the devices recommend, not what you learned from a friend or on the Internet.

## Self-Belaying with a Single Fixed Line

With a single fixed rope system, you'll want to be extremely cognizant of sharp edges, especially if you're working the same sequence of moves over and over again. Since the rope is tied off, and the only movement is rope stretch, during falls one section of rope is repeatedly exposed to abrasion and cutting over an edge. Judicious use of a rope protector is indicated here, as there's no backup to your main line. For your rope you'll want either an EN 892 (dynamic) or EN 1891 (low-stretch) rope with a minimum 10mm diameter used in conjunction with two PCDs. My preference for rope soloing is the 10mm diameter Sterling Safety Pro (EN 1891 certified), which has superior abrasion resistance to a dynamic rope and about 4 percent stretch in a rope solo fall.

To prevent the PCDs from colliding with each other and potentially malfunctioning, both devices should not be clipped into the belay loop together. Petzl recommends rigging one PCD or ascender to the belay loop with a locking oval carabiner and the second PCD rigged with a chest harness and attached to a quickdraw sling with a locking oval carabiner, connected to the two harness tie-in points with a steel quick link.

You'll want to lightly weight the bottom of the rope so that when the devices slide upward, they don't pull the rope hanging below up with them.

In a fall, don't grab the rope (this keeps the device from loading) or grab the device, which may cause it to malfunction.

While many Yosemite climbers routinely "mini trax" with two Mini Traxions on a single fixed line, Petzl does not recommend this: "Petzl has studied the current usage of the Mini Traxion as a self-belay device on a fixed rope. Serious accidents and many handling errors have been reported.

"The risk of using the device with the cam held open is significant, as well as the possibility of accidental opening of the cam when climbing. Consequently, the Mini Traxion must be paired with a different ascender: Ascension, Basic, Microcender . . .

"Petzl does not recommend using a system consisting of only two Mini Traxion for self-belayed solo climbing with a fixed rope."

## Self-Belaying with Two Ropes

The advantage of using two ropes is redundancy. If one rope is cut, you have a backup. Using a chest harness, you can rig your top PCD with a quickdraw sling attached to the two harness tie-in points with a steel quick link. The lower PCD or ascender can be clipped to your belay loop with a locking oval carabiner.

Without a chest harness, one PCD or ascender can be clipped to the belay loop with a locking oval carabiner, and a second device can be attached to the backup rope with a quickdraw sling and locking oval carabiner attached to the two harness tie-in points with a steel quick link.

The device on the quickdraw sling should not have sharp teeth, since a fall on this system has the force of a miniature fall factor 2 and can generate more impact force. Petzl estimates that more than 4 kN of force can be generated in this mini fall factor 2, which can rip and tear off the sheath of the rope. Instead of a device with sharp teeth, use one with a cam-locking mechanism (like the Petzl Rescucender) for any PCD attached via a sling, quickdraw, or lanyard, used without a chest harness.

With a two-rope system, another method is to use one or two PCDs on one rope, backed up with knots on the second rope (figure eight loops clipped to your belay loop with a locking carabiner). The disadvantage of this system is the difficulty in stopping to tie knots and clip them in; you'll also be dragging up the weight of the rope that's hanging below you. The extra carabiner clipped to your belay loop may also interfere with the functionality of the PCD during a fall.

*Todd Gordon rappels off the Long Dong Silver Spire, Utah.*

PHOTO BY GREG EPPERSON

*John Mallery belays Tom Callahan on Separate Reality (5.12a), Yosemite.*

# CHAPTER 10

# Belaying

Belaying involves three major elements: managing the slack in the rope, maintaining a brake hand on the brake strand of the rope, and stopping the fall. Belaying is a big responsibility; if you take on the task, you should be competent and alert, and you should know the proper safety checks and belay signals.

## The Hip Belay

I began climbing before the advent of the belay device. Back in the 1970s we used the "hip belay" technique to catch a fall, which was simply wrapping the rope around your waist to generate enough friction to stop a fall. Catching a climber on a big "whipper" was painful indeed, and I often ended a hard day of climbing with a black streak singed across the back of my waistline. The hip belay is still useful today in situations where there is so much rope drag that you can barely pull the rope, in alpine rock situations (e.g., exposed Class 3 and Class 4) where the rope is running over considerable terrain, and when the rock itself can be used as a giant friction brake. The hip belay can be made more secure by clipping the non-brake strand into the front of the belayer's harness, which keeps

*The hip belay is the most elemental form of belay. To take in rope, start with the brake hand at your hip and the guide, or "feel," hand extended.*

*To take up slack, the brake hand goes out as the guide hand comes in.*

*The guide hand reaches above the brake hand and pinches the rope . . .*

*. . . so that the brake hand can slide back.*

*In the event of a fall, the brake hand brings the rope in front of the waist for maximum friction.*

the rope at the belayer's waistline in the event of a fall. If tied in and anchored with the rope, the tie-in strand to the anchor should be on the non-brake hand side of the belayer's waist.

## Manual Braking Devices

The most commonly used belay/rappel device is a manual braking device (MBD), essentially a tube or slot device (with two slots so it can be used for both belaying and rappelling on a doubled rope). When the two strands of rope (one going to the climber, one to the belayer's brake hand) are held parallel, in front of the belay device, there is little friction; but when the brake strand is held at a 180-degree angle relative to the strand going to the climber, the device affords maximum friction, making it relatively easy to hold the force of a falling climber.

Learning the proper hand movements is key to becoming a safe belayer. There are many techniques acceptable for a safe belay with an MBD,

*Black Diamond ATC XP in high-friction mode, with the brake strand on the teeth side.*

and they all have this in common: They effectively manage the slack, while still maintaining a brake hand on the brake strand side of the rope, and generate enough friction to stop a fall and safely lower a climber.

Over the last decade, advances in technology have allowed manufacturers to produce thinner ropes, and belay devices have evolved along with the ropes. When buying a belay device, check the manufacturer's specifications and make sure it's appropriate for the diameter of your climbing rope. The most popular MBD is the Black Diamond ATC (tongue in cheek for "air traffic controller"), which also comes in a more versatile version with teeth on one side (the ATC XP) that gives the belayer two options: a regular friction mode when the brake strand is on the non-teeth side, and roughly twice the amount of friction when the brake strand is on the teeth side.

## Multipurpose Devices: Autoblocking Devices

Several manufacturers make hybrid tube devices (e.g., the Black Diamond ATC Guide and the Petzl Reverso) that have both a manual braking mode and an autoblocking mode, making them versatile choices that can be used for both belaying and rappelling in the regular manual mode, or for belaying directly off the anchor in the autoblocking mode. For multipitch climbing, they allow you to belay two followers at the same time. The main disadvantage to these multipurpose devices is the difficulty in lowering a climber when the rope is under tension.

*Black Diamond ATC Guide in autoblocking mode.*

# Assisted Braking Devices

Assisted braking devices (ABDs) with self-locking cams have become popular for sport climbing. The most widely used models include the Petzl Grigri and the Trango Cinch. These devices are designed to lock when suddenly weighted, as during a fall, but might not lock under certain circumstances: if there is a slow and accelerating pull, when the handle is pressed against the rock or carabiner, when the belayer grabs the rope on the non-brake hand side, or when the belayer grabs the device incorrectly and holds the cam down, preventing it from locking. For these reasons it is important to remember, even though ABDs are self-locking, that a brake hand should always be maintained on the brake side of the rope. These devices are far from foolproof, and many accidents have occurred with ABDs, typically when someone is being lowered, the handle is pulled all the way open, and the belayer loses control of the brake hand. The Petzl Grigri Plus is a new design that addresses this problem with a built-in anti-panic function that essentially locks the device when the handle is opened too far when lowering.

As with any belay device, the cardinal rule to remember is this: Always maintain a brake hand!

If for some reason you need to take your brake hand off the rope, tie a backup knot (e.g., overhand loop) on the brake strand side of the rope.

ABDs are very useful for direct belays. Their main advantage over multipurpose devices is that they allow an easy lower when the rope is under tension. When lowering with a direct belay using an ABD, the brake strand should be redirected. I'd recommend using gloves when belaying with ABDs, since they'll allow you to put more weight on your brake hand for smooth lowers.

*Petzl Grigri in lowering mode.*

*Trango Cinch in lowering mode.*

## Plaquette Devices

A plaquette is essentially a flat plate with two slots. The most popular models are the Kong Gigi and the CAMP Ovo. They are most widely used by professional guides when leading two clients up multipitch routes, as they allow a direct belay of two followers at the same time, and the rope is much easier to pull through the device than it is through an ATC guide or Petzl Reverso. Many guides have discovered this the hard way, with tendinitis from belaying after a season of multipitch guiding. Other disadvantages to these plaquettes are that they are poor choices for

*Kong Gigi. Note the position of the carabiner, which is the recommended orientation for direct belaying with a single rope of 10mm diameter or less.*

## Standard Climbing Signals

Proper use of the universal climbing signals, along with a methodical safety check, are integral parts of a safe climb. Ambiguity in the use of climbing signals has led to many tragic accidents, simply because of lack of communication between the climber and belayer. One infamous tragedy occurred in a toprope setup at a popular ice climbing area when the climber reached the top of the climb (at the top of the cliff) and the anchor. The climber yelled, "I'm OK!" but the belayer thought he heard "Off belay." The belayer unclipped the rope from the belay device and took the climber off belay, thinking he was going to walk off the top. The climber leaned back to be lowered, and fell to his death.

On a yo-yo toprope climb, it's important to be vigilant at the transition from the climb up to the lower down. This is where most accidents due to improper communication and climbing signals occur. There should be no ambiguity. If I'm the climber, I always hold onto the strand of rope that goes back down to my belayer until I am sure he or she has heard my command and is in the brake position and ready to hold my weight. In most cases you'll be within visual contact, so in addition to hearing the verbal commands, you'll want to look down over your shoulder and visually verify that the belayer is being attentive, with his or her hand in the proper brake position, alert and ready to lower you safely. In situations where you are climbing with other parties around you, it's best to include your partner's name in the signal (e.g., "Off belay, Bob.") to prevent confusion, although I once saw a leader who was in the middle of a pitch on a crowded multipitch crag get taken off belay when someone else yelled "Off belay, John," and there was more than one John. So be vigilant and be heads up.

# Standardized Climbing Signals

Here are the standardized climbing signals I've used for over thirty years in my climbing school:

**On belay?** Climber to belayer, "Am I on belay?"

**Belay on:** Belayer to climber, "The belay is on."

**Climbing:** Climber to belayer, "I'm beginning the climb."

**Climb on:** Belayer to climber, "Go ahead and start climbing; I have you on belay."

**Up rope:** Climber to belayer, "There is too much slack in my rope. Take up some of the slack." (Too much slack in the belay rope will mean a longer fall. Remember that rope stretch also contributes to the total distance of a fall, especially when there is a lot of rope out in a toprope scenario.)

**Slack:** Climber to belayer, "Give me some slack; the rope is too tight."

**Tension (or Take):** Climber to belayer, "Take all the slack out of the rope and pull it tight; I am going to hang all my body weight on the rope." (This could be a situation where the climber simply wants to rest by hanging in the harness while weighting the rope, or a toprope situation where the climber is getting ready to be lowered back down a climb.)

**Tension on (or I've got you):** Belayer to climber, "I've taken the rope tight, and my brake hand is now locked off in the brake position, ready to hold all your weight."

**Lower me:** Climber to belayer, "I'm in the lowering position (feet wide, good stance, sitting in the harness, weighting the rope, and leaning back), and I'm ready to be lowered."

**Lowering:** Belayer to climber, "I'm proceeding to lower you."

**Off belay:** Climber to belayer, "I'm safe. You can unclip the rope from your belay device and take me off belay." (Never take someone off belay unless you hear this signal. The universal contract between belayer and climber is that the belayer must never take the climber off belay unless the climber gives the belayer the "off belay" command.)

**Belay off:** Belayer to climber, "I've unclipped the rope from my belay device and have taken you off belay."

**That's me!** Climber to belayer, "You've taken up all the slack in the rope, and the rope is now tight to my harness."

**Watch me!** Climber to belayer, "Heads up! Be attentive with the belay—there is a good chance I'm going to fall right here!"

**Falling!** Climber to belayer, "I'm actually falling; go to your brake position and lock off the rope to catch my fall!" (A fall can happen so fast that the climber might not be able to shout this signal during a short fall, but it helps the belayer react more quickly, especially in situations where the belayer can't see the climber.)

**ROCK!** Climber to belayer and others below, "I've dislodged a rock and it's now free-falling below me—watch out below!" (The equivalent signal to "Fore!" in golf, "ROCK!" should also be yelled when the climber drops a piece of equipment.)

---

belaying the leader and are more complicated to use for lowering a climber, especially when the rope is under tension. They are not the most versatile rappel devices either, and for this reason many guides carry a second device, like an ATC, for rappelling.

Plaquette devices can be tricky to use, so as with any belay device, read the manufacturer's guidelines carefully. Also, seek proper instruction from a certified guide or experienced climber if you have any doubts about how to use the device or the proper technique to use when belaying with the device. Someone's life is, literally, in your hands; and if you're the belayer, it's your responsibility to know what you're doing.

## Belaying on a Toprope

The best way to belay from the base of a climb in a toprope situation is to attach the rope and belay device directly to the belay loop on your harness with a locking carabiner. The rope then runs through the top anchor and back down to the climber. Your body weight serves as part of the anchor, and the added friction at the toprope anchor makes it relatively easy to catch a fall, hold a climber who is hanging on the rope, or lower a climber back down. The belay device is right in front of you and easy to manipulate. In situations where the climber far outweighs the belayer, or when the belayer is precariously perched in uneven terrain, the belayer should have a ground anchor. *A direct belay (directly off the anchor) is not recommended for toprope belaying from the base.*

*1. The BUS (brake under slide) method of belaying on a toprope. Start by clipping the rope into the slot in the belay device closest to the spine side of the carabiner and orient the rope so that the brake side is down.*

*2. To take up rope, pull the rope up with your brake hand (palm down) as you simultaneously pull the rope down with the other hand . . .*

*3. . . . then brake the rope down under your belay device.*

*4. Take your non-brake hand and grasp the rope below your brake hand.*

*5. . . . then slide your brake hand back up under the belay device, and return the non-brake hand to it's starting position above the belay device. In a fall, remember the brake position is down.*

## The Ground Anchor

The worst accident I've had in forty years of rock climbing happened when I was belaying in a toprope situation without a ground anchor. I was belaying from the base of the climb in a relaxed position about 15 feet out from the base of the cliff. Between the ledge I was belaying from and the cliff itself was a deep chimney. My partner was climbing on a toprope and suddenly fell while attempting an overhang about 50 feet above me. He swung wildly in the air. I easily caught the fall and locked off my belay device in the brake position, but I was pulled off my stance, swinging 15 feet straight into the wall like a pendulum. I braced for the impact with an outstretched leg and sustained a severely sprained ankle. A simple ground anchor would have prevented this accident. Belaying accidents are common, and in almost every case they have the same element: no ground anchor.

When should you use a ground anchor? When belaying a leader, it's always a good consideration. Clip into your ground anchor with your rope, and allow about 3 feet of slack. If there's a high enough impact force to pull you tight against the anchor, this movement will serve as a great counterweight to lessen the impact force on the piece the leader has fallen on, but the ground anchor will keep you from losing control of the belay or slamming into the cliff.

In a toprope situation, if both the climber and belayer are roughly the same body weight and the terrain at the base of the cliff is flat, a ground anchor is unnecessary. But if the climber far outweighs the belayer, a ground anchor should always be considered. If the climb is vertical or overhanging, more force will be exerted by the falling climber than a fall on a low-angle climb. It is especially important to establish a ground anchor

*After you've mastered the BUS method, a more advanced technique is to brake under and switch the brake hand, alternating back and forth with either hand. As a professional guide, in a day's belaying I can pull over a thousand feet of rope, which can really work your shoulders, especially if there's rope drag. I prefer this method, as I can alternate arms/shoulders rather than tiring out one arm or shoulder.*

## *Two-Rope Toprope Setups*

When rigging long topropes of more than half a single rope length, two ropes can be tied together using a double fisherman's knot or figure eight bend knot. With such a huge amount of rope out between the climber and the belayer, rope stretch is a major concern, especially if you are using dynamic ropes. Remember that even a short fall in a toprope situation will stretch a dynamic rope about 10 percent, so tighten up the rope when belaying someone just off the ground or just above a ledge.

There are two methods that can be used to deal with the knot joining the two ropes. The simple solution, also the best if there will be no stance for the climber to stop at, avoids the knot pass altogether. With the knot joining the two ropes at the anchor, tie a figure eight loop and attach it to the climber's belay loop with two locking carabiners (gates opposed and reversed). When the climber reaches the anchor, the knot will be just above the belayer's device, so no knot pass is required.

Another solution is to use two belay devices. The climber ties into the end of the rope as usual. The belayer anticipates the knot pass and has a second belay device clipped to his belay loop, at the ready. When the knot reaches the belayer, the belayer alerts the climber to find a good stance, then ties a backup knot (figure eight loop) on the brake hand side of the belay device. The belayer steps forward to create a bit of slack, then clips the rope into the second belay device on the climber's side of the knot, leaving the first belay device clipped in. If another person is available, he or she can assist the belayer simply by holding the rope with both hands under a little tension above the belay device as the belayer accomplishes this. When the climber reaches the anchor, the belayer lowers him until the knot is almost to the belay device, and the process is reversed: The climber takes a stance, the belayer unclips the second belay device (first double-checking that the first belay device is still clipped in and has the backup knot), then unties the backup knot and lowers the climber as normal.

for the belayer in uneven terrain, particularly if the belay stance is perched high on top of boulders, or is some distance away from the base of the cliff.

A good system to rig a ground anchor is to start with the belayer tying into the end of the rope. Not only does this "close" the rope system, but it allows the belayer to use the climbing rope to connect to a ground anchor with a clove hitch, which can be easily adjusted to suit the stance.

Natural anchors are obvious choices for ground anchors, like a sling or cordelette around a tree or a large block of rock. A single bomber cam or nut in a crack will also suffice.

If you are the belayer in a toprope scenario, anticipate that you will be pulled in a line directly to the toprope anchor master point, and anchor and brace yourself accordingly. If you're belaying the leader, you'll be pulled in straight line between the ground anchor and the leader's first piece of protection. Ideally, the ground anchor will be low and directly behind or beneath you or just slightly to the side. Remember your ABCs: anchor, belayer,

*In the single-pitch environment, it's critical to always close your rope system, either by tying into the end of the rope, or tying a stopper knot like this.*

climber. There should be a straight line between the anchor, the belayer, and the direction of pull created by the climber.

## Belaying from the Top

Whether on a single-pitch or multipitch climb, when belaying the follower, the belayer can choose from a variety of belay methods, depending on the situation.

### Belaying Off the Harness: The Indirect Belay

Using the indirect belay method, the belayer clips the rope and belay device into a locking carabiner attached to the belay loop on her harness. The belayer is "in the system," which means that if the climber falls, the belayer's body will absorb the force of the fall to some extent. I call it "indirect," since the force generated in a fall does not necessarily go directly onto the anchor. For example, if the belayer

*Belayer ground anchored in uneven terrain. Remember ABC: The anchor, belayer, and climber's direction of pull should all come into a straight line. Her tie-in strand is on her brake hand side, so she won't spin awkwardly if the system is loaded.*

takes a sitting stance and braces with her legs against a rock outcropping, and the climber falls, the belayer can absorb the force of the fall without transferring any load onto the anchor, accomplishing this by the stability of the stance aided by the friction of the rope running over the surface of the rock and at the belay device itself. When using the indirect belay, the anchor and stance are important because if the belayer gets pulled off-balance, or pulled sideways, she can easily lose control of the belay. The belayer should be anticipating the direction she will be pulled if a fall occurs and position herself accordingly, tight to the anchor. The ABC acronym works in this situation: The belayer should be in a line between the anchor and the climber (anchor-belayer-climber).

While the indirect belay is commonly used by most recreational climbers, it is rarely used by trained, professional guides—for a number of reasons. One is that the belayer is trapped "in the system," and if a climber falls, the climber's weight is hanging directly off the belay loop of the belayer, making it difficult for her to even move. Once in

*Belaying with an indirect belay. The belayer is in a good seated stance, with his rope clipped to the anchor's master point. The ATC XP belay device is attached to his belay loop. If the climber below falls, the belayer will have to absorb all the force and bear the full weight of the falling climber onto his harness. The braking position will be awkward, and since the belayer is slightly out of line from the direction of pull to the anchors, he will get pulled into that line. The belayer should simply position himself in line (anchor-belayer-climber, or ABC) to remedy this potential problem. My choice in this situation would be to belay with a direct belay, using my Grigri.*

*Here the belay device is clipped into both the belayer's belay loop and the rope tie-in loop. If the climber below falls, his weight will go mostly on the anchor, not the belayer. If belaying a leader, this method is not recommended, since the belay becomes less dynamic, thereby increasing impact force on the leader's protection.*

*Belaying*  **203**

1. The old-school "pinch and slide technique" is commonly used as an indirect belaying technique when belaying from the top of a cliff. Start with the brake hand (the right hand in these photos) next to the belay device, with the left hand extended out.

2. Pull the rope in with the left hand and simultaneously pull rope out with the brake hand.

3. Move the brake hand back behind the braking plane (more than 90 degrees from the angle of the rope going to the climber) and pinch the rope above the brake hand with the left hand . . .

4. . . . then slide the brake hand down toward the belay device.

5. Move the left hand back to the extended position and repeat the process. The cardinal rule to remember with this method is to always keep the brake hand on the rope.

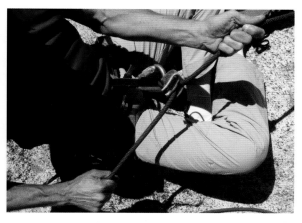

1. *Another belay method for an indirect belay from the top of the cliff is a variation of the BUS (brake under slide) method, but instead of braking down, the brake position is up and back. The belayer's right hand is the brake hand in these photos. Starting with the brake hand palm down, the brake hand pulls the rope out as the left hand pulls rope in.*

2. *Next, the brake hand pulls the rope back into a brake position.*

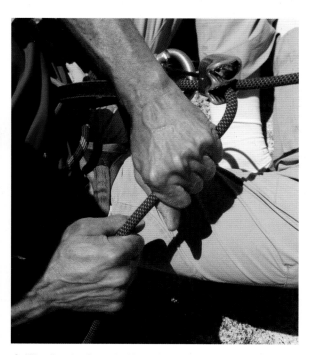

3. *The left hand grasps the rope, palm down on the brake strand, just below the belay device.*

4. *The brake hand slides back toward the device without releasing its grip on the rope. The left hand extends again and grabs the non-brake side of the rope to repeat the process.*

# Escaping the Belay

If you are belaying with the belay device clipped to your harness (indirect belay) and need to escape from the system, follow these steps:

1. Tie off the belay device with a mule knot.

2. Tie a friction hitch (klemheist or prusik) on the load strand going to the climber.

3. Attach the friction hitch to a locking carabiner and tie a Munter/mule/overhand with the climbing rope (off the back side of the knot connecting you to the anchor).

4. Tie a backup knot (eg. figure eight loop) on the load strand, and clip it to your anchor with a locking carabiner.

5. Release the mule knot on your belay device, and transfer the load to the Munter/mule/overhand. You are now free to "escape the belay." What you do next depends on the situation. To raise a climber, if you don't have a Grigri, build a 3:1 raising system using a prusik knot at the anchor as a ratchet, and another prusik knot on the load strand going to the climber.

this position, it is awkward for the belayer to hold the fallen climber, particularly if the stance is bad. Lowering the climber from the top of the cliff using an indirect belay can be difficult, if not dangerous, particularly if the cliff is steep and the climber far outweighs the belayer.

The indirect belay is also the worst method to use if the belayer needs to provide any assistance (like a raising system) to the climber below, since the belayer is trapped in the system and would need to perform a "belay escape" in order to get out of the system and convert it to a raise.

If this sounds complicated, that's because it is! I detailed these steps to illustrate a point: An indirect belay is a poor choice for belaying a second. The only situation where I would consciously seek to use an indirect belay is when the anchor is marginal and I don't trust it. I'll still clove hitch my rope to the anchor's master point with a tight connection, but then I'll take the best stance I can and brace myself so that my stance, and the falling climber's weight on my harness, absorbs the force of the fall, not the anchor.

## The Redirected Belay

This technique utilizes the additional friction generated by running the rope back through the anchor to help assist in catching a fall. Clip your

*The redirected belay. If the climber below falls, the force on the belayer will be directly in line to where the rope is redirected through the anchor. The friction of the rope running over the redirect carabiner will absorb some of the force.*

belay device into your harness belay loop, then run the rope back through a locking carabiner at the anchor master point. If you're using a cordelette-style anchor setup, you can also redirect the rope through a locking carabiner clipped to the "shelf," which is defined as all the loops in the cordelette just above the master point knot. If your partner falls, you'll be pulled toward the anchor, so brace yourself for a pull in that direction. Because of the rope's friction through the redirect carabiner, you only have to hold about two-thirds of the force generated in the fall. The redirect nearly doubles the force on the anchor (just like in a toprope rig), so if you decide to use a redirected belay, the anchor should be bomber. The drawback to this technique, like the indirect belay, is that if any rescue or assistance skills are required, it's more complicated to rig any raising system.

### *The Direct Belay*

The method preferred by most professional guides when belaying a follower is the direct belay. In a direct belay the belay device is clipped directly to the anchor, and in the event of a fall, the anchor, not the belayer, bears the brunt of the fall and holds the climber's weight.

Using an MBD like an ATC *is not recommended for use in a direct belay*, because unless the device is positioned below your waist level, the braking position will be very awkward, and you will be in a weak and dangerous position to hold a fall. If the master point is above your waist level, the Munter hitch works well, since the braking position for maximum friction is when the two strands of rope are parallel to each other, with the brake position down below the carabiner, not above it.

The best way to set up a direct belay is to use an ABD like a Grigri, an autoblocking device like the ATC Guide or Petzl Reverso, or a plaquette device attached directly to the master point on the anchor. The advantage of a Grigri or similar device is that

**The direct belay. A Grigri is clipped directly to the master point. As long as the anchor is bomber, this is my preferred method.**

in the event of a fall, the Grigri simply locks off and the anchor holds the climber's weight. When using a Grigri in the direct belay mode, take care when the device is close to rock, as anything that presses against the handle (i.e., the rock) will release the locking mechanism. Be sure to position the handle away from the rock.

Remember, an MBD or similar non-autoblocking device is *not recommended* for use in a direct belay.

*Detail of a direct belay setup using a quad rig.*

*Another method of rigging a quad for a direct belay.*

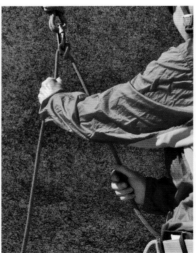

*A direct belay with a Munter hitch. Here the belayer's right hand is her brake hand. The starting position (left photo, position 1) is with the brake hand at the top and the guide, or feel, hand at the bottom. Pull the rope down with the brake hand as the guide hand goes up. Feeding the rope up with the guide hand, rather than pulling the rope down tightly with the brake strand, puts fewer kinks in the rope. The brake hand stays on the rope as the guide hand grabs below it. Then return to position 1. Unlike a manual braking tube device, maximum friction with a Munter hitch is when the two rope strands are parallel.*

## The Rope Direct Belay

If the belay anchor is initially built well back from where you can see your follower, and you want to belay from a stance to maintain a visual on the person who's climbing up from below, you can use the climbing rope and a rope direct belay technique, which is essentially belaying off an extended master point. Clip your climbing rope to the master

*Another method of rope direct belay rigging useful for belaying from the top on a single-pitch climb. The belayer is on the right strand of rope, attached to the master point with a clove hitch to a locking carabiner. Off the back side of the clove hitch, the rope is clipped back to a separate carabiner with a figure eight loop. Off this strand, the Grigri is clipped to another figure eight loop. Here the distance is fairly close to the anchor, but this rigging technique is most useful for greater distances between the anchor and your desired belay stance, limited only by the length of available rope. The big advantage is visual contact with your climber in situations where the anchor is some distance back from the edge.*

*Guides often use this rope direct method in single-pitch situations where the anchor is well away from the edge and they want to position themselves to better watch their clients, and perhaps lower them back down when they reach this point. It is essentially an extended master point, created by running the lead rope through carabiners at the anchor's master point (I prefer two lockers, opposed and reversed), lowering down to the preferred position, then tying an overhand knot on both strands, creating another two-loop master point. While the loop extending up to the anchor is not redundant, it's monitored, and it's your full rope strength.*

point on the anchor with two locking carabiners, opposed and reversed, then lower yourself to your preferred stance (you can remain on belay for this process), then tie a BHK. The master point loops on the BHK should be within arm's length so that you can easily belay from these with an ABD. I call this method "rope direct" because you are essentially belaying directly off the anchor, albeit extended whatever distance is required to position you at the edge. Using a device like a Grigri, you'll have the

*Rope direct belay using the "Atomic Clip." This is a great method to use for a two-bolt anchor on a single-pitch climb, or a multipitch sport climb if you're swinging leads. Tie a double-loop bowline, equalize it to the two anchor points, then tie a figure eight loop off the back side of this knot. Tie the figure eight loop so that it's about arm's length above you, and belay with an ABD. To belay the leader, switch the belay device to your harness belay loop.*

benefit of a quick and easy conversion to a raising system if required, and it's easy to lower someone on this setup by redirecting the brake strand on the Grigri (see "Lowering" in this chapter).

## Lowering

It's often easier and quicker to lower someone back down a single-pitch climb than to have her rappel. Depending on the belay device you're using, the lowering procedure can range from simple to relatively complicated, so have this in mind when considering which belay device will work best for a particular situation.

### Lowering with a Grigri

My first choice is always to lower someone using a Grigri. Since it has a built-in autolock, there is no need to back it up with an autoblock. Petzl sells the Freino, a carabiner that has a special gate on the side for the brake strand to be clipped into, to facilitate lowering. Without the special carabiner, you can redirect the brake strand back up through a separate carabiner clipped to the master point (or, on a cordelette anchor, up to the shelf). The big advantage of the Grigri is that once the rope is clipped in, you can use it for lowering (just remember to redirect the brake strand!) or belaying (as the climber climbs back up), and it's all set to rig a 3:1 hauling

*A Grigri in the lowering mode with the brake strand redirected using the Petzl Freino carabiner, which is specifically designed for this application.*

*A Grigri rigged for lowering with the brake strand redirected through a carabiner clipped to the master point.*

system if your climber needs some assistance on the way back up.

## Lowering with a Munter Hitch

Flake the rope at your feet so that if there are any tangles, you can get to them. If you're anchored with a clove hitch, it's adjustable, so you can fine-tune the length of your tie-in as required. If the stance at the anchor allows you to see down the cliff and watch the climber as you lower him, clip another locking carabiner (a large, pear-shaped carabiner works best) to the master point and tie a Munter hitch. Back it up with an autoblock clipped

to a locking carabiner at your belay loop, and you're ready to lower your climber.

### MULE KNOT

The mule knot is used to tie off a Munter hitch. The great advantage of the Munter/mule combination is that it can be tied off and released when the rope is weighted and under tension, making it one of the key knot combinations for many rescue applications.

## Using an Autoblock Knot as a Backup When Lowering

Whenever you are lowering a climber with a manual braking device or Munter hitch, it's best to back

*The belayer is ready to lower the climber with a Munter hitch on a locking carabiner clipped to the master point, backed up with an autoblock clipped to a locking carabiner attached to the belayer's belay loop.*

*Lowering with a Munter hitch and an autoblock. The belayer is holding an autoblock backup that's clipped with a locking carabiner to his belay loop.*

up your brake hand with an autoblock knot clipped to a locking carabiner attached to your belay loop.

Some guides call the autoblock the "third hand," because if you take your brake hand off the rope when you're lowering or rappelling, the autoblock grabs the brake strand of your rope like your hand would. The autoblock adds an extra level of safety, especially when there are tangles in your rope that you need to untangle as you lower your climber or descend on a rappel.

In a single-pitch setting, if the stance at the anchor does not allow you to see down the cliff and watch the climber as you lower him, you can rig the rope direct belay system to position yourself at the edge to maintain visual contact. As a guide, I always strive for visual contact with my clients whenever belaying or lowering them.

### Lowering with a Redirected Manual Braking Device

To lower a climber with an MBD like an ATC, you can clip the ATC to your harness and redirect the climber's strand back through the anchor at the master point. This adds friction and makes it easier to hold the climber's weight but increases the load on the anchor—in fact, it nearly doubles it. Also, if the climber far outweighs the belayer, it can be very awkward and difficult to lower the climber, because the belayer is getting pulled into the anchor.

A better technique is to clip the ATC directly to the anchor master point and redirect the brake strand back through a locking carabiner at the master point (or, on a cordelette anchor, the shelf, which is all the loops in the cordelette just above the master point knot), to maintain the proper angle (for maximum friction) on the brake strand. Back it up with an autoblock attached to your belay loop with a locking carabiner. If you're using a manual braking device like an ATC or similar tube device, remember, *do not use an MBD for a direct belay* as the braking position would be weak, awkward, and dangerous.

*A manual braking device (Black Diamond ATC XP) rigged with a redirect for lowering. The climber's end is coming out of the left side of the belay device, and the brake strand is redirected up through a carabiner clipped to the shelf.*

## Lowering with an Autoblocking Device

If you're using an autoblocking device (like the ATC Guide or Petzl Reverso) and belaying a second with a direct belay in the autoblocking mode, if the second falls, the device locks off. Lowering from a locked device under tension presents a

*For very short lowers, or to provide slack, you can simply grab the blocking carabiner firmly and ratchet it up and down. Make sure you have a firm grip with your brake hand on the brake strand.*

challenge, and there are a variety of solutions based on the situation.

For longer lowers, if the climber is weighting the rope and the device is under tension, follow these steps.

1. Tie a catastrophe knot on the brake hand side of the rope.

*For a short lower of a few body lengths, you can use a small carabiner (it's a good idea to have one dedicated in advance for this application) clipped to a small hole in the autoblocking device. Autoblocking devices can be unpredictable, and can release suddenly, so an autoblock backup is recommended. Tie the autoblock knot on the brake hand strand, and clip it to your harness belay loop with a locking carabiner.*

2. Redirect the brake strand to the master point or up to the shelf.

3. Tie the autoblock knot on the brake hand strand, and clip it to your harness belay loop with a locking carabiner.

*Setup for lowering with an autoblocking device, backed up with an autoblock knot on the brake strand side. To lower, slide the autoblock knot down and hold it with your brake hand while pulling down on the sling, keeping a firm grip on the rope with your brake hand.*

4. Using a double-length (48-inch) sling, clip it to the small carabiner you've clipped to the small hole in the device, then redirect the sling through a carabiner up higher on the anchor.

5. Untie the catastrophe knot.

6. Using the sling like a pulley, lean back to release the tension and autoblock function, and proceed to lower the climber.

*1. Redirect the brake strand, then tie an autoblock knot on the brake strand and attach it to your harness belay loop with a locking carabiner.*

If you are using a direct belay with an auto-blocking device and the plan is for your second to be lowered once he or she reaches your stance, you can easily convert the autoblocking device to the MBD mode once the climber reaches the ledge or stance and is ready to be lowered.

*3. Now you're ready for a smooth lower in the manual braking mode, brake strand redirected and backed up with an autoblock knot.*

*2. Clip another locking carabiner to the master point, and clip in the autoblocking locking carabiner on the device (carabiner to carabiner; check that both are locked).*

# Rappelling

## Rappelling Safety: Preventing Rappel Accidents

Although rappelling is a simple technique, statistically a high percentage of rappelling accidents end in a fatality. Why is this? Perhaps rappelling is so rudimentary that the fine points of safety are sometimes overlooked. Analyzing rappelling accidents tells us what can go wrong. Let's take a look at two scenarios.

### Scenario 1: Rappelling Off One or Both Ends of the Rope

Believe it or not, this happens with some regularity, and almost every year there are several fatal rappelling accidents in America in which someone has simply rappelled off the ends of a rope. Usually it happens when the ends are uneven on a doubled-rope rappel. When the short end passes through the rappelling device, only one strand of the doubled rope remains in the device; the climber's body weight rapidly pulls the rope through the rappel anchor, quickly dispatching the climber to the ground. A simple solution is to tie stopper knots separately in both ends of the rope. It's a simple solution, and a key safety habit in the single-pitch and multi-pitch environment, no matter what you're using the rope for.

### Scenario 2: Not Clipping Both Strands of the Rope into the Carabiner

This is an easy mistake to make if you're not alert and double-checking your system. If you thread both strands of rope through your rappel device, but only clip one strand into your locking carabiner, when you lean back and weight the rope, you'll descend as rapidly as in the first scenario, with equally injurious or fatal results. A good safety habit is to first clip in with a sling to the rappel anchor, rig your rappel device, then weight the rappel system and double-check everything *before* unclipping the sling.

Always go through a mental checklist before rappelling—ABC:

**A** is the rappel anchor. Take a look at the anchor, slings, chains, etc., and make sure the rappel rope is threaded properly through the anchor. The anchor should be redundant all the way to the point where your rope is threaded through the anchor. This means you should not rely on a single piece of gear in your anchor system, whether it is a single cord, sling, or rappel ring.

**B** is for buckles on your harness—double-check to make sure they are buckled properly and doubled back appropriately.

**C** is for carabiner. Make sure the locking carabiner that attaches your rappel device to your harness is being loaded properly on the long axis—and check to make sure it is locked!

### Rappel Belays

If you're teaching a beginner who is rappelling for the first time, it's best to belay him on a separate rope. Another technique to back up somebody on rappel is called the fireman's belay. This is done by having someone down below attentively holding both strands of the rappel rope (in a double-rope rappel). When this person pulls down on the ropes

*Fireman's belay.*

the prusik, you might need the skills to perform a mini self-rescue.

The modern rappel backup utilizes the autoblock knot, rigged *below* the rappel device. There are two distinct advantages to this method. One is that for the autoblock knot to grab, it needs to hold only a very small percentage of the rappeler's weight, since it is on the braking side of the device, and the device itself is holding most of the weight and providing most of the friction. It is essentially like your brake hand squeezing and gripping the rope; for that reason, some instructors refer to it as the "third hand," like an angel grabbing your rope and averting a catastrophe if, for some reason, you've lost control of the brake. The second big advantage of the autoblock method is that it is

and applies tension, the rappeler will stop on a dime—he cannot move down the rope when it is under tension.

## Rappel Backups

In the old days the most common method for a rappel backup was using a prusik knot on the ropes *above* the rappel device, connected to the harness with a sling. The non-brake hand would cup the prusik knot and hold it in a loosened position during the rappel, allowing it to slide down the rope. Letting go of the knot allowed it to slide up and grab onto the ropes, stopping the rappel. There are two drawbacks to this method. One is that for the prusik to lock off, it must hold all the rappeler's weight. The second is that once the prusik is weighted, the rappeler must remove all his body weight from the knot in order for it to be released—not an easy task if you're on a free-hanging rappel. In essence, to take your weight off

*Black Diamond ATC XP rigged for rappelling with a three-wrap autoblock backup clipped to the leg loop with a locking carabiner.*

*By positioning your autoblock carabiner on the inside of the leg loop strap, you can gain a bit more separation between the autoblock and your rappel device.*

*Proper use of an extended rappel device with autoblock backup. A double-length nylon runner is threaded through the harness tie-in points and tied with an overhand knot for redundancy. The rappel device is the Black Diamond ATC Guide in the rappel mode. The autoblock knot is clipped to a locking carabiner attached to the belay loop.*

releasable under tension (i.e., when you've weighted it and it's grabbing onto the rope). As you rappel down, you simply take your thumb and forefinger, forming a circle (like the OK sign), and push the autoblock down as you go, allowing the rope to slide freely through the knot. When you let go, the autoblock knot rides up and grabs onto the rope, like your brake hand squeezing the rope. To release the autoblock, even with your weight on it, is as simple as sliding it back down and holding it in the "open" position with your fingers. It's a beautiful thing, and easy to rig.

The disadvantage of clipping the autoblock to your leg loop is that if for some reason you were

*Here's a close-up look at an extended rappel device with autoblock backup.*

to go unconscious and flip upside down, the auto-block could ride up and come in contact with your rappel device, which would prevent it from grabbing, much like sliding it down and keeping it "open" with your fingers. In recent years, professional guides have developed a method to safeguard against this simply by extending the rappel device with a sling attached to the harness and rigging the autoblock clipped into the belay loop. I like to rig a double-length sewn nylon sling threaded through

*In a pinch, the Munter hitch can be used for rappelling, although it will put some kinks in your rope. Position the gate of the carabiner opposite the braking side of the Munter hitch so the rope doesn't rub against the gate mechanism.*

both points at the front of my harness (where your rope tie-in goes through) and tied with an overhand knot, to gain redundancy at the sling. I prefer to use a fat nylon sling over a thin Spectra or Dyneema sling for this application because nylon has a higher melting point. If the rappel rope is running across the sling, it could potentially create some heat due to the friction, which could damage the sling and reduce its breaking strength in later applications.

## Multipitch Rappelling

Climbers use multipitch rappelling techniques to descend from long routes, normally with two ropes tied together, allowing them to descend the length of a standard rope (60 or 70 meters) on each rappel.

The first thing to check on a multipitch rappel is the condition and soundness of the anchor, as in most cases the rigging will already be in place, having been left by a previous climbing team. The most common anchors will be two bolts, a single tree, or a solid, wedged block of rock. If I know I'll be descending a long route via multiple rappels, I'll bring extra nylon webbing, rap rings, and a knife—in case I need to cut away a nest of old slings and rerig an anchor. On obscure climbs in Yosemite, I've come across old nylon webbing bleached pure white by the sun, only to flip it over and find the other side bright red. Over time UV exposure will weaken nylon and Dyneema/Spectra webbing,

I came across this natural anchor several hundred feet up a route on Tahquitz Rock, near Idyllwild, California. Someone had obviously rappelled from it, probably to escape an afternoon thunderstorm. Although the anchor has two basic components, each "trunk" is less than 3 inches in diameter, and the master point you'd thread your rappel rope through is a nonredundant, single aluminum rappel ring (albeit rated at 3,000 lbs.). The real problem I have with this rappel anchor is simply the size of the "tree" itself. I'm glad I didn't have to rappel from it!

SMC rap rings are light (11 grams) and strong (14 kN, or 3,147 lbs.), a good choice for carrying on long multipitch climbs where weight is a factor and the descent will involve multiple rappels. They are not a good choice for high-use fixed anchors, as aluminum wears quickly.

*Typical rigging found at many climbing areas: two separate 1-inch nylon webbing slings, each tied with a water knot, and two rappel rings. I've rappelled off this tree many times over the years, as it grows on one of my favorite climbs at Suicide Rock, California. Although the trunk is over 12 inches in diameter and the tree is alive and healthy, notice the crack it grows out of— barely 2 inches wide! I always back it up with a separate anchor until the last climber is down.*

*This sturdy rock bollard is attached to the main structure of the cliff, and the rigging is redundant, with two separate 1-inch tubular nylon slings and two rappel rings. Bomber.*

so carefully inspect any existing slings you might decide to use. If the sling is stiff and the color faded from UV exposure, it has probably lost most of its strength. Also, if the sling shows a burned (blackened) or glazed mark where a rope has been pulled across it, the sling should be retired; the friction from the rope being pulled over the sling created enough heat to melt it slightly, and its strength will be severely compromised.

Whenever you're not tied into the climbing rope, always protect yourself by tethering to the anchor with a nylon sling or PAS (personal anchor system) like the Metolius PAS or Sterling Chain Reactor. Remember, a traditional daisy chain with bartacked pockets is not recommended as a tether or for rappel extensions, because clipping a carabiner into two loops is a very weak connection (only 3 kN, or 674 lbs.).

Girth-hitch the PAS or sling through both tie-in points on your harness, then clip in with a locking carabiner directly to the anchor whenever you're going to untie from the rope and rig the rappel. The loop-to-loop design of the PAS allows you to conveniently adjust the length. Be cautious when using slings or a PAS not to climb above the anchor; if you slip you'll generate a high-impact force on both yourself and the anchor—essentially a mini fall factor 2 (total distance of the fall divided by the length from the anchor)—and since the sling or PAS has virtually no stretch like a rope would have, you can generate a surprising amount of force. I prefer the Sterling Chain Reactor since

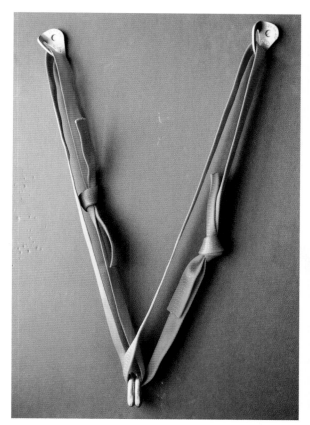

*The most common fixed anchor you'll encounter is a two-bolt anchor. An easy and bomber pre-equalized rappel rig is a simple V configuration. Thread two separate 5-foot lengths of nylon webbing through each bolt hanger and two rap rings, then tie each sling with a water knot.*

it is made of nylon, with at least a modicum of stretch compared to other designs made of Spectra or Dyneema, which have virtually no stretch—like clipping in with a wire cable.

The first person down a rappel should be prepared for rope tangles, especially if there are ledges or bushes on the cliff. Rigging an autoblock backup allows you to let go of your brake hand and have both hands free to deal with rope tangles and clipping in when you reach the next rappel stance. It's

*Two-bolt anchor rigged with cord. Thread a length of cord (7mm nylon here) through both bolt hangers, then tie into a loop using a figure eight bend. Pull the cord down between the bolts, tie with a figure eight loop, then add two quick links.*

important that the first person down be especially aware of the danger of rappelling off one or both ends of the rope if no end knots are in place. When the first person down arrives at the next anchor, she should clip in with a sling or PAS, then unclip from the rappel device and yell "Off rappel" as a signal to let the next person know he can proceed down. If it's a hanging stance, the first person down should prepare an equalized clip-in point for all members of the team to clip into when they arrive at the stance. The quad system works great for this application.

For multipitch rappels, many climbers don't tie knots in the ends of their ropes for fear the knots

*Multipitch rappelling efficiency with a party of three on a two-rope rappel. I arrived first at this anchor, rigged a quad, and clipped in with my personal tether. Mike and Lori Satzberg each rappelled down and did the same. Then I pulled the ropes down, at the same time threading one of the ropes through the anchors for the next rappel. We all clipped our rappel devices in, then I removed the quad, leaving Mike and Lori pre-rigged with rappel extensions. I'm now rappelling down to the next anchor station, where I'll set up a quad rig, clip in, then have them rappel, one at a time, to the station, where we'll do it all again.*

*The quad rigging allows for two separate and redundant master point clip-ins for multipitch rappelling, convenient for two-bolt anchor stations. The red sling is her rappel extension, which also serves as her personal tether. Her rappel device is at the ready for the next rappel. Lori Satzberg on Walk on the Wild Side, Joshua Tree.*

may jam in a crack, especially in windy conditions where the ropes may blow out to the side.

For me it just feels unsafe (and unnerving) to be high off the ground on a rappel with the free-hanging end of my rope swaying in the breeze and no stopper knot in the end. My philosophy for multipitch rappelling is this: Always tie stopper knots in the ends of the rappel ropes as your routine practice, and only leave them untied if there is a very, very compelling reason to do so, such as the high probability of the stopper knot getting

*Rappelling with butterfly coils reduces the chances of the rope snagging in windy conditions.*

*Here the PAS (a Sterling Chain Reactor) was clipped to the anchor for a tether while the rappel rope was threaded through the rings. The ATC rappel device was extended and clipped into two loops of the PAS. An autoblock backup was rigged using a Sterling Hollow Block, clipped to the harness belay loop with a locking carabiner. Before unclipping the PAS, go through the ABCDE checklist and weight the system. If everything is AOK, unclip the tether from the anchor and clip the locking carabiner into the harness belay loop. Since the rappel device has been clipped into two loops of the PAS, this now makes the PAS itself redundant. Note: Never use a daisy chain for a rappelling tether. A carabiner clipped into two loops is an extremely weak connection!*

jammed in a situation where a jammed knot would be catastrophic.

A simple and safer solution is to tie stopper knots in the two rope ends, then butterfly coil each rope separately, drape over a sling, and clip in at both hips, holster style, letting the coils out as you rappel down. While this may seem time-consuming, good rope management practices will save you time in the long run.

As the second rappeler comes down, the first person can prepare by threading the rope to be pulled down through the next anchor, tying a new stopper knot in the end. If there is concern about the rope getting hung up on obstructions (blocks, bushes, etc.) on the way down after you pull the rope through the anchor, rig the two ropes so that you pull down on the thinner of the two lines. This way you'll have most of the thin rope already down before you must let go of the other end, and the thicker rope will be the last to come down. I've

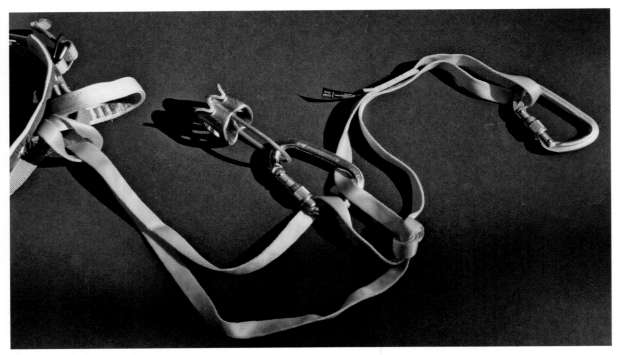

*Another method for rigging a tether/rappel extension with a sling. Start with a double-length (48-inch) sling and girth-hitch it through both tie-in points on the harness. Tie an overhand knot about halfway down the length of the sling, adjusting the knot so that when you clip it back into the harness belay loop with a locking carabiner, the length to the overhand knot is equalized. Clipping the locking carabiner of your rappel device into both loops you've created in the sling makes the sling itself redundant when it's clipped back into the harness belay loop.*

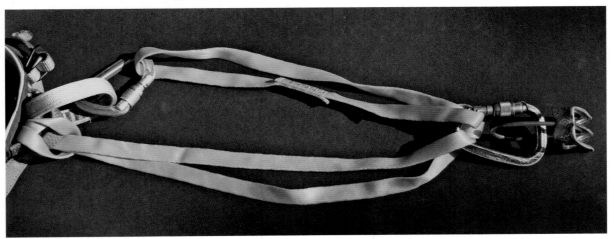

found that a thicker rope is less likely to get tangled or hung up than a thinner rope.

Beware if rapping on ropes of drastically different diameters (say, 10.5mm with 7mm) and ropes with different percentages of stretch (such as a dynamic paired with a static), as this can cause the ropes to shift at the rappel anchor and change the lengths at the end points—another good reason to knot the ends. Also, use metal rap rings instead of rope over webbing, as the friction of a shifting rope creates heat that can melt the webbing.

When the second rappeler arrives at the stance, she clips in with her tether before unclipping from the rappel device, holding onto the ropes. The stopper knot is untied, and the rope is pulled down through the anchor. Once the rope comes down, a new stopper knot is tied in the end and the procedure is repeated.

## Tandem Rappel

This simple yet effective technique allows two people to rappel at the same time, from the same rappel device, with one person controlling the brake hand. Primarily used in rescue scenarios, the tandem rappel method is also a viable technique when taking a novice who is intimidated and fearful of rappelling on his first rappel, where, like a tandem skydive, a more experienced person controls the situation. The advantage of the tandem rappel is that you're right there with the other person, to calm his fears or, in the case of a rescue, to attend to his needs. For multipitch rappelling on long alpine routes, the tandem rappel saves time and limits exposure to rockfall caused by your partner rappelling above you.

To rig a tandem rappel, connect two separate slings (or cordelette) to each rappeler's harness and clip them both to the same locking carabiner at the rappel device. An MBD (like an ATC) will work best. Rig an autoblock backup and attach it to your belay loop with a locking carabiner so that you

*Tandem rappel rig rigged with slings. Note the autoblock backup.*

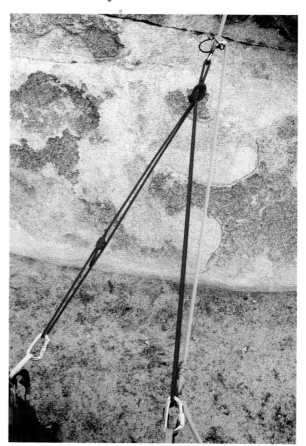

*Tandem rappel rig rigged with cordelette and autoblock backup.*

have hands-free control if you need to stop and deal with rope tangles, rig an anchor, etc.

## Simul Rappel

This technique is used by experienced climbers and military special forces to facilitate a more rapid descent. Using this method, two people can rappel at the same time, each on a separate strand of rope, using the other person's body weight as a counterbalance. In climbing situations, the rope is typically threaded through an equalized anchor, and it is important to rig the rope through metal rappel rings, quick links, or carabiners and *not* over webbing or cord—the rope may saw back and forth and slice through the webbing or cord due to differences in rope stretch and body weight. Also, the two rappelers should stay close together—within sight of each other—watching carefully for the other person to complete the rappel before unclipping, as unweighting one side of the rope leaves the other side unanchored. An additional safety measure is to take a long sling or cordelette and attach it to both rappelers with locking carabiners. Utmost care should also be taken to account for the rope ends, which absolutely should have stopper knots. Be forewarned that many accidents have occurred during simul rappels by inattentive climbers, usually resulting in a single or double fatality. *Simul rappels should only be undertaken by experienced rappelers who are fully aware of all the necessary precautions.*

My first simul rappel was not by choice but necessity. John Long and I had just completed the first ascent of an obscure arch formation in the Utah desert, and after I hand drilled a bolt anchor for the rappel at the top, John plucked the bolts out with his bare hands. The soft sandstone had a consistency more like mud than rock, so to descend with no fixed anchor, we decided to simul rappel, each off opposite sides of the arch. We each clipped our rappel devices into the same rope. Facing each other, eye to eye, we leaned back, the rope taut between us. We used each other's body weight as an anchor, intently mimicking each other's steps as we paced backward, away from each other, before stepping over the edge. Once the rope was firmly seated on the broad back of the arch, I breathed a sigh of relief; after descending to the open window of the arch, we enjoyed a free-hanging rappel, gently spinning in the air about 30 feet apart.

## Rappelling with a Heavy Pack or Haul Bag

Rappelling with an extremely heavy pack or haul bag can be dangerous. The weight of the pack can make a long rappel strenuous and more difficult to control or, worse, flip you upside down. An easy solution is to hitch a sling to the pack or haul bag, then clip it with a locking carabiner to the locking carabiner on your rappel device (carabiner to carabiner). This takes the weight off you and puts it on the rope, making it much easier to manage. Make sure the sling is hitched to a bomber loop (or, better yet, two points) on the pack. More than one climbing team has had the misfortune of dropping all their gear when the attachment point to their pack ripped out. You can put the pack between your legs and straddle it as you rappel down, or use a long sling to rig the bag just below your feet, keeping it out of your way.

## Rope Management

### Tossing the Rope

There is an art to tossing a rope. The key is preparation—taking a little time for rope management will save you time in the long run. Several methods work well. One is to flake about half the rope (coming from the anchor) right at your feet, then butterfly coil the bottom half. Before you toss the rope, check that no climbers are directly below so that you don't toss the rope right on

*"Rope!" is the universal signal to use before tossing down a rappel rope. To prevent tangles, butterfly coil the rope first. At crowded climbing sites, when people are down below, a better method is to simply lower the rope from the ends until the entire rope is down.*

top of them. Make sure there are no loose rocks where you've flaked your rope, as the rope will launch any loose stones. If there are people directly below, yell "Rope!" and give them enough time to move out of the way before you toss it down. If there are trees at the cliff base, be careful not to throw the rope too far outward and get it hung up in a tree.

## Retrieving the Rope

One of the best days of climbing in my entire life was nearly ruined by a careless retrieval of a rappel rope. My exuberance faded to grave concern in the time it takes a tear to flow down a cheek. I had just rappelled to the ground after completing one of the most difficult free climbs I'd ever done, in Eldorado Canyon, Colorado. I pulled my rappel rope to retrieve it, and just as the end of the rope passed through the rappel anchor rings, I called "Rope!" to alert my wife and partner, Yvonne, that the rope was coming down. She looked up, and the end of the rope, now whipping down with the sound of a fast jump rope slicing through the air, hit her squarely in the eye, temporarily blinding her. Luckily it wasn't a serious eye injury, but it could have been much worse.

I learned an important lesson that day; and after that near-miss, I've always been more vigilant whenever I pull a rope down. First I make an assessment on where the rope will go; if anyone is in the path, I explain that I'm going to pull a rope and ask them to move out of the way beforehand.

If it's windy, note the wind direction and where it will take the rope. Calling out "Rope!" as the rope comes sailing down is too late for anyone to move out of the way.

Before you begin pulling the rope down, look up and make sure there are no twists in it. If it's a long rappel, it's important for the last person down to safeguard against any twists and to be careful to separate the strands when unclipping the rappel device. If two ropes are tied together, make sure everyone in the party is clear on which rope to pull before you head down (e.g., "pull red"). If there is any chance of rope drag hampering the pull, do a test pull when the first person rappels down to ensure the rope can be pulled without jamming, and make any necessary adjustments (e.g., a longer sling extended over an edge) before the last person comes down.

There is a technique to pulling a rappel rope down, and it takes a little practice to get a feel for it. First double-check that there are no knots, kinks, or twists in the end you'll be pulling up toward the anchor. As the end approaches the anchor, slow your pull so that you can feel when the weight of the rope coming down toward you starts to pull the free end of the rope up toward the anchor without your assistance. Wait a second—for the end to pass through the anchor—then make an instantaneous sharp, forceful outward tug on the rope, which should fall away from the rock. Beware that a pulled rope can knock rocks off the cliff face, so be alert for rockfall. If all goes well, the rope will be lying in a big pile on the ground.

## Dealing with Stuck Ropes

Early one summer morning I came across a curious scene at the base of a multipitch climb on Tahquitz Rock in Idyllwild, California. There was a doubled rope, seemingly abandoned, hanging from the first pitch of a moderate climb I was planning on taking my client up. I pulled on one end of the rope. It didn't budge. At the base of the climb were telltale signs of a nighttime epic: a dozen cigarette butts, an empty pint bottle of gin, and a few discarded

*Facing page: Instructor Erin Guinn rappelling a single fixed line with a Grigri at Joshua Tree. If you take your brake hand off the rope, tie an overhand loop as a backup knot as shown here. If the Grigri slips (as it will when unweighted), the knot will jam.*

batteries. Upon reaching the ledge at the top of the pitch, I found the rope was simply wedged deeply in a crack—jammed solid, but easily extracted from my position.

A stuck rope can be your worst nightmare. Visualizing and anticipating what might happen when you pull your rope will prevent most mishaps; be especially vigilant for situations where your rope can get pulled into a crack. If you have two ropes tied together, the joining knot is what you need to watch out for on the pull-down; using the flat overhand will present a cleaner profile (with the tails pointed away from the rock) if you're concerned about the knot getting stuck.

Any twists in your rope at the anchor can make pulling the rope difficult, even impossible if there is friction with the rope running over a ledge or contacting lots of rough rock.

If your rope is stuck at the anchor and you have both strands available, and both strands are still through the rappel anchor, then the solution is relatively simple and fairly straightforward: Prusik up both strands of the rope, fix the problem, and rappel back down (see prusiking in chapter 12).

If you have only one strand of rope at your position, and the rope is jammed somewhere above you, then you face a risky proposition and the worst-case scenario. Prusiking up a single strand

with the other strand jammed on who knows what is not advisable. You can use what rope you have to lead up (placing protection) and hopefully reach the jam. If you're on the ground with little rope length available, you may want to abandon the rope and return with another rope to properly re-lead up to the jammed one.

Again, be aware that many rockfall accidents occur when a rappel rope is being pulled down a cliff. Sometimes the rope jams behind blocks or loose rocks, and the vigorous pulling to free the rope launches a barrage of rocks on those below.

## The Reepschnur Method

This technique is the most common rigging method to block a rappel rope when two ropes are tied together. It allows you to rappel with your Grigri on a single strand. The larger rope is threaded through the anchor and tied to the thinner line with a flat overhand—or a bulkier knot if needed. Remember, the knot must be bulky enough to jam into the rappel rings, chain links, or quick links. Below the jamming knot, a figure eight loop is tied on the thinner line and clipped to the rappel strand with a locking carabiner. *This critical backup is the key to safely rappelling with the Reepschnur Method.*

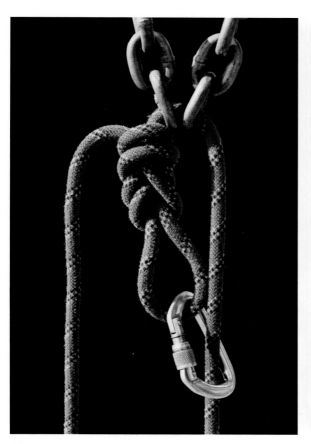 

*The Reepschnur knot block with one rope. This technique allows you to rappel on a single line using a Grigri (in this example, on the right strand), retrieving your rope by pulling on the left strand.*

*The Reepschnur Method with two ropes. The blue rope is the rappel line and the green line is the tag line for retrieval. Always tie a safety backup—shown here with a figure eight loop clipped into the rappel strand with a locking carabiner. If the flat overhand knot pulls through the rings, your rappel line will still be attached.*

*Practicing counterbalance ascension to rescue a fallen climber.*

# CHAPTER 12

# Rescue and Assistance Skills

## Improvised Rope Ascending: Prusiking

One of my favorite movie scenes is in the James Bond classic *For Your Eyes Only*, where Bond makes a preposterous roped solo climb up a towering rock formation in Meteora, Greece. Before he can reach the enemy stronghold, he (of course) takes a monstrous fall, which was performed by stuntman and climber Rick Sylvester. Rick was a bold climber, and the first person to ski off El Capitan (and pop a parachute) before it was illegal. Rick performed the same stunt in the opening of the Bond flick *The Spy Who Loved Me*, skiing off Mount Asgard on Baffin Island and popping a Union Jack parachute for the 4,000-foot ride down. But I digress.

In *For Your Eyes Only*, Rick performed a 165-foot fall tied into two 11mm diameter ropes that were rubber-banded together. In the movie, after Bond takes the catastrophic plunge, he dangles like a dazed spider for a moment, collects himself, then unties his shoelaces to use for prusiking up the rope. At the top he encounters a bad guy trying to bang out his sole anchor piton with a gun, so Bond hurls a piton at him, knife-thrower style, which pierces the guy's chest and sends him over the brink.

"Prusiking" is a verb for the act of ascending a rope using friction hitches. It's a generic term, since the prusik knot was the first friction hitch used for such purposes, although it's still called prusiking if other friction hitches are used.

When rock climbing, there are a few situations where improvised rope ascending skills will prove indispensable. One situation is when you take a leader fall on a multipitch overhanging route that leaves you hanging in midair. Falling off a traversing climb, where you can't climb up to get back on route would leave you in a similar predicament. In either case, all you need to do is prusik back up the line to get back to your last piece of protection. Your rope tie-in is your backup if the friction hitches slip, and you can also tie a figure eight loop and clip it into your belay loop with a locking carabiner below the prusiks as an additional backup as you proceed upward if you so desire.

Another situation is during a rappel, when something gets stuck and jammed in your rappel device, like an article of clothing or long hair. You'll be unable to proceed, and to fix the problem you'll likely need to take the weight off your rappel device. If the rappel is low angle, it may be as simple as standing on the rock to unweight your rappel device and yanking it out. If it's a steep or overhanging rappel, you'll need to perform a basic self-rescue. First make sure you've backed up your brake hand, because you'll need both hands free to perform this maneuver. If you have previously rigged an autoblock backup, simply slide the autoblock up until it engages. If you don't have an autoblock backup rigged, a simple and fast backup is the leg wrap (see photo). Better yet, tie a figure eight loop on the rope below you and clip it to your belay loop with a locking carabiner. Tie a friction hitch (e.g., prusik or klemheist) on the rope about a foot above your device, then take a double-length (48-inch) sling, or two 24-inch slings girth-hitched together, and clip it to the friction hitch. Stand in the sling so you can unweight your device. Don't grab the friction hitch itself, which can cause it to slide down the rope.

Another situation is when you've completed a double-rope rappel, proceed to pull on one strand to retrieve your rope—and the rope is hopelessly jammed. This can happen when the rope is twisted a few times below the anchor, or if the rope is wedged tight in a crack. You'll need to prusik back up the ropes to fix the problem.

*Demonstration of basic prusiking technique to ascend a double rope as in a stuck rappel rope scenario. With the top friction hitch slid as high up the rope as possible, hang in your harness and put your foot in the sling attached to the lower friction hitch. (Left) Stand up in the foot sling and slide the top friction hitch as high up the rope as you can; then (right) hang in your harness and repeat the process. As a backup as you ascend, tie an overhand loop on both strands and clip it to your harness belay loop with a locking carabiner.*

Another scenario is on a multipitch rappel where you've lost your way and can't find the next anchor, you've rappelled past the anchor, or your rope is too short to reach the next ledge or anchor. In all these cases you'll need to prusik back up the rope to resolve the situation.

In each scenario you're dealing with a doubled rope (two stands), and the best method is simply to tie friction hitches around both strands of rope. A prusik or klemheist knot is a good choice for rope ascending. If you don't have any prusik cord at your disposal (a 5mm or 6mm soft nylon cord works best) and only have slings, the klemheist knot is preferable. A nylon sling is a better choice than a Dyneema or Spectra sling for a friction hitch, since nylon grips better and has a higher melting point than either Dyneema or Spectra.

There are myriad prusiking methods, but I'll describe only one here, because I believe it is the fastest, simplest rig, requiring the least amount of gear. All you'll need are two prusik cords, three regular length (24-inch) slings, and three locking carabiners.

The basic setup for improvised rope ascension is to tie two separate friction hitches—the top one attached directly to your harness with a 24-inch sling, the other used with a foot sling (also attached to your harness with a sling). The procedure is a simple, inchworm-like technique. Stand on the bottom sling and slide the top friction hitch as high as you can reach, then immediately sit back in your harness, with your weight on the top friction hitch. Now that you are more or less comfortably hanging in your harness, move the bottom friction hitch up until your leg in the foot sling is bent at a 90-degree angle at the knee. Stand up in the sling, using your hands for balance by grabbing the rope with both hands below the top friction hitch, and slide the top friction hitch up again as high as you can reach. Remember, don't grab the body of the friction hitch itself—this can loosen the hitch and cause it to slide down the rope.

*Prusik rig with cord. The top cord was rigged by taking a 5-foot length of 6mm nylon cord and tying a loop in both ends, with the top loop large enough to tie a prusik knot. The bottom length of cord is 11 feet long, tied with loops on both ends and a larger loop in the middle to accommodate the prusik knot.*

Although it may sound complicated, and can be a little awkward, the technique can be mastered quickly with a bit of practice. To back up the friction hitches, simply take both rope strands together and tie a figure eight loop below the friction hitches, then clip the loop into your harness belay loop with a locking carabiner. This is known as "clipping in short" and should be done at regular intervals (every 15 feet or so) when you're ascending a long way.

## Ascending a Single Fixed Rope

To ascend a single strand of fixed line, the same methods just described apply, although you may need an extra wrap with your friction hitch to add a little more friction on a single rope. For example, if ascending a doubled 10mm diameter rope with a prusik, two wraps of your prusik cord (i.e., four strands) will probably suffice, where on a single cord three wraps (six strands) are usually optimal. When ascending a single 10mm diameter rope with a klemheist knot, with either cord or sling, I usually go with four wraps.

If you have an ABD (like a Petzl Grigri) or an autoblocking belay/rappel device (like the Petzl Reverso or Black Diamond ATC Guide), there is a very simple system you can use to ascend a single-strand fixed rope. Clip the Grigri or ABD device into your harness belay loop; if you're using an autoblocking belay device, clip it into your harness belay loop in the autoblocking mode. Tie a friction hitch (prusik or klemheist) on the rope above your device and attach a 48-inch foot sling to the friction hitch. Slide the friction hitch up until your foot sling is positioned at the height where your leg is bent 90 degrees at the knee. Grab the rope above you with your non-brake hand and stand up in the sling, simultaneously pulling the rope through the device at your waist by pulling straight up on the brake strand with your brake hand, then sit back and rest in your harness on the locked-off device. When you're hanging in your harness, slide the friction hitch up again until your knee is bent at a 90-degree angle, then repeat the process. Tying

a slip hitch for your sling foot helps your foot stay put. As a backup, clip in short every 15 feet or so by tying a figure eight loop and clipping it into your harness belay loop with a locking carabiner. This is

*Instructor Lisa Rands demonstrates ascending a fixed line with a friction hitch and a Grigri. As she straightens out her left leg and stands up, she'll pull up on the brake strand side of the rope above the Grigri, then sit in her harness tight to the Grigri as she slides the klemheist back up.*

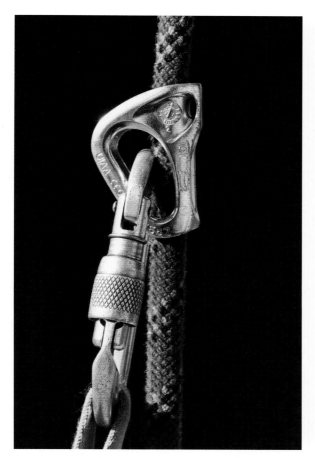

*Mini ascenders like the Petzl Tibloc (left) and the Wild Country Ropeman (right) are much faster and efficient than friction hitches for rope ascending.*

an easy and quick method for a short rope ascent, but if you plan on extensive fixed-line ascending, then mechanical ascenders are the way to go (see chapter 8).

## Assistance from the Top

### 3:1 Raising System

One reason to use the direct belay technique with an ABD when belaying is that it is easily converted to a 3:1 raising system (aka the Z system) in a

matter of seconds. As a climbing guide, the direct belay is always my first choice, providing the anchor is bomber, because it allows me to anticipate and prepare for any eventuality, like a quick lowering or raising of the climber. I use my Grigri, clipped directly to the master point or extended master point (using the climbing rope).

If you're direct belaying with an autoblocking device (e.g., Black Diamond ATC Guide or Petzl Reverso), the 3:1 system enumerated here will still work, but you'll have way more friction in the system, which will make the raise much more difficult.

To set up a 3:1 raise, follow these steps:

1. Tie a backup knot (overhand loop) on the brake strand side of the Grigri. Now I'm "hands free" and can take my brake hand off the rope.

2. Tie a friction hitch (prusik or klemheist) on the load strand going down to the climber.

3. Clip the brake strand side of the rope (from the Grigri) to a locking carabiner clipped to the friction hitch. Now untie the backup knot and pull up on the brake strand side of the rope. Pulling 3 feet on your end raises the load 1 foot. Friction is your enemy when raising with a 3:1. If the rope going to the climber is

in contact with a large surface area of rock, the raise will be correspondingly more difficult. A pulley at the friction hitch carabiner reduces friction and makes it easier to pull. Remember,

Also known as the Z system, the 3:1 raising system is easy to rig if you're already using a Grigri for a direct belay. The Grigri is the ratchet (which locks off when you need to reset), and the friction hitch (in this example, a klemheist knot) is your tractor (which moves up and down the field).

A 3:1 raising system using a Grigri and klemheist knot.

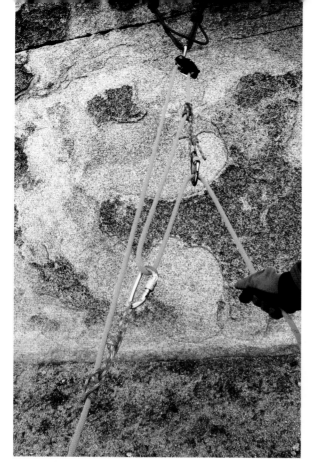

*A 5:1 raising system with two friction hitches.*

this technique is for assisting a climber, helping him get past a tough spot, not for hauling up a severely injured or unconscious climber.

4.  When the friction hitch is all the way to the Grigri, reset the friction hitch by sliding it back down toward the climber. The Grigri's built-in ratchet will lock off and hold the load as you do this. Then continue the raise.

*By building a 3:1 on top of a 3:1, you get a 9:1. When you pull 9 feet of rope, the load is raised 1 foot. But be careful here; whatever force you're pulling with is multiplied about eight times on the anchor. In most scenarios a 3:1 is more than adequate to do the job if the climber you're trying to pull up is assisting by climbing the rock as well as she can.*

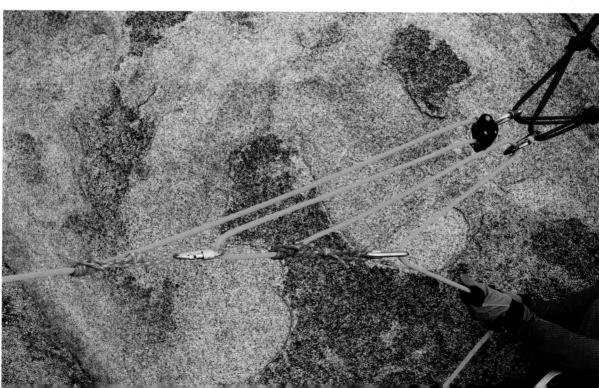

### 3:1 Assisted Raise from a Direct Belay

For this method the climber must be close enough that you can throw her a bight of rope. The climber clips the rope into her harness to assist in the raise. Using this system allows both the climber and rescuer to work together, and makes it much easier for the rescuer to raise the climber.

If you are the belayer/rescuer, the steps are as follows:

1. Tie a backup knot (overhand loop) on the brake strand side of your ABD or autoblocking device.

2. Toss a bight of rope down to the climber and have her clip it into her belay loop with a locking carabiner.

3. Identify which strand the climber should pull on by shaking it.

4. Untie the backup knot.

5. The climber pulls down as you pull up on the brake strand side of the rope. Warn the climber to watch her hands so they are not pinched in the carabiner as you pull.

## Assistance from Below

In more than thirty years of professionally guiding thousands of clients in toprope situations, I've only had a few instances where I actually had to go up on the rock and bring a climber down—all

*A 3:1 assisted raise. With the climber also pulling, you get a tremendous mechanical advantage, making it far easier to raise someone than with an unassisted 3:1 raise.*

*Basic assistance skills will allow you to assist your partner if needed.*

of them being in toprope situations with young kids who were overcome by fear and mentally lost control, afraid to lean back and weight the rope so they could be lowered back down. Having the knowledge and skills to go up the rope and bring a climber down is important in case you ever have to assist an injured climber, even in a toprope situation.

## Climber Pickoff on a Toprope

I call this technique the "climber pickoff," and it is essentially the same technique you can use to rescue a fallen lead climber who is injured and can't be lowered. The difference in a toprope situation is that you're dealing with a bomber anchor, not just the one piece of gear that held the leader's fall. If you

practice this technique in a benign toprope setup, and get it completely dialed in, you'll have more "tools in your tool box" if, God forbid, you ever need to rescue a fallen leader who can't be lowered.

The climber pickoff is most easily accomplished with an ABD, like a Grigri. I highly recommend carrying a Grigri as a part of your basic personal rescue package, as it streamlines and facilitates all the basic rescue techniques described here. To me it's worth its weight in gold. My second-best choice would be an autoblocking device, like an ATC Guide or Petzl Reverso. I'd also recommend first learning the climber pickoff with a Grigri before trying it without one. The climber pickoff utilizes a counterbalance ascension and counterbalance rappel technique. Basically, you ascend the rope to the climber, then rappel down with him. The beauty of this system is that it requires minimal equipment and can be done very quickly.

All you need is the following equipment as your rescue package:

- 1 ABD (Grigri) with locking carabiner
- 1 double-length (48-inch) sling with locking carabiner
- 1 prusik cord (5mm or 6mm soft nylon cord, 4 feet long, tied into a sling with a double fisherman's knot)

If you are already belaying with a Grigri, here are the steps:

1. Start by tying a backup knot (overhand loop) on the brake strand side of the Grigri.

2. Tie a friction hitch (klemheist or prusik) with your prusik cord on the load strand going up to the climber, and attach your double-length sling to it with a locking carabiner.

3. Ascend the rope by sliding the friction hitch up so that when you put your foot in the sling, your knee is bent at a 90-degree angle. You can tie a knot in the sling to shorten it as needed. Stand up in the sling, and as you straighten your leg, simultaneously pull the slack through

the Grigri (pulling straight up on the brake strand) and hang in your harness off the Grigri. Alternate standing up in the sling, then hanging in your harness, tight to the Grigri. About every 15 feet or so, tie a backup knot (overhand loop) on the brake strand side of the Grigri.

4. When you reach the climber, transfer the friction hitch from your side of the rope onto the rope above the climber you're assisting. Take the double-length sling and thread it (basket style) through your belay loop, and clip both ends of the sling to the locking carabiner attached to the friction hitch. Where you position the friction hitch (klemheist or prusik) will affect where the assisted climber will be positioned. If the friction hitch is as high as you can slide it, the climber will remain at that position as you both rappel. If you position the friction hitch just above the knot, the climber will move up and slightly above you before you both descend.

5. Rappel with the Grigri, untying the backup knots as you descend.

If you are belaying with an MBD (like an ATC) or combo device (like an ATC Guide or Petzl Reverso), the sequence will be as follows:

1. Tie off your belay device with a mule knot.

2. Tie a friction hitch (prusik or klemheist) on the load strand (going up to the climber) of your rope.

3. Thread (basket style) the double-length sling through your belay loop, and attach it to the friction hitch with a locking carabiner.

4. Tie a backup knot (figure eight loop), and clip it to your belay loop with a locking carabiner.

5. Release the mule knot, and create slack at your belay device—the tension will now be transferred to the friction hitch, with you essentially becoming an anchor.

6. If you have a Grigri, unclip your belay device and replace it with the Grigri. If you're belaying

*Counterbalance ascension using klemheist and Grigri.*

with an autoblocking device (e.g., ATC Guide or Petzl Reverso), switch it to the autoblocking mode and clip it to your belay loop with a locking carabiner.

7. Transfer the weight of the hanging climber from your friction hitch/sling to your ABD or

autoblocking device by taking up all the slack in the rope and pulling upward on the brake strand side of the rope, using your body weight as the anchor.

8. Unclip one end of the sling from the locking carabiner at the friction hitch.

9. Ascend the rope by sliding the friction hitch up so that when you put your foot in the sling, your knee is bent at a 90-degree angle. You can tie a knot in the sling to shorten it as needed. Stand up in the sling, and as you straighten your leg, simultaneously pull the slack through the Grigri (pulling straight up on the brake strand) and hang in your harness off the Grigri.

*Counterbalance pickoff using an ATC Guide. On the way up, she used her ATC Guide in the autoblocking mode in lieu of a Grigri, then converted it to manual rappelling mode, backed up with an autoblock, for a counterbalance rappel descent.*

*Counterbalance rappel.*

Alternate standing up in the sling, then hanging in your harness, tight to the Grigri. About every 10 feet or so, tie a backup knot (overhand loop) on the brake strand side of the Grigri.

10. When you reach the climber, transfer the friction hitch from your side of the rope onto the rope above the climber you're assisting. Take the double-length sling and thread it (basket style) through your belay loop, and clip

both ends of the sling to the locking carabiner attached to the friction hitch. Where you position the friction hitch will affect where the climber you are bringing down will be positioned. If the friction hitch is as high as you can slide it, the climber will remain at that position as you both rappel. If you position the friction hitch (klemheist or prusik) just above the knot, the climber will move up and slightly above you before you both descend.

11. Rappel with the Grigri, untying the backup knots as you descend. If you're using an autoblocking device, convert it to manual mode, and back it up with an autoblock knot on your brake hand side. You'll need an additional prusik/klemheist on your side of the rope, above the device, to make this conversion. Make sure you've backed everything up with a figure eight loop attached to your belay loop with a locking carabiner.

If you're using an MBD, and don't have an ABD or autoblocking device at your disposal, you can still use this system, but you'll need an additional prusik and slings (see the improvised rope ascension discussion above).

### Rescuing a Fallen Leader

When I'm teaching self-rescue skills, students often want to go straight to a worst-case scenario: How do I rescue a fallen leader?

In most cases it's one of the easiest scenarios: The leader falls and sustains an injury, but is not incapacitated, and his top piece is less than 100 feet above your belay. Solution: You simply lower him back down.

In cases where the leader's top piece is more than 100 feet above your belay, the first option, as long as the leader is not too badly injured, is to lower him to a point less than 100 feet above you— to a good ledge or stance—where he can build an anchor, transfer to it, pull his lead rope, and rig a

rappel to get back down to your belay stance or the ground.

But that's asking a lot if the leader is dealing with a distracting and painful injury.

The scenario gets increasing complex if the leader is more than 100 feet above you and is so severely injured that he is not able to perform tasks like building an anchor, rigging a rappel, etc.

This is where your assistance from below comes into play.

Before attempting to rescue a fallen leader, your initial consideration should be the viability of the piece the leader fell on, since you'll both be using it as your anchor. It's a given that it held the fall, but is it a #2 Camalot or a #2 stopper? How far below is the next piece that backs it up? And how many pieces are between you, the rescuer, and the top piece. These are all important factors to consider before you proceed, as you are now putting yourself at greater risk too.

The initial goal is for either you or the fallen leader to reach a ledge or stance with a solid anchor less than 100 feet below the top piece the leader has fallen on. The fastest way to accomplish this is for you to tie off and back up your belay device (tie a figure eight loop and clip it your harness belay loop with a locking biner) then climb up as the leader is lowered down to a point where he can clip into a solid piece. You can switch to rope ascending mode at any point to reach his position.

Another option, if the leader is moderately incapacitated, is for you to ascend the rope while the leader stays in place as a counterbalance. If you're on a multipitch climb, cleaning the gear from the anchor and a few pieces as you ascend upward will give you some gear to help build a higher anchor, but if possible you'll want to leave at least a few pieces between you and the top piece for safety.

Once you get to that point less than 100 feet from the top piece, build an anchor and lower the leader to join you. From here you can proceed with a counterbalance or tandem rappel.

*Having the right tools in your rescue "toolbox" will allow you to perform self rescues no matter what the scenario.*

If you're ascending all the way to the fallen leader, he can provide additional security for you, if you can unweight the rope, by clipping your side of the rope into a piece of gear with a clove hitch or loop knot or, if you can't unweight the rope, with a friction hitch.

In situations where the leader exhibits sustained unconsciousness, possible spinal cord injury, or other critical injuries, you're going to need help from a rescue team, and possibly a helicopter evacuation. Every situation is different, and obviously if you're in a remote setting, help from a rescue team may be a long time coming. Having the right rescue tools in your climbing "tool box" will help you improvise in even worst-case scenarios.

If you're interested in studying more advanced self-rescue techniques, I highly recommend *Self-Rescue,* second edition, by David Fasulo (FalconGuides).

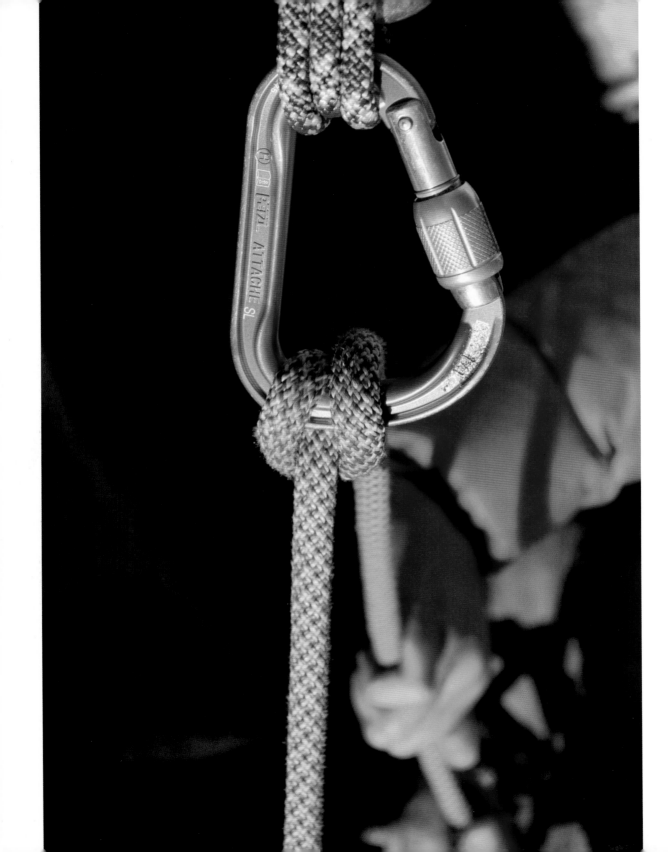

# Knots

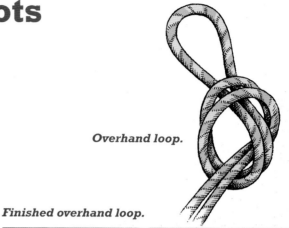

*Overhand loop.*

*Finished overhand loop.*

## Loop Knots

Loop knots are tied by taking two strands of rope (called a bight) and wrapping them back over themselves so that the knot does not slide, or by taking the end of the rope and tying it back over the standing part so the knot does not slide. Loop knots are used to clip the rope into a carabiner, or to tie around an object.

### Knot Terminology

**Bend:** Two ropes tied together by their ends.

**Bight:** Two strands of rope where the rope is doubled back on itself.

**Load strand:** The strand of the rope that bears all the weight.

**Hitch:** A knot that is tied around another object (such as a carabiner or rope).

**Standing end:** The part of the rope that the end of the rope crosses to form a knot.

**Tag end:** The very end of a rope, or the tail end that protrudes from a knot.

### Overhand Loop

This is the simplest knot you can tie to form a loop. It requires less rope to tie than the figure eight, which makes it useful on cordelettes when you don't quite have enough length to tie the master point with a figure eight loop. For most applications, however, the figure eight loop is superior because it tests about 10 percent stronger than

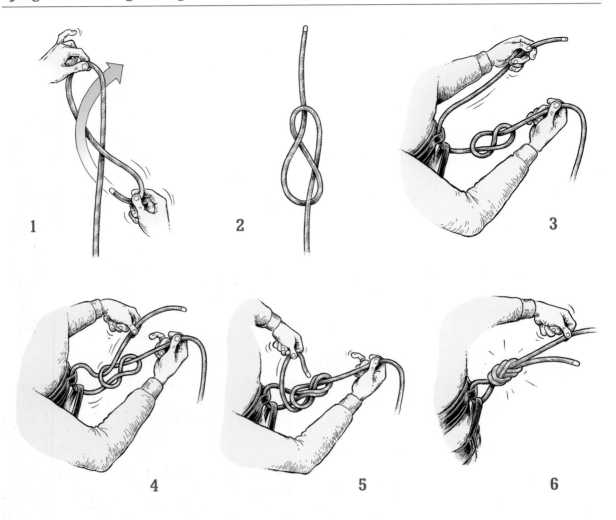

1

2

3

4

5

6

*Check your harness manufacturer's guidelines for information on how to properly tie the rope to your harness. For harnesses with belay loops, you generally follow the same path as the belay loop, which goes through two tie-in points on the harness. Tie the figure eight so that its loop is about the same diameter as your belay loop. The figure eight knot does not require a backup knot.*

the overhand loop and is easier to untie in small-diameter cord.

### Figure Eight Follow-Through

The standard knot for tying the rope to your harness, it can also be used to tie a rope around an object like a tree or through a tunnel. Tie it with a 5-inch minimum tail, and tighten all four strands to dress the knot.

### Figure Eight Loop

Another standard climbing knot, the figure eight loop is used for tying off the end of a rope, or for tying a loop in the middle, or bight, of a rope. It is also commonly referred to as a "figure eight on a bight."

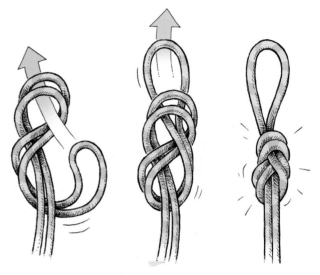

*How to tie a figure eight loop.*

*Finished figure eight loop clipped to an anchor.*

*Tucked figure eight. Sport climbers often use this variation of the figure eight follow-through, which makes the knot easier to untie after hanging/falling.*

## In-Line Figure Eight

### Tying the In-line Figure Eight (aka Directional Figure Eight)

*1. This knot, like the clove hitch, can be used with the extension rope to attach to a series of anchors in a line. It takes some practice to master this knot, but after you do, you may find it easier to use than a clove hitch. Cross the strands to form a simple loop.*

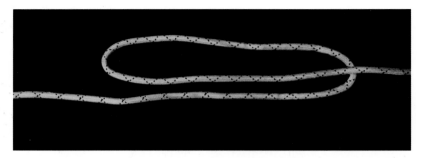

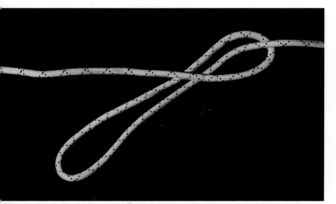

*2. Cross a bight under the single strand.*

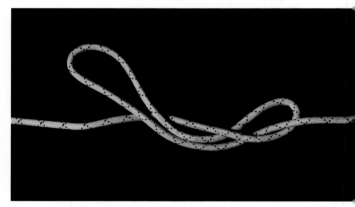

*3. Cross the bight over the strand.*

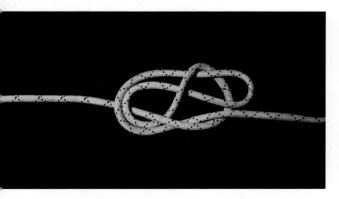

*4. Thread the bight back through the loop you've just formed.*

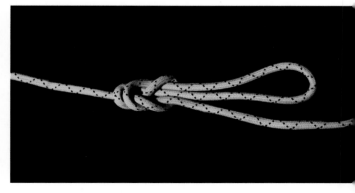

*5. Finished in-line figure eight.*

## Bowline

If you were a Boy Scout, you learned this knot with the saying "the rabbit comes up through the hole, around the tree, and back down through the hole." The bowline is very useful to tie the rope around something, like a tree, block of rock, or tunnel in the rock.

*The bowline knot with fisherman's backup.*

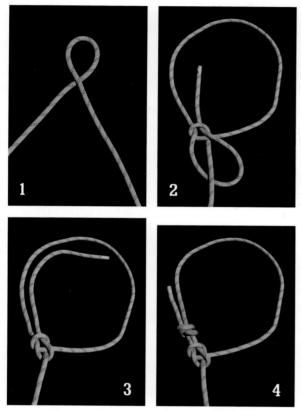

*Tying the bowline. The bowline should always be tied with a backup, shown here with half a double fisherman's knot for the backup (photo 4).*

*Rethreaded bowline. Tie a regular bowline, but leave the tail long enough to go all the way back around the object you're tying around, then retrace the start of the knot, like you would on a figure eight follow-through, finishing with a fisherman's backup. This is a great knot to use for tying a rope around a tree or through a tunnel, because you end up with two loops, adding strength and redundancy to your rigging.*

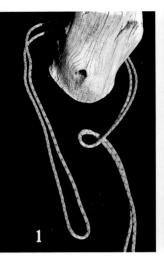
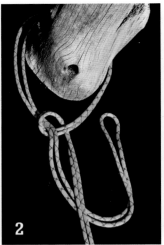

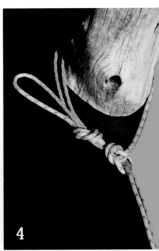

*Tying a bowline with a bight (not to be confused with the bowline on a bight also known as the double-loop bowline). The big advantage of the bowline with a bight is that you can tie around an object anywhere down the length of the rope without having to pull the tail all the way through. It's essentially the same configuration as a simple bowline, but tied with two strands of rope—very useful for tying to trees if using the Joshua Tree System for a toprope rig. Back it up with an overhand (photo 4).*

It is important to note that a bowline knot *requires* a backup, as weighting and unweighting the knot easily loosens it. *Always* tie half a double fisherman's knot to back it up. One advantage of the bowline is this same feature—it is very easy to untie after it has been weighted, so it's used regularly by professional riggers. Be aware that an unsecured bowline used as a tie-in knot (without the backup knot) has been responsible for several climbing accidents when it came untied.

*Toprope setup using the Joshua Tree System on rock horns. The top horn is tied with a simple bowline, backed up with half a double fisherman's knot. The bottom horn is tied using a bowline with a bight, backed up with an overhand. The master point is tied with a BHK. This is a great system to use on two trees.*

## Double-Loop Knots

### BHK

BHK is an acronym for "big honking knot." Technically, it's an overhand knot tied on a doubled bight. It's commonly used to rig a redundant master point when rigging toprope anchors with an extension rope.

*1. Tying a BHK. Start with a bight of rope and double it.*

*2. Tie an overhand knot on all four strands.*

*3. Thread the two loops back through the single loops you've created . . .*

*4. . . . or incorporate all three loops into the master point carabiners.*

## Double-Loop Figure Eight

This knot is very useful for pre-equalizing two anchor points. Note that if the two loops are used together to form a master point, they are not redundant due to the rewoven configuration.

### Tying the Double-Loop Figure Eight

*1. Take a bight of rope and cross it back over itself, forming a loop. (above left)*

*2. Take two strands of the bight and wrap them around the standing part, then poke them through the loop. (above right)*

*3. To finish, take the loop at the very end of the bight and fold it down and around the entire knot you've just formed. (right)*

*The double-loop figure eight is a great knot to use to equalize two gear placements. You can manipulate the knot by loosening one strand and feeding it through the body of the knot, shortening one loop, which makes the other loop larger. Unlike the double-loop bowline, the double-loop figure eight does not require a backup knot.*

## Double-Loop Bowline
## (aka Bowline on a Bight)

This is another great knot for pre-equalizing two anchor points. It's very handy for clipping into a two-bolt anchor. Back it up with half a double fisherman's knot if the tail end is near the body of the knot, as it can shift a bit when weighted.

## Tying the Double-Loop Bowline

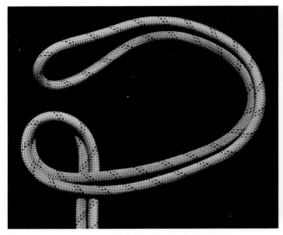

*1. Take a bight of rope and cross it over the standing part.*

*2. Thread the bight through the loop you've just formed.*

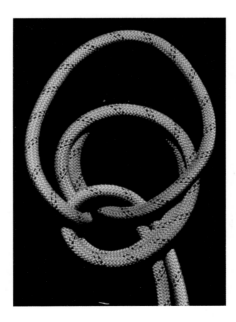

*3. Configure the end of the bight in a loop above the rest of the knot.*

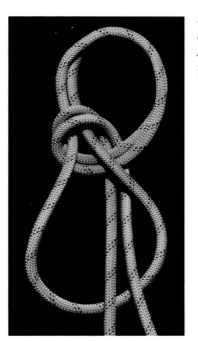

**4. Flip the loop down like a hinge behind the rest of the knot.**

**5. Pull on the two loops until the end of the bight tightens at the base of the knot.**

**6. The two loops can be adjusted by feeding one strand into the body of the knot, which alternately shortens one loop and lengthens the other.**

## Knots for Webbing

Nylon webbing is a slick material that should be tied with caution. There have been many accidents where poorly tied knots in nylon webbing have failed. The two recommended knots for tying nylon webbing into a loop are the water knot (also known as the ring bend) and the double fisherman's knot (also known as the grapevine knot). When tying the water knot, your finished tails should be a minimum of 3 inches in length. It is important to tighten the water knot properly, as it has a tendency to loosen if tied slackly in a sling that is being used over time.

Why would you even use nylon webbing tied with a knot as opposed to a sewn runner? A sewn nylon runner is stronger than the same material tied with a knot. The answer is for rappel anchors

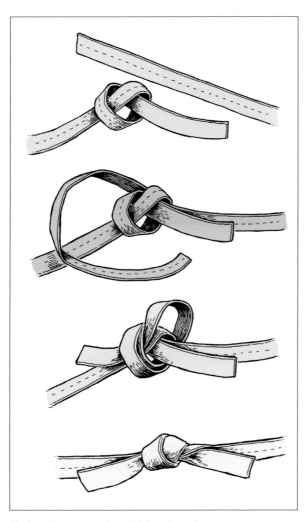

*Tying the water knot (ring bend).*

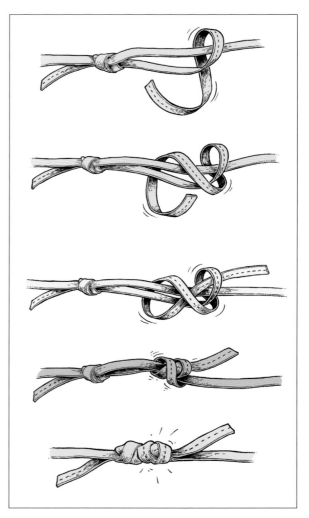

*Tying nylon webbing with a double fisherman's (grapevine) knot.*

*The water knot.*

when you tie slings around a tree or through bolt hangers. It is also sometimes useful to untie the knot, thread it through something (like a tunnel), and retie it.

The double fisherman's knot is also a good knot to use to tie nylon webbing into a loop, although it does require more length of material to tie and is very difficult to untie after it has been seriously weighted.

## Bends

A bend is a knot that joins two ropes or lengths of cord together. These knots are used to tie your cordelette into a loop, and also to tie two ropes together for toproping or rappelling.

### Figure Eight Bend

A variation of the figure eight follow-through, this knot can be used to tie two ropes together. It has superior strength and is easy to untie after it has been weighted. It is simply a retraced figure eight. On 9mm to 11mm diameter rope, tie it with the tails a minimum of 5 inches long.

*The figure eight bend.*

## Double Fisherman's Knot

This is the preferred knot to use for joining nylon cord into a loop to make a cordelette. It is also a very secure knot to tie two ropes together for a double-rope rappel, but it can be difficult to untie.

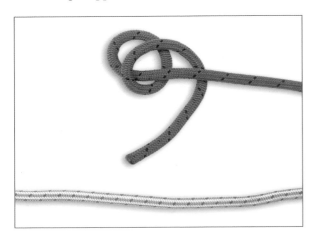 

*Tying the double fisherman's knot (aka grapevine knot). When tying 7mm nylon cord, leave the tails about 3 inches long.*

*The double fisherman's knot.*

## Triple Fisherman's Knot

For 5mm and 6mm diameter high-tech cord (e.g., Spectra, Dyneema, Technora), a triple fisherman's knot tests slightly stronger than the double fisherman's.

*To tie a triple fisherman's knot, make three wraps before feeding the cord back through.*

*Completed triple fisherman's knot.*

## Knots for Joining Two Rappel Ropes

Standard knots for joining two ropes include the double fisherman's knot and the figure eight bend. The double fisherman's is more difficult to untie than the figure eight bend once weighted; the figure eight bend, while relatively easy to untie, is bulky. Tie these knots with a minimum of 5 inches of tail, and carefully tighten the knots before using

them. A stiff rope makes it harder to cinch the knots tight, so be especially careful with a stiffer rope.

Which knot you use should be based on several variables. If the ropes differ drastically in diameter, or are very stiff, the most foolproof knot is the figure eight bend, backed up with half a double fisherman's knot on each side. This is a bulky knot, but it gives you a real sense of absolute security.

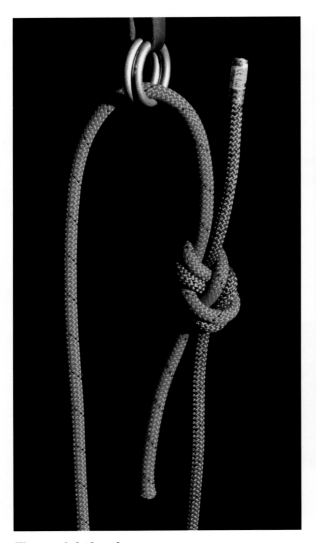

*Figure eight bend.*

*Figure eight bend with fisherman's backups.*

## Flat Overhand (aka Euro Death Knot)

How this knot received the "Euro Death Knot" moniker is unclear. Most likely the knot was initially adopted by Europeans and deemed unsafe when first seen by American climbers unfamiliar with its use. As far as I know, it has been responsible for only one rappelling accident in recent times (in the Tetons, September 1997), when it was sloppily tied with too short a tail. Ironically, in July of that year, former *Rock and Ice* magazine editor George Bracksieck had written that "the one-sided overhand knot (tails parallel and together) remains the best knot for rappelling. . . . Be sure to leave plenty of tail and to set it snugly."

After analyzing the accident, Grand Teton ranger Mark Magnusun wrote: "I intend to do some additional research in an effort to gain information on the overhand knot used for joining ropes, the origin of the 'Euro-death' nickname, and incidents of other failures."

From 1999 to 2009 various tests revealed the flat overhand knot to be roughly 30 percent weaker than the double fisherman's for tying two ropes together, but still plenty strong for rappelling situations. Testing also revealed that it was virtually impossible to get the knot to fail—as long as it was tied with a suitable-length tail and properly tightened.

*Flat overhand knot.*

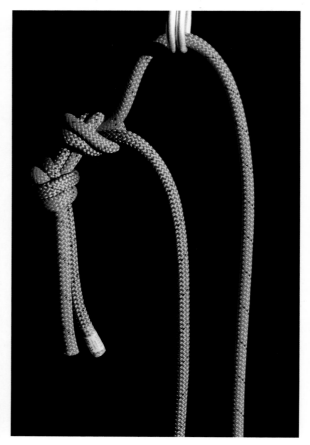

*Flat overhand with overhand backup.*

Petzl, a leading manufacturer of rappelling devices, recommends the flat overhand as the knot to use for joining two rappel ropes together, if the ropes are of similar diameter and the tail is a minimum of 20 centimeters (8 inches).

The flat overhand has become widely adopted as *the* knot for joining two rappel ropes of similar diameters because it is easy to tie and easy to untie after it has been weighted, and it presents a clean profile when pulled down the cliff as the ropes are retrieved, thus less likely to jam in a crack. Multi-pitch guides often tie their cordelettes with a flat overhand so that the knot can be easily untied and the cordelette used for other applications. For added security it can be easily backed up simply by tying another flat overhand right on top of the first one, although this adds bulk.

There are a few cautions, however: The flat overhead knot is not recommended for tying together two ropes of drastically differing diameters (e.g., 7mm to 11mm), or for use on very stiff ropes. The bottom line is that the knot should be used with discretion, well tightened (pull as hard as you can on all four strands), and tied with a long tail (minimum of 8 inches). Personally, I use the flat overhand (with a second overhand backup) in situations where I'm concerned about the knot possibly jamming in a crack when I pull the rope down for retrieval. Otherwise I use a figure eight bend or double fisherman's.

The flat overhand is a very poor choice for use with nylon webbing, and it has been responsible for numerous rappel anchor failures where it was tied in webbing with a very short tail. An even worse knot for rope and webbing, and a knot responsible for numerous accidents, is the flat figure eight, which inverts at shockingly low loads as the knot rolls inward and capsizes. The flat eight is a knot to be avoided and is very dangerous if tied with short tails, especially in nylon webbing.

**EBGBs (5.10d), Joshua Tree.**

# Hitches

A hitch is a knot that is tied around something. The clove hitch is used to fasten a rope to a carabiner. A friction hitch is a knot tied with a cord or sling around another rope, utilizing friction to make the knot hold when it is weighted, but releasable and movable without untying when it is unweighted.

## Clove Hitch

The clove hitch is tied around the wide base of a carabiner. The beauty of the clove hitch is easy rope-length adjustment without unclipping from the carabiner, making it a truly versatile knot for anchoring purposes—for anchoring a belayer, tying off an anchoring extension rope, or tying off the arms of a cordelette.

Get in the habit of tying the load-bearing strand on the spine side of the carabiner; you'll ensure that you're loading the carabiner in the strongest configuration. Make sure you tighten the clove hitch properly by cranking down on both strands, and you're good to go.

*Tying the clove hitch.*

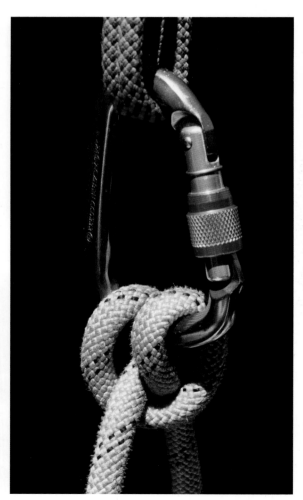

## Munter Hitch

Tied on a carabiner, the Munter hitch can be used for belaying, lowering, and rappelling. It can be tied off and released under tension, a benefit that makes it a key knot for rescue and assistance applications. The Munter can be tied off and secured with a mule knot.

### Tying a Munter Hitch on a Carabiner

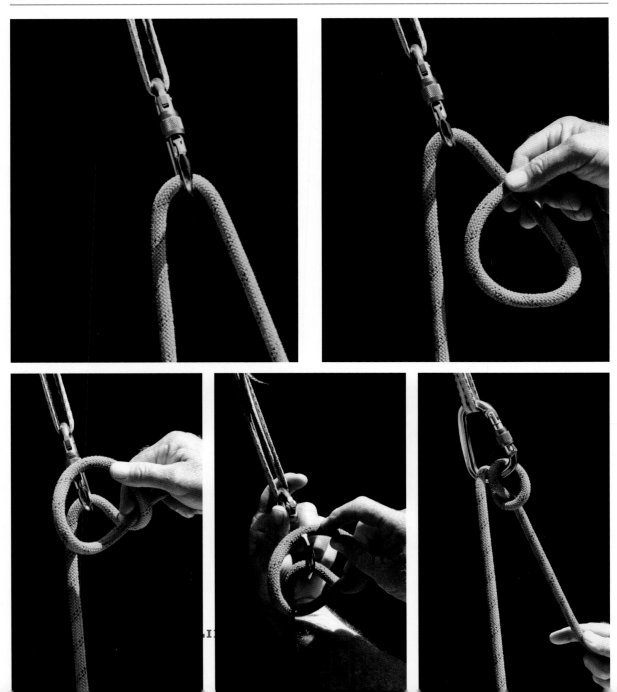

## Tying a Munter Hitch

**1. Grasp a single strand of rope with both hands, with thumbs pointing toward each other.**

**2. Cross the right-hand strand on top of the left-hand strand, and hold the two strands where they cross with your left thumb and forefinger, then slide your right hand down about 6 inches.**

**3. Now bring the right strand up and behind the loop.**

**4. Clip a locking carabiner where the forefinger is shown here, below the top two strands.**

*1. When tying a mule knot, be aware that when the rope is under tension (holding a climber's weight), you'll need to keep a firm grip on the brake strand.*

*2. Keeping the load and brake strands parallel, form a loop on the brake strand by crossing it behind while still maintaining your grip with your brake hand.*

3. With your non-brake hand, take a bight of rope and pass it through the loop you've created with the load strand in between the loop and the bight. Snug the mule knot up tight against the Munter hitch.

4. Pull some slack, and finish with an overhand loop backup.

*1. Pass a bight of rope (from the brake hand side) through the belay carabiner.*

*2. Tie a mule knot above the device on the load strand of the rope going to the climber.*

*3. Finish by tying an overhand backup on the load strand.*

*1. Pass a bight of rope through the carabiner and form a loop. If the device is under tension, pinching the rope against the device with the opposite hand will help lock it off.*

*2. Pass a bight of rope through the loop you've created, with the spine between the loop and the bight.*

*3. Finish with an overhand loop backup on the load strand in front of the device.*

## Prusik Knot

A prusik knot is used for rope ascending and as a component in many rescue systems. It can be loaded in either direction. To tie a prusik, first make a "prusik cord" out of a 4- to 5-foot length of 5mm or 6mm diameter nylon cord tied into a loop with a double fisherman's knot, which gives you about a 16-inch loop. Buy the softest, most pliable nylon cord you can find, because a softer cord will grip best. To tie the prusik, simply make a girth-hitch around the rope with your cord, then pass the loop of cord back through the original girth-hitch two or three more times. Dress the knot to make sure all the strands are even and not twisted—a sloppy friction hitch will not grip as well. Test the knot before using it. A thinner cord will grip better, but below 5mm in diameter, the cord will be too weak for many rescue applications. To slide the prusik after it has been weighted, loosen the "tongue," which is the one strand opposite all the wraps.

Tests on various friction hitches reveal that the prusik consistently has the most holding power in a wide array of cord and rope combinations. Use the prusik in scenarios (like 3:1 raising systems) where it will be loaded with more than body weight.

*A four-wrap prusik.*

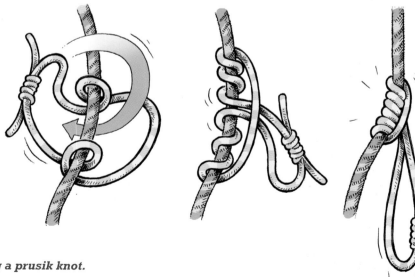

**Tying a prusik knot.**

LOAD

## Klemheist Knot

This is another useful friction hitch that is quick and easy to tie—a good choice as a rope-ascending knot, or if you're forced to use a sling rather than a piece of cord to tie a friction hitch. If using a sling, pick a nylon one (preferably 18mm/¹¹⁄₁₆-inch width) over a Spectra or Dyneema sling; nylon grips better and is less susceptible to weakening if it gets hot (nylon has a higher melting point). Four wraps of 6mm cord (or ¹¹⁄₁₆ nylon) tied on a single 10mm diameter rope usually work well. After the hitch has been weighted, loosen the tongue (the one strand opposite all the wraps) to slide it more easily.

## *Tying the Klemheist Knot*

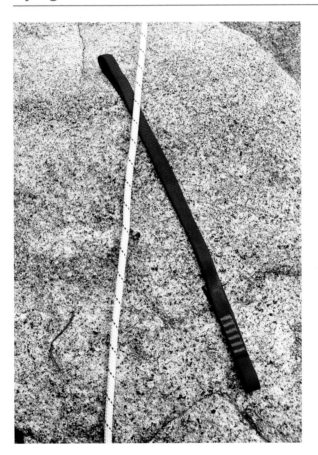

*Completed klemheist knot.*

## Autoblock

Sometimes called the "third hand," the autoblock is used to back up your brake hand when lowering someone, or to back up your brake hand when rappelling. Tie it with your loop of 5mm or 6mm diameter nylon cord wrapped three or four times around the climbing rope. When I tie it on a single strand of 10mm diameter climbing rope (as in a lowering situation), I usually make four wraps. For a rappel backup on a doubled 10mm rope, I usually go with three wraps.

*The Sterling Hollow Block, shown here wrapped in an autoblock configuration, is a 100 percent Technora sling designed specifically for use with friction hitches.*

*The autoblock with nylon cord. To construct an autoblock, I've found that a good length of cord is 3-foot 9-inches, tied with a double fisherman's knot. Select the softest, most pliable 5mm or 6mm nylon cord you can find.*

# Stopper Knot

This knot is used as a safety knot in the end of a rope. It is essentially half a double fisherman's knot tied on one strand of rope. A stopper knot prevents the end of a belay rope from passing through the belay device, and prevents rappelling off the end of the rope if rappelling with a plate, tube, or assisted braking (e.g., Grigri) device. When using two ropes, I tie a separate knot at the end of each rope, as tying both ropes together can cause the ropes to twist around each other.

## *Tying a Stopper Knot*

*It sounds almost too simple, but the best way to avoid rappelling off the end of your rope is simply to tie a stopper knot in the rope's end. The stopper knot can, however, pass through a figure eight descending ring, so if you're rappelling with that particular device and want a safety knot at the end of your rope, you'll need to use a bulkier knot that cannot pass through it.*

# CHAPTER 14

# Risk Management

In 1980 my partner and I started up the Salathe Wall of El Capitan, planning to veer off up higher and climb the infamous Shield route—a smooth, overhanging headwall of granite climbed via a 600-foot incision that splits the wall.

On our way up the Free Blast, the first twelve pitches of the Salathe Wall up to Mammoth Terrace, we climbed smoothly and efficiently, and in no time, we were only a few pitches shy of the terrace, where we planned to bivy. Suddenly I heard faint calls for help, muffled by the afternoon breeze. Soon, from the valley floor, came a broadcast through a bullhorn: "Climbers approaching Mammoth Terrace. If you can hear us, raise your right arm." It was the YOSAR, the Yosemite Search and Rescue team rangers, who had their telescope trained on us. The conversation went back and forth like a game of charades: "Climbers on Mammoth Terrace, if you're in need of a rescue raise your right arm." When we reached the ledge and found the two climbers, they looked strung out. They'd been up there for two nights, with no food or water. One of the guys had stretched his T-shirt down to his ankles, and he looked cold and grim. The first thing he said was "You don't smoke, do you?" And I didn't.

Their plan had been to climb the Triple Direct route, then base jump off the top. They planned on fixing lines down from Heart Ledge, but made a serious mistake by putting five ropes in a single pack. The nonredundant strap on their pack broke under the weight when they clipped it in, leaving them only one rope—and no food or water.

With various questions via bullhorn from YOSAR and various responses with raised arms from us, we agreed to assist the stranded climbers.

We agreed to abandon our climb and rappel with the two unfortunates to the ground. Down on the valley floor they proceeded to give me their rack as a gift, and swore they'd never climb again.

Afterward, YOSAR chief John Dill asked if I'd like to join him for dinner. After a thorough debrief John asked if I'd like to join the YOSAR team. I guess my partner and I saved them a lot of work.

And so began a serendipitous period in my life where I worked to help unlucky climbers who'd been in accidents. The perks: free unlimited camping at the Camp 4 rescue site in addition to high wages during actual rescues.

## Anatomy of an Accident

Proper risk management in the rock climbing environment involves identifying and assessing hazards, then making the right decisions to avoid them. If the hazards can't be completely avoided—climbing is not without hazards and risk—then controls to mitigate or minimize the risks should be implemented.

*Joshua Tree Search and Rescue Team in action at Joshua Tree National Park, California.*

Every year the American Alpine Club publishes *Accidents in North American Mountaineering*, a comprehensive analysis of all the climbing accidents for the year. Studying what happened to other climbers can heighten your awareness of what to watch out for to avoid a mishap.

John Dill studied the most serious climbing accidents that happened in Yosemite Valley from 1970 to 1990. During that time fifty-one climbers died in accidents, 80 percent of those accidents, Dill estimates, "easily preventable." In his article "Staying Alive," Dill points out that state of mind is the key to safety: "It's impossible to know how many climbers were killed by haste or overconfidence, but many survivors will tell you that they somehow lost their good judgment long enough to get hurt. It's a complex subject and sometimes a touchy one. Nevertheless . . . at least three states of mind frequently contribute to accidents: ignorance, casualness, and distraction."

Ignorance is being unaware of a potential danger. Casualness is not taking things seriously enough—complacency reinforced by repeatedly getting away with practicing poor safety habits and having nothing go wrong. Distraction is when something takes your mind off the important task at hand, and your brain simply moves on to the next task without completely checking what you've just done.

My friend Kevin Donald, who used to run the International Alpine School in Eldorado Canyon, Colorado, had a business card he'd pass out to Hollywood producers when we worked together as mountain safety officers for film shoots. The slogan on his card: "Gravity Never Sleeps." I took that adage to heart, especially after a close friend of mine busted nearly half the bones in his body and almost died after a 30-foot fall onto a concrete floor during a seemingly mundane rigging job for a commercial shoot in an airplane hangar.

## Inattentional Blindness

"Inattentional blindness" is a term psychologists use to describe the neurological phenomenon that occurs when the brain fails to see something obvious, when attention is distracted or focused on something else. Psychologists who study multitasking have found that most of us aren't the multitaskers we think we are. Our brain is simply switching back and forth from one activity to another, deactivating one area of focus to process the other task. Think about it. When you make a mental error during the course of your day, it's almost always because you were thinking about something else, not the task at hand.

In my role as an examiner for guides' certification exams, I've seen examples of inattentional blindness many times during complicated technical scenarios, where the guide has moved his or her focus without seeing an obvious error, such as a carabiner unlocked at a key belay or rappel device. It's as though the mind skipped a step, or the brain said that everything was correct and complete, when in fact it wasn't—a cognitive blind spot.

Psychologists theorize that once the brain determines what is important, it fills in the picture with whatever your expectations believe *should* be there. These failures of awareness happen to all of us at one time or another, but we're not aware of them, so we don't realize what we've missed! A systematic and routine checklist is helpful, but what we really need to look for is what might be wrong, not what looks right.

Don't be distracted when performing crucial tasks, and don't engage in conversation when tying in, clipping into anchors, rigging, making transitions, and performing technical scenarios. Get in the habit of double-checking your systems before engaging.

*Jo Whitford leads Midterm (5.10a), Yosemite Valley.*
PHOTO BY GREG EPPERSON

Pat Ament, the great Colorado climber of the 1960s and 1970s, writes in his book *Rock Wise*: "As with all of climbing, it is attitude that saves or kills. There is no better beginning than within the mind, in the form of complete concentration. There is no room for oversight or for dismissing what is logically understood. Keen intuition must evaluate all which strikes both mind and eye."

## Rockfall

The closest call I've had in more than forty years of rock climbing was due to rockfall. It's been said that when the human brain is under the influence of adrenaline, memories become more embedded than during its normal state. In my case, I believe it, since the rockfall incident I'm recalling happened seventeen years ago, but I can replay the moment like it happened a few hours ago. It was during the first ascent of a new route in Yosemite Valley. I was clipped tight to a two-bolt belay anchor. My partner had nearly completed the pitch, 120 feet above me, and was moving over a series of ledges, seeking a good crack for an anchor. It was his rope that dislodged the rock. You can usually judge the size of a falling rock by how loud your partner yells "ROCK!" I had one partner who would say "Pebble" for anything smaller than a golf ball. But in this case, it was more of a blood curdling scream, which he repeated three times: "ROCK! ROCK! ROCK!" It was roughly the size of a minifridge, and the moment I saw it, my brain quickly calculated that the block would bounce off the wall and squarely hit me if I didn't get out of its way. Tethered to the anchor, I moved sideways as far as I could, and the rock barely grazed my shoulder. If my partner hadn't warned me, by the time I saw the rock, it would have been too late. A split second can make all the difference.

At multipitch areas known for rockfall, it's simply not a good idea to climb below other parties. On ledges on multipitch routes, and clifftops at single-pitch crags, be especially vigilant when pulling your rope around near the edge of the cliff. In many cases, it's the movement of the rope that causes the rockfall.

## Closing the System

In both single-pitch and multipitch environments, the rope system should always be closed. That should be your default. This simple protocol will prevent many accidents during lowering and rappelling. If a climber is rappelling and one rope end is too short, she can rappel off the short end, which results in her pulling (rapidly!) the now free short end through the rappel anchor, quickly dispatching her to the ground. Another common accident occurs during lowering. If the belayer has wandered out a bit from the cliff, and the rope is too short and he's not paying attention to the end of the rope, the rope can travel through the belay device, resulting in a dropped climber.

A closed system means that both ends of the rope have a knot in them—either the end is tied into someone's harness, or a stopper knot is tied on a free end. This simple safety habit prevents the end of the rope from ever going through a belay or rappel device. What I teach is *always close the system unless there is a compelling reason not to do so.* An example of a compelling reason? If you know you're going to be pulling the end of the rope back up the cliff, since the knot can potentially jam in a crack as you're pulling it up the rock.

## Safety Checks

If you haven't developed a safety check protocol, now is a good time to start. For me as an instructor, it's become second nature, and I'm a little shocked when I see recreational climbers who haven't developed the habit. I start with ABC: Check the ground anchor (if used), check the belayer, then check the climber. A proper safety check should be both visual and verbal.

## Anchor

Check the ground anchor to make sure the belayer is in a line between the direction she will be pulled in the event of a fall and the anchor itself. A best way to attach the belayer to the ground anchor is with the rope, since it stretches, rather than a sling. The belayer is tied in, as normal, then clove hitches the rope to a locking carabiner attached to the ground anchor.

## Belayer

Check the belayer's harness to make sure it is buckled properly. Check the figure eight follow-through knot to make sure it is (1) tied properly and (2) threaded through the correct tie-in points at the front of the harness. Check the belayer's belay device, to make sure the rope is properly threaded through the device. Lastly, check the belayer's locking carabiner on the belay device to make sure that it is locked. Check that the belayer is wearing her helmet.

## Climber

Check the climber's harness to make sure it is buckled properly. Check the climber's figure eight follow-through knot to make sure it is (1) tied properly and (2) threaded through the correct tie-in points at the front of the harness. Check to ensure the climber is wearing his helmet.

These safety checks are simple, but you'd be surprised how many times I've caught students making a mistake somewhere along these lines. Do these checks before every climb. It's that simple.

One acronym to help you remember what to look for is BARCK:

**B** buckles on the harness

**A** anchor (check the ground anchor)

**R** rope

**C** carabiners locked

**K** knots

Whatever system you use, know what to check for, and be methodical with your safety checks.

*Peter Croft begins his day of climbing with Figures on a Landscape (5.10b), Joshua Tree, California.*

# CHAPTER 15

# Leave No Trace Ethics

You can practice Leave No Trace principles from the moment you step out of your car. The following simple steps will help keep the climbing sites we all share as clean as possible, with minimal degradation to the climbing area and the surrounding environment:

- At popular climbing areas, use the outhouses located at most parking areas before you embark on your approach to that day's chosen cliff.

- Always use marked climber's access trails where they are available. If there is no marked trail to the cliff, minimize your impact by walking on durable surfaces (e.g., a sandy wash, rock slab, or barren ground).

- At popular, easy-access crags, avoid making a beeline from the parking lot straight to the crag without first looking for an established path or trail. Walking off-trail can significantly impact vegetation and cause soil erosion if enough people do it over time.

- If traveling in a group in more remote, pristine areas where no trail exists, fan out instead of walking in single file, and try to walk on the most durable surfaces, avoiding fragile vegetation. Don't leave rock cairns to mark the path—this takes away the challenge of route-finding from those who prefer to experience it on their own.

- If nature calls and you're far from any outhouse, deposit solid human waste well away from the base of any climbing site or wash by digging a cathole 4 to 6 inches deep. Cover and disguise the cathole when you're done. Pack out all toilet paper and tampons in a ziplock bag. Urinate on bare ground or rock, not plants. Urine contains salt, and animals will dig into plants to get at it.

- Leave no trace means just that: Pack out everything you bring in, including all trash and food waste (that means apple cores and orange peels too). Set an example for your group by picking up any trash you find. Plan ahead; always carry a trash bag with you when you go out to the crag.

- Don't monopolize popular routes by setting up a toprope and then leaving your rope hanging on the climb, unused. If your climb begins from a campsite and the site is occupied, ask permission to climb from the campers there.

- Minimize your use of chalk, and if you're working a route, clean off any tic marks with a soft brush after you're done.

- Protect everyone's access to a climbing area by being courteous, beginning with parking only in designated areas and carpooling whenever possible.

- Noise pollution can be a problem, from blasting tunes on a boom box to yelling and screaming while attempting a hard climb. Be considerate and aware of those around you, and limit your noise production to a reasonable level.

- Pick up all food crumbs, and don't feed any wild critters; this habituates them to human food and encourages them to beg and scavenge, sometimes even chewing holes in backpacks to get at food.

*Bivouac on Cosmos,*
*El Capitan.*
PHOTO BY GREG
EPPERSON

- Consider leaving your dog at home—dogs dig and root up vegetation and stress native wildlife in rural areas. If you do bring your dog, be sure to remove any dog poop from the base of the cliff and the approach trail.

- Leave all natural and cultural objects so that they can be experienced by everyone in their natural setting. If you are climbing in a national forest or national park, obey all regulations concerning the gathering of firewood and other objects.

For more information on Leave No Trace ethics, visit www.lnt.org.

# Index

open-handed grip, 11
overhand loop, 249–51

**P**

pendulums and tension
    traverses, 179–81
Peterson, Charlie, 32, 171
pickoff, climber, 243–46
pitons, 70–71, 91–93
plaquette devices, 197–99
pre-equalized cordelette system,
    104–10
protection
    avoiding flakes, 62–65, 82,
        83, 129
    bolt replacement for, 98–99
    evolution of chockcraft,
        70–79
prusik knot, 275
prusiking, 235–38
push/pull technique, 13–15

**Q**

quad, the, 116–19

**R**

Rands, Lisa, 9, 238
rappelling, 217–33
    assistance skills. See rescue
        and assistance skills
    backups, 218–20
    belays, 217–18
    counterbalance techniques,
        228, 234, 243–46
    fireman's belay and, 217–18
    with heavy pack/haul bag,
        228
    joining two ropes for,
        264–66
    lowering and, transitions,
        138–43
    mistake scenarios, 217–18

multipitch, 220–27
    Reepschnur Method,
        232–33
    retrieving rope, 230
    rope management, 228–33
    safety, preventing accidents,
        217–18
    safety checks, 217, 220
    simul, 228
    stuck ropes, 230–32
    tandem, 227–28
    tossing rope, 228–30
    transitioning from rigging
        to, 128–29
    transitioning from toproping
        to, 141–43
redirected belay, 206–7
Redundancy, Equalization,
    and No Extension (RENE)
    principal, 103–4
Reepschnur Method, 232–33
Renn, Beth, xv, 216
rescue and assistance skills,
    235–47
    ascending single fixed rope,
        238–39
    assistance from below,
        242–47
    assistance from top,
        239–42
    climber pickoff on toprope,
        243–46
    El Capitan incident
        example, 281
    improvised rope ascending,
        235–38
    prusiking, 235–38
    rescuing fallen leader,
        246–47
    3:1 assisted raise, 242
    3:1 raising system, 239–41
    See also risk management

"ring lock"/"finger stack,"
    25–26
risk management, 281–88
    anatomy of an accident and,
        281–82
    closing the system, 284
    inattentional blindness and,
        282–84
    rappelling safety and backups,
        217–20
    rockfall hazard, 284
    safety checks, 133–37, 217,
        220, 284–85
    sport climbing safety,
        133–37
    standard climbing signals,
        192–93
    See also rescue and assistance
        skills
Robinson, Doug, 71, 131, 153
rock assessment, 61–65
rockfall hazard, 284
rope direct belay, 209–10
ropes, 37–50
    care and use, 42–43
    CE EN 1891 ratings, 40–41
    coiling. See ropes, coiling and
        uncoiling
    cord, cordelettes and, 53–55
    diameter and sheath
        percentage, 41
    dry or non-dry, 41
    dynamic, certifications,
        39, 41
    dynamic types, 39
    fall forces and. See fall forces
    half rope, 39
    history of, 37–38
    kernmantle, 39
    knots for joining, 264–66
    length of, 42
    low-stretch, 40, 41

**W**

water knot, 51, 260–61
Watts, Alan, 132
webbing. *See* slings and webbing

**Y**

Yosemite Method of big wall
climbing, 173

Yosemite Method of jumaring,
177–79
Yosemite Method of leading,
170–73
Young, Wills, 9–10, 12, 13–15

**Z**

zipper effect, 156–57

# About the Author

**Bob Gaines** began rock climbing in Southern California in the 1970s. Since then he has pioneered more than 500 first ascents at Tahquitz and Suicide Rocks and Joshua Tree and Yosemite National Parks. Bob began his career as a professional rock climbing guide in 1983 and is the owner of Vertical Adventures Rock Climbing School, which offers classes at Joshua Tree National Park, California. Vertical Adventures was voted the number-one rock climbing school in America by *Outside* magazine.

Bob has worked extensively in the film industry as a climbing stunt coordinator. He has coordinated more than forty television commercials and was Sylvester Stallone's climbing instructor for the movie *Cliffhanger*. Bob doubled for William Shatner in the movie *Star Trek V: The Final Frontier* as Captain Kirk free-soloing on El Capitan in Yosemite.

He is an AMGA Certified Rock Instructor and is the coauthor of *Rock Climbing: The AMGA Single Pitch Manual*, the textbook for the AMGA's single-pitch instructor program. He has worked extensively training US military special forces, including US Navy SEAL Team 6, and is known for his technical expertise in anchoring and rescue techniques. Bob is also the author of *Best Climbs Joshua Tree National Park, Best Climbs Tahquitz and Suicide Rocks, Toproping,* and *Rappelling* and is coauthor of *Climbing Anchors* and the *Climbing Anchors Field Guide* (with John Long). Bob's other passion is fly fishing. He currently holds eleven International Game Fish Association world records.